Pontypridd at War

1939–45

Pontypridd at War
1939–45

The Second World War at Home

Don Powell

MERTON PRIORY PRESS

First published 1999

Published by
Merton Priory Press Ltd
67 Merthyr Road, Whitchurch
Cardiff CF14 1DD

ISBN 1 898937 32 X

Dedication

*To all the men and women and boys and girls
of Pontypridd during The Second World War*

Printed by
Hillman Printers (Frome) Ltd
Handlemaker Road
Marston Trading Estate
Frome, Somerset, BA11 4RW

Contents

Acknowledgements

This book tells the story of the events at home in Pontypridd and its villages during the valiant years of the Second World War, 1939–45. To give a fuller picture, it also tells of many things that happened in the way of life here in the years of the 1930s immediately before the outbreak of hostilities, and continues into the few years of the aftermath of war. And there are a few memories of other times. Every effort has been made to ensure accuracy of the facts researched.

As with my earlier book *Victorian Pontypridd* (Merton Priory Press, 1996), my thanks to the former Mid Glamorgan County Libraries and the present Rhondda-Cynon-Taff County Borough Council Libraries for the many facilities accorded to me during my several years research of the local collection at Pontypridd Library; and to the staff at museums, libraries and other places in Wales for their help and courtesy. To my family and many friends for their encouragement and support. And to the men and women of Pontypridd with whom I have spoken in the preparation of the book.

Some of the photographs included are from my own collection. For others, I am indebted to and acknowledge with thanks the courtesy of the Rhondda-Cynon-Taff County Borough Libraries, Local Collection; Pontypridd Historical & Cultural Centre; the Trustees of the Imperial War Museum, London; Crown Copyright material from the Central Office of Information, London; Crown Copyright material from the Ministry of Agriculture, Fisheries and Food, Surbiton; Valentines of Dundee Ltd; and my son Graham Powell for some modern photographs.

My special thanks to the following people of Pontypridd for the loan of photographs: Mrs Betty Carter, Charles and Annice Crockett, Ken and Marilyn Davies, Malcolm and Cathy Davies, Colin Gibbon, Kerry Greenaway, Mrs Jean Griffiths, Mrs Thelma Jones, Ted and Bette Mantle, Reginald and Edna Phillips, Jim and Corinne Rees, Bill and Marie Reeves, Stanley Wells. I apologise to anyone to whom acknowledgement may be due but, inadvertently, has not been given.

Pontypridd   Don Powell
January 1999

CHAPTER ONE

Air Raid Precautions

Thirties scene

Living conditions were not easy for people of the terraces and streets of
Pontypridd and its villages in the depression years of the 1930s.
Coal-burning fires heated the ovens in which housewives did all their
cooking. A kettle was boiled on the fire and a stock-pot usually hung
over the coals, or a saucepan of stew warmed on the hob. But the grates
shone from being regularly black-leaded and polished with pride. Some
houses still had gaslight in the downstairs rooms. Candle-lit bedrooms
stayed unheated. If there were firegrates in bedrooms, they were usually
lit only in cases of illness. Someone getting out of bed first placed one
foot gingerly on the icy cold linoleum and then braved it down the stairs
to light the fire. The more fortunate could undress downstairs in front of
it. The morning chore meant shivering while raking out the ashes, setting
the sticks and banking the coal. And you normally needed a sheet of
newspaper placed across the fireplace for enough draught to coax the
flames. Few households could afford the luxury of an electric fire to take
the chill off the room first.

People had simple expectations from life in the harsh years. They
readily helped each other through shortages and it seemed as though
neighbours could always borrow anything from a bowl of sugar to a
bucket of coal. Families stood at the windows watching for the unemployed breadwinner to come home with his 'dole' money so that food
could be bought at the corner shop. Mrs Evelyn Davies and her husband
Glyn and their then five children who lived in a two-up one-down house
in Old Park Terrace (Tub Row) in Treforest were typical of the families.
Their eight-year-old daughter Barbara often skipped down to Plowman's
shop on the corner of nearby Saron Street to buy a fragile gas mantle in
its tiny cardboard box. Plowman's was one of many general shops in the
villages that supplied much of a family's needs.

Another occasional errand was to H.G. Joshua's ironmongery in Park
Street for a galvanised bucket or, more likely, for a rubber-backed
washer to repair the old leaky bucket. The bucket was put on a single
gas ring to boil the family washing. Also bought were rubbing soap for
use on the ribbed washboard, scrubbing brushes, and a 'slate square' for

cleaning the doorstep. To power their wireless sets, the nearby villagers in Treforest had to take their heavy batteries or 'accumulators' to another shop in Park Street for recharging. Mrs Kate Griffiths's shop in Queen Street sold groceries. Evelyn Davies, like hundreds of other Treforest residents, would leave the shop with a small basket or brown-paper carrier bag of goods, feeling uplifted by the courteous service received and the pleasant smiles exchanged on the little outing. Going home, Evelyn had to pass a little temptation of a shop in the parlour of a house in Queen Street which sold home-made toffee and crunchie.

If you were in Pontypridd town, you could treat yourself to a few pennyworth (or penn'orth) of pork dripping at Scudamore's shop on the corner of Market Street and Church Street. Nearby you found kippers at a penny or so a pair. In Trallwn, many mothers sent their children round to the Hopkin Morgan bakery in East Street where they could get a large bag of broken biscuits or cake pieces and trimmings for a few coppers. To recall the old currency: four farthings made one penny, 240 pennies or pence equalled one pound. A pound or twenty shillings was written £1 or 20*s*. The tiny silver threepenny bit was called a 'joey'. A sixpenny bit was known as a 'tanner' (6*d*.). Twelve pennies made a shilling or a 'bob' (1*s*.). The half-crown was 2*s*. 6*d*. A guinea was 21*s*. A shilling in decimal coinage is 5p. In addition to the large, white £5 notes then in circulation were the £1 and 10*s*. notes (first issued in 1928). The only time many Pontypridd families saw banknotes was when men, dressed in dowdy and well-darned or patched clothes, drew their dole or unemployment benefit, which in 1936 was just under 30*s*. a week for a married couple with three children.

In Pontypridd and the valleys the 1930s were unrelenting years of hunger and scraping for pennies. Public Assistance officials checked the homes where 'means tests' had been conducted to ensure that the value of any little luxuries that may have been acquired was deducted from their money. Those who remember the years speak of small things and significant things which create a mosaic of life in Pontypridd in those times before the war: seemingly constant sunshine and hot summers; groups of despairing, idle men standing on street corners; the ship-builders who had no ships to build but carried their petition for jobs on their 1936 Jarrow Crusade march to London, and before them the marchers from the Rhondda; and the local street marches against unemployment in 1935 which involved some protesters from the 300,000 communist-led Unemployed Workers' Movement in South Wales. The national working population in June 1939 was nearly 20 million men and five million women. More than one million workers in Britain were unemployed in 1939. For people in work, the Holidays with Pay Act of

1938 increased the number of people entitled to paid holidays from half a million to eleven million.

Evelyn Davies helped to make ends meet in bringing up her family by making baskets out of the cardboard tops from milk bottles: she put a blanket stitch of raffia through the centre holes of two tops placed together, which were then sewn all round with raffia to cover them. They were linked with raffia to form the basket which had plaited raffia handles. It took days to make one but the task earned a few shillings. Jack Whiles, of Hopkinstown, an agent with the local Refuge Insurance Company, noted that rag mats were made in many houses in Treforest, Graig and Glyntaff to cover part of the stone-slab floors. Another agent for the company, William (Bill) Jones of Oakland Terrace, Cilfynydd, found a frequent scene to be housewives using Singer sewing machines with treadles, that once belonged to their mothers or grandmothers, making clothes for their large families. Women could not afford health care: they were not insured workers and had no entitlement to free health care services. Home remedies for those families who could not see a doctor included onion juice for coughs or severe colds; and gargles of salt water for throat infections. Bill Jones of Cilfynydd often noticed brown paper coated with goose grease used on the chests of children who were obviously suffering from flu or bronchitis. Local doctors made up medicines in their own dispensaries: one of them was Dr Tudor Williams at his surgery at 'Dundella' in Cilfynydd. He often waived the 2*s*. or 2*s*. 6*d*. fee for his consultation from villagers who were not able to afford it. The insurance agents knew of the terraces where window blinds were drawn in nearly every house when there was a death. Usually, a well-practised neighbour laid out the body in a coffin placed in the small front parlour to await the hearse and burial.

Washing days in the 1930s and the wartime years meant a long day of drudgery in many households, especially for the poorer housewives with big families. A Treforest lady, who had no boiler, used to put a bucket of water with Persil on a gas ring to take the first load of sheets and pillow slips and towels. She agitated these with a stick and then lifted them out with a wooden tongs and placed them in a tin bath raised up on two chairs by the wall tap for rubbing on a metal washboard. (In some houses the heavy, steaming buckets were tipped straight into the kitchen sink—which she did not have.) She rinsed the washing which had to be wrung out tightly by hand, for there was no mangle. A load of shirts, loose collars and tablecloths underwent the same programme before being swished with a net holding a small Reckitt's blue block to whiten them and then immersed with water containing granules of Robin's starch, as many ladies will remember. More bucketfuls would follow on the gas ring to leave only the chore of the ironing, on a 'board' of folded blankets on the table, with flat irons heated in rotation on the gas ring and placed now and then on a trivet or an upturned enamel mug.

Outside lavatories, and perhaps one cold water tap in the kitchen, served many houses in Pontypridd villages. If you could afford to buy a house, new semi-detached ones along Cardiff Road in Hawthorn would have cost you £450. Families bathed in a tin bath (filled from many boiling kettles) in front of the kitchen fire: a daily ritual for many miners who did not attend pithead baths. Cilfynydd people saw the opening of pithead baths erected at the Albion Colliery by the Miners Welfare Committee in January 1939 at a cost of £25,000. You could have the luxury of a turkish bath at an establishment on the Graig if money didn't matter.

At schools, nurses checked through classes for fleas, and for hair infections of nits—the eggs of lice which were treated by smearing them with a substance which stuck them to the hair; or sometimes with a solution of iodine. The highly contagious skin disease of scabies was often detected and children were then disinfected at the clinic in Ynysangharad Park and given itch-soothing ointment. The nurses sometimes suspected the children's disease of rickets caused by a lack of vitamin D and not enough sunshine. Many children had free meals at school (where the cane was used in the classroom or, for serious cases, in the headmaster's study). In hot weather, many houses needed some twelve hours of smelly fumigation to obviate the menace of bed bugs.

In Ynysangharad Park, musicians gave evening performances at the bandstand. Hundreds of people sat or sprawled on the lawns near the Evan James and James James memorial to enjoy the music. Elsewhere, the signs 'Keep Off The Grass' gave you warning; and at one time the park-keeper, Mr Facey, would blow on his whistle to attract your attention before sometimes setting off in pursuit of offenders. Children wandered among the music lovers and held out small biscuit tins while asking, 'Got any cigarette cards, please, Mister?' One series of 50 cards featured Air Raid Precautions (ARP) illustrations. Players cigarettes cost 6*d*. for a packet of ten, while Woodbines cost 4*d*. for ten, or you could buy an open-topped paper packet of five for 2*d*. from vending machines outside many shops. On occasions, the residents of Ivor Court and Llewellyn Court adjacent to the Ivor Arms Hotel (beer 2*d*. a pint) sat on the roofs of their cottages, situated on the site of today's mini golf course in the park, and watched boxing matches staged in the Fairfield (now part of the car park below the YMCA) on the other side of the River Taff. The hotel and all the cottages, close to the Old Maltsters

Arms off Bridge Street, were demolished in 1936–7 and some of the residents moved to the new Oakland Crescent in Cilfynydd.

The turnstiles to the park swimming baths groaned and revolved constantly. Timed 'sessions' of an hour often became necessary so that the sweltering queue of bathers waiting outside could get into the water. Many bathers would swim in local pools: in Cilfynydd, in the ice-cold Albion Colliery lido in the beautiful Cwm near the Cilfynydd RFC social club building. Some villagers claim that the tranquillity of the Cwm is disturbed by the ghostly white lady that haunts its quiet paths. Children and adults from Glyntaff, Treforest and Rhydyfelin in particular could dive into the canal to cool off. At cold times of the year, they made use of the section known as the 'hotties' where hot water was discharged into the canal from the adjacent gas works. Clusters of children often dammed a local stream with boulders and clods of earth and turf to create a pleasant pool where everyone could enjoy long hours of bright sunshine—until a spoilsport landowner or tenant farmer appeared like a Barnes Wallis bouncing bomb and made a devastating breach in the dam.

Pontypridd Royal Welsh Ladies Choir was formed by Madame Muriel Jones of Treforest in 1927. The choir dressed in traditional Welsh national costume and sang before royalty more than 20 times. They sang before Princess Helena Victoria in Pontypridd in July 1929, for the Duke and Duchess of Kent in Cardiff in October 1937, and for the Duke (later, George VI) and Duchess of York and the two young princesses at Windsor in April 1935. Pontypridd celebrated the Silver Jubilee of King George V and Queen Mary in 1935 when many buildings in the town were decked out with portraits, bunting and flags. (King George V died on 20 January 1936. He made the first Christmas Day wireless broadcast to the Empire in 1932.) In December 1936 came the abdication of Edward VIII so that he could marry Mrs Wallis Simpson, an American divorcee. People listened intently to his emotional broadcast when he spoke the well-remembered words, 'I have found it impossible ... to discharge my duties as king as I would wish to do so without the help and support of the woman I love'. In earlier years, when Prince of Wales, he had made his 'something must be done' visit to the depressed and hungry valleys of South Wales. The couple became Duke and Duchess of Windsor. There was disquiet when they visited the German chancellor Hitler in 1937. The Duke was remembered in South Wales for another connection: on the day of his birth, 23 June 1894, the Prime Minister preceded his announcement of welcome in the House of Commons for this new prince and great-grandson of Queen Victoria with an expression of sympathy for the stricken families of Cilfynydd—an explosion at the Albion Colliery on that day had killed 290 miners.

1. View of the Tumble and the centrally situated Clarence Hotel, with Taff Street right and the bus terminus in Sardis Road left, in the 1930s.

2. Single-decker trolley bus in Taff Street, in the 1930s.

3. *Above:* Evelyn Davies of Old Park Terrace, Treforest, with her children: Ted, Barbara, Eira, Bill, Marie (Baby Jean was in her pram), 1941. *Below:* Sewing machinists at James Badcock's factory on Treforest Trading Estate, 1945–6: left to right: Pamela Betty, Milly Lenox, Barbara Davies, Eluned Jones. Note the turban to avoid hair being caught in machinery.

4. Treforest Silver Band, 1936. Fifth left in second row from bottom is bandmaster Tom Crockett. Also included are his sons Charles, fourth left, with Cyril and Billy fourth and fifth left in front row.

5. Glyntaff in the 1940s, showing Dr Mitchell's surgery at the end of the Machine Bridge, Llanbradach Arms (largest building), and bridge over the filled-in Glamorganshire Canal. Gwern-y-Gerwn far left of centre.

Many local people tuned into their wireless sets on 12 May 1937 for live broadcasts of the coronation of King George VI and Queen Elizabeth. Street parties were held throughout Pontypridd and the villages to celebrate and seating accommodation set up in Market Square near the New Inn for the royal visit on 14 July 1937. In October 1937 more than a thousand people attended Pontypridd's Great Exhibition at the Arcade where the highlight was a ten-valve Marconi wireless set with an improved output. Some enthusiasts still used sets from the 1920s such as the two-valve Marconiphone V2 or even a Brownie tube-type crystal set with headphones. Tom Evans, a railwayman and First World War veteran of Lock Street in Abercynon, enjoyed listening to his large HMV table gramophone in its wooden case. You wound it up frequently, changed the steel needle after playing every twelve-inch shellac record, and heard the music coming out of a large metal horn. But it still clearly reproduced the great tenor and soprano and other voices of the twenties and thirties or popular tunes like 'Bells Across the Meadow'. On 20 October 1938 the Duke of Kent officially opened the Treforest Trading Estate, soon to turn to wartime production of aircraft accessories and the manufacture of other vital components for the fighting services.

The romance of ballroom dancing blossomed at several halls in Pontypridd town during the 1930s, including the Star Ballroom situated above what recently became the new main post office (the former Swalec showrooms) in Mill Street; the New Inn Hotel in Taff Street, where dancers reached the ballroom from the magnificent, wide staircase built in 1922 by a carpentry firm from Cardiff at a cost of £750 which gave a view of a grand stained-glass window; and the ever-remembered, but now demolished, Coronation Hall on the corner of Church Street and St Catherine Street. The hall had access steps next to the top entrance of the Arcade from Market Square. Everyone flocked to the 'pictures': to the County Cinema in the High Street, now the Castle Leisure bingo hall; the Palladium, now the site of the Somerfield supermarket in Taff Street; the White Palace, which stood in Sardis Road; the Park Cinema, once at the lower entrance to the park; the Town Hall, at the market; the Regent in Hopkinstown; and the Cecil Cinema in Treforest. All were easy to get to by bus. Prices at the end of 1939 in the County were 6*d.* and 1*s.* ground floor and 1*s.* 3*d.* in the balcony.

In September 1930 trolley buses started running between Treforest and Cilfynydd and replaced the electric trams which had served on the route for 25 years. The single- and double-decker trolley buses provided a frequent early morning to late at night service for the next 27 years. The *Pontypridd Observer* reported that the trolley buses were fitted with air brakes and could stop very quickly. The newspaper warned local car drivers not to follow them too closely. The new service could not cope initially with the demands of the route and for a time some of the trams played nursemaid and ran in conjunction with the trolley buses. The residents of Treforest and Cilfynydd and places along the route complained to the council that the passing trolley buses played havoc with their wireless sets. On their journeys through a two-way Taff Street traffic system, the trolley buses knew virtually no hold-ups and, because they all had conductors on board, caused no delays themselves at bus stops in the town.

Petrol buses operated on the old Pontypridd to Trehafod tram route and the Pontypridd Urban District Council (PUDC) Transport Department ran cheap and effective services to the surrounding villages. The PUDC buses and those of the Rhondda Transport on the Trehafod and Porth routes negotiated a two-way system in Mill Street. Coming to the town, these buses turned right into the High Street and then reversed to their waiting place outside the Park Hotel, now the premises of the Midland Bank and Woolworth's. Another terminus for buses on routes west of Pontypridd was in Sardis Road, alongside the Clarence Hotel (Angharad's) where paperboys stood and called out the last editions for their *Echo* readers to 'read all about it'.

Motor cars seen in Pontypridd in the 1930s included the Riley Kestrel, Austin 7 and in 1936 its development the Austin Ruby; Austin 8 and 12, Sunbeam Talbot 10, Rover 10, Morris 8, 10 and 12; the Ford 8 model Y introduced in 1932 which sold for £100 in 1935 when petrol was about 1*s*. 2*d*. a gallon; Flying Standard 12 saloon which cost £260 in 1936; Ford Prefect 8 and 10, Hillman Minx 10, Vauxhall 10, Singer 9, 10 and 12, the MGTB and many other models and manufacturers. The Ford 8 was very popular in 1937 when it cost £140. In that year, 17-year-old John James drove his Ford 8 into the Palais de Danse (now Badman's furniture warehouse) in Mill Street as part of R.J. Bown's garage exhibition being held there.

In 1932 the Model Y Ford of eight-horsepower at £100 captured the market. It did 40 miles to the gallon and could reach 60 mph. At this time there was no speed limit. Motorcycles were sought after in Pontypridd and often seen with sidecars about the town and country roads. There were also the two-stroke bikes of low power, smelly, and called 'stinkwheels' among other names. The Road Traffic Act of 1930 abolished the 20 mph speed limit for motorcycles. Crashes grew more frequent on the open road. A draft Highway Code was issued in 1930 and, over the years, there came traffic lights, road signs, cat's eyes, roundabouts; small traffic islands like those on the Tumble and in Tabernacle Square at the junction of Bridge Street and Taff Street; and

Belisha crossings—pedestrian crossings with orange flashing beacons named after the minister who introduced them. You were allowed to drive at the age of 17. Compulsory driving tests started in 1935 and the 30 mph urban speed limit was enforced. Three-letter car numbers were introduced in 1932.

Shopping basket

Service with a smile was the motto in the shops. Some of those in the town were the Direct Trading Company, Star Supply Stores, John Bull, Liptons, Home and Colonial, Morgan Harris, Melias, Thomas and Evans (of Corona pop fame), John's Cafe and a number of other enjoyable Italian cafes. Several grocery shops were similar to the Pontypridd shops of the Victorian and Edwardian days: shoppers walked up to wide counters lined down to the floor with biscuit tins fitted with hinged glass tops so that the contents could be viewed and sampled. Some counters were formed from marble slabs. Wooden counters were scrubbed daily with scalding water. Some floors were wooden and sprinkled liberally with sawdust; some were tiled. The assistants in white coats, and often wearing hats, welcomed you. You watched as they weighed out tea from new chests into stout blue packets, ladled sugar with a horn scoop from sacks into small blue bags, and dug butter from large slabs before patting it into shape on a sheet of grease-proofed paper and weighing it on shiny brass scales with a selection of small weights. As well as being lit by electricity, some shops still had their Victorian gaslights or oil lamps and their smells mingled with those from hanging sides of bacon, from hams, coffee, cocoa, a barrel of apples, strings of onions, and cheeses set out to be tasted and selected by customers. In some shops in town, the assistants totted up your bill and placed it with your payment into a metal ball which was sent along an overhead wire to a small cash office at the back of the shop and your receipted bill and any change returned along another wire.

Chris Thomas recalls some of the depression years and early wartime years in the locality:

> I got on my bike in the late 1930s and pedalled through the years as an errand boy for a few shops in our mining village of Cilfynydd and in Ponty's Taff Street when they were extra busy. Shops like the Meadow Dairy and Evans and Tucker in Richard Street in Cil were filled with atmosphere. I sometimes helped out in the Meadow by patting-up butter. The wooden butter-pats were

kept in a wooden bowl of water. Large Cheddar cheeses laughed at me as I tried cutting them with a taut wire; and I was too unreliable to be trusted anywhere near the danger from the bacon slicer. So, mainly, I packed the made-up orders into large baskets for delivery on my bike. There wasn't always a lot to deliver: money was short in those years of depression and most of the villagers had to scrimp for pennies.

Customers waited patiently for their turn to be served. The grocer would bring each purchase from shelf to counter and take a pencil—usually an indelible one which he chewed—to jot down the prices of a few items at a time on a sheet of grease-proofed paper. Gossip of the day circulated among the groups standing about. I overheard the whisperers. Once, in my ignorance when their eyes were bright and hands were rubbed after a young woman had just left, I had to look up the word 'pregnant' in a dictionary.

A basket on my bike could be loaded with fresh dairy products and meats, sugar and tea, chocolate drinks that Ovaltiney girls and boys sang about on the wireless, golden syrup, soap flakes, swiss rolls, and an array of packets and tins with famous brand names seen on some of the enamel advertising signs in the village. And always condensed milk, which made a change of spread from the bread and marge—or even lard—that we had sometimes.

The wages were small and the bike was big. On hot summer days when I reached the top of one of the long, steep terraces which clung to the hillside, I could drink from an ice-cold stream that tumbled down into Oaklands from the Eglwysilan mountain towering over the village. Riding back to the shop was easy—you whistled down the wind of the terraces at speed. Until the time I buckled my bike when I ran into a baker's van in Jones Street near the Albion colliery and frightened the old Co-op horse even more than I did myself.

Cold winter weather took its stinging effect on skinny errand boys in short trousers. Mending a puncture with hands in slushy wet mittens was a chilling experience. During one skid into a wall, I was horrified when a paper bag of six eggs fell from my basket and ended up as a Humpty Dumpty splodge in the frozen snow—a mishap that would have spelt disaster in the coming days of food rationing. During the Second World War, strange additions appeared in my delivery basket: besides a family's meagre rations were tins of Household Milk in dried powder form; cans of American spiced ham or Spam; large tins of American sausage meat and red tins of dried egg which meant that omelettes and scrambled eggs were always on the menu, if little else.

It was sometimes perilous to ride in the blackout, for my bicycle lamp was fitted with a curved mask which gave only a small slit of light to show the way ahead. When I carried a basket, my torch had to be masked with tissue paper and always shone downwards not to attract enemy bombers. I joined the casualty list of people who bumped into gaslamps. I'd panic about the paper bag with its couple of eggs on top of my basket. Air raid sirens sounded many times in the village during the Battle of Britain. The local ARP warden, Mr Smith in Wood Street, often ordered me home, or wagged a warning finger because I'd left my gas mask in the shop. I was more careful of going about after a bomb fell on Cilfynydd Common—not far from the landslide of December 1939 when a large section of the tip, formed from buckets of spoil continually running on overhead lines from the Abercynon colliery, rolled down the slope and cut off the road over the common and also the Glamorganshire Canal to the height of the telegraph posts. It was a miracle that nobody was buried, but there wasn't a lot of motor traffic in those days.

Some of the larger stores in Pontypridd were the Co-operative, Burtons, Gwilym Evans, Woolworth's 3*d*. and 6*d*. stores where you could buy six-inch 78 rpm Eclipse gramophone records made from shellac for 6*d*.; and Rivlins on the site later occupied by Marks & Spencer. In contrast, near the Fountain in Taff Street was the tiny Penny Bazaar with its bursting counter displays fronted by small fences of wire mesh. Supermarkets were unheard of and all local villages had their main street of shops, or just corner shops and some little general shops dotted here and there in the front parlours of houses in the terraced streets.

Street ways

There was a strong smell of horses in the streets when carts went rumbling by carrying their deliveries of coal, meat, eggs, fruit and vegetables. And the horses in shining harness that hauled the drays of beer for the more than a hundred Victorian pubs and inns in Pontypridd town and its villages. Milk was delivered in bottles, sealed with cardboard discs, crated in a horse-drawn float; although several milkmen serving the Pontypridd villages had tiny carts that carried a full churn of milk and metal cans of a gill or quarter pint, half pint, and pint measures for milk to be poured into your jug on the doorstep or at the cart. Among the milk traders for many decades were Thomas John Lewis of Graig-yrHelfa Farm, Harry Tong of Pontypridd, and a lady from Mason's Farm in Treforest. The baker usually had a rounded-top van for the deliveries of his freshly baked bread that sent its aroma wafting along the terraces. There was a distinctive smell from carts carrying bundles of neatly chopped firewood bound with a twist of wire; and from the containers of paraffin. The dustmen came and tipped the bins and buckets, mainly filled with surplus ashes not wanted for garden paths or for throwing along back lanes, into a horse-drawn cart or into a lorry with sloping sides that slid back like a giant bread bin.

Sounds in the streets came from combs wrapped in paper and held to tingling lips, from kazoos or 'gazhooters', and from the clacking of two slivers of slate flicked in your fingers; the shouts and whistles of drovers guiding their flocks and herds to the cattle market behind today's Taff Street shopping precinct; the calls and laughter of boatmen on the Glamorganshire Canal unloading their cargoes, taken by a hoist high up in the Corn Stores near the busy lock at the Queens Hotel; the blasts from pit hooters and the occasional 'honk honk' of a motor horn; the sounds of creaking carts, horses hooves, and the clip-clop of children clad in outsize boots or wearing Mam's shoes as they played hopscotch and 'kit you're on it', or spun skipping ropes to favourite jingles like 'Salt, vinegar, mustard, pepper'; the steam trains clattering constantly through the town and the villages and the valleys; loud yells from expectant youngsters calling 'Chuck out! Chuck out!' for pennies and ha'pennies to be thrown from a wedding party in a house down the street; the ringing of handlebar bells and the shrill whistling by errand boys on their carrier cycles laden with grocers' baskets hurrying here and there in the terraced streets. The boys were often forced to brake or swerve to avoid thimble-sized cap bombs thrown high above them to land close by with a bang: provocations that frequently led to fist fights.

Raucous shouts of the rag and bone men often echoed in the streets. The men gave out things like balloons in exchange for your unwanted tatters of clothing. But sometimes you had to scurry back to the house for a jam jar of water for your prize of a goldfish, though it rarely seemed to survive for long. A pedlar's call of 'Pots and pans—get your kettle here!' often screeched from his cart. A gypsy asked you at your door to 'Buy my lucky white heather, dear'. She would carry a tray of other lucky charms, pins and needles, lace, elastic, and whittled pegs made from two pieces of willow fixed by a small piece of tin and a nail. Or dolly pegs—little girls loved to draw faces on the rounded, wooden tops and dress them. The ice cream man strenuously rang the bell on his push bike with its black panel white lettering that said 'Stop Me and Buy One'. You could wallow in a big, sumptuous cornet if only you had a penny.

Gaslight still lit many streets in the villages of Pontypridd, and the familiar figure of a lamplighter always drew knots of curious watchers when he came by at dusk. You heard a click as he raised his long lighting pole into the glass lampshade. A chain was pulled down, and the lamp quickly glowed. You would then watch him from afar as he lit up your terrace. When the wartime blackout was enforced, editor Percy Phillips suggested in the *Pontypridd Observer* that all the local lamp-lighters should be given jobs as labourers. The postman always had children tracking him: would there be a letter for your house? Would there ever be a—parcel! Letters were delivered three times a day from the then main post office built on the Tumble in the 1930s. In Pontypridd and the district in 1939 there were Merry Christmas GPO deliveries on Sunday (Christmas Eve) and on Christmas morning, but none on Boxing Day. The red public telephone box was designed in 1935 and appeared in the town and district. The telephone emergency 'Dial 999' system started in July 1937.

Boys and girls raced through the village streets with their iron hoops guided by a stick or hooked rod of iron. Some made 'bowlies' and 'bogey carts' from old bicycle wheels which forced people to step aside quickly. While some children talked to each other through two tins joined by a taut string, others climbed up the gas lamp posts to swing on its two short arms (keeping a wary eye out for the local policeman) and more sped along on a single roller skate or created colourful rings and patterns with their spinning tops made of tin. Whose top would spin the longest? Everyone competed, too, with whip and top. Crack! And the pear-shaped wooden tops whirled from the lash. Yelling kids pitched marbles on the roads and pavements. In a bigger version of the game, wooden balls once used at a coconut shy when Danter's funfair came to Pontypridd were kicked against kerbs and walls by scuffed shoes. The wearers would be in trouble with Mam when they got home.

The game of 'cattie and doggie' became a craze in the 1930s: the cattie or short piece of wood with pointed, whittled ends was placed on the ground and hit smartly with a stout stick (the doggie). The cattie then flew up and was hit again in flight to hurtle away—sometimes into a window pane and suddenly the street would be empty and silent. For many children, in time, the cattie became an enemy bomber and the doggie a vengeful Spitfire or Hurricane with machine guns blazing.

Duplicate cigarette cards were swapped or the children placed a line of unwanted cards up against a kerb or wall while competitors flicked a thick wad of stuck-together cards at them to knock down the prizes. More children fought battles in the timeless game of shiny conkers on strings. 'My fourteener will smash your niner any day!' Such a proud boast often ended up in bits. Children played in complete safety in country lanes and deep woods. Pirates boarded ships with crow's nests in high oaks. Red Indians pounced on a passing wagon train—usually some tranquil horse and cart. An irate local farmer once discharged a shotgun in defence of his scalp, and caused a stampede of panicky braves back to their reservation in the village. Countless Robin Hoods fought injustice with home-made bows and arrows and often with the help of demure or rough-and-tumble Maid Marions. Soon there would be invaders bearing swastikas to vanquish. Outdoor adventures sometimes included dangerous escapades such as dangling from the old swing bridge over the River Taff north of Cilfynydd; or clinging to loaded drams, or trams, as they ascended the steep incline above the village to send ever more pit waste in black clouds on to the growing threat of the Albion Colliery spoil tip looming over the village.

Children spent their hours at home reading, often by candlelight or oil lamps, the many illustrated books available from Pontypridd Free Lending Library, poring over jigsaws, putting together collections of cigarette cards into the special albums available from the cigarette manufacturers, creating little stamp albums, making up scrapbooks from pictures cut out from mail order catalogues, playing board games such as ludo, draughts, snakes and ladders; or building Meccano models and other creative hobbies from kits of metal or wood. For some children, Sunday evenings at home after church or chapel meant a warm fireside and a gathering round the piano where a family created its own entertainment.

Peace for our time

From about 1937 Britain at last faced up to the menace of the jackboot and the fact that she must rearm, for in Germany the Nazi Government had created a vast war machine. Britain and France had pledged to assist Poland against any aggression by Germany. But rearmament stayed slow while Britain stood ill-prepared and faced the danger of invasion in any conflict. The Prime Minister, Neville Chamberlain, who replaced Stanley Baldwin on 28 May 1937 (the month when the German airship Hindenburg exploded in a fireball whilst mooring in the United States), announced that he was going to Berchtesgaden to see Hitler on 22 September 1938 because 'personal conversation between him and myself might have useful results'. He returned to Downing Street on 24 September to cheering crowds. Then off he went to Germany again and he and Daladier of France met Hitler at Munich on 29 September. Chamberlain accepted Hitler's slightly modified terms of the Munich Pact and returned to London with the worthless 'Peace for our Time' scrap of paper agreement which he fluttered in the wind at the airport. The Lord Mayor of Cardiff flew the Nazi Swastika flag alongside the British flag from the mast above the City Hall on 30 September. Some councillors protested and the Swastika was hauled down—only to be hoisted again the following day. A mock air raid staged in Cardiff on 19 October 1938 included an anti-aircraft gun firing from outside the City Hall.

In May 1938 advertisements appeared in the newspapers calling for volunteers for the Air Raid Precautions scheme. They were wanted for first aid parties, staffing first aid posts, ambulance services, messengers, decontamination squads, administrative staff; and squads for rescue, demolition and clearance of debris. The volunteers would be given general air raid precautions training and also specialised training for their particular service. Persons willing to offer the use of vehicles for the scheme were asked to register their private cars, vans, or lorries for carrying wounded or men and materials in time of emergency. The response to the appeals for volunteers brought initial disappointment to the authorities. In April 1938 the Chancellor of the Exchequer, Sir John Simon, presented his Budget which put 6*d*. on income tax (making it 5*s*. 6*d*.) to pay for rearmament. He added £3½ million to his defence budget for air raid precautions. The Government announced plans for ration books and regulated prices, and an urgent national survey to locate suitable premises that could be turned into air raid shelters.

Chamberlain announced in June 1938 that there would be compulsory military service if war came. In South Wales, Bank Holiday Monday in August 1938 was one of the hottest on record. On such a lovely day it was laughable to consider the threat of war. After the burial of the Unknown Warrior in Westminster Abbey on 11 November 1920 and the march of mourners past the first Cenotaph in Whitehall, war memorials inscribed with the names of the fallen were erected in towns and villages all over Britain. Poppy Day was held for the first time in 1921. And every year at 11 a.m. on 11 November, Pontypridd and all its villages remembered their own sacrifice in the two-minute silence when everything stopped in the streets and in the factories and in the homes. And then wreaths were laid in honour at the monument on the Common and elsewhere. Surely war could never come again.

Later, on that glorious Bank Holiday Monday, the rains came: the

South Wales Echo reported that it was 'one of the most ferocious storms in local history bringing an evening of sky-shaking thunder, frightening lighting, and floods'. Nightmare thunderstorms swept the West Country. But Britain was in a relaxed mood: in the Test Match, England piled up 903 for seven declared against the Australians while Len Hutton batted for 13 hours and 20 minutes for his 364. In 1936, Fred Perry won the Wimbledon singles title for the third successive year—the year that the liner *Queen Mary* set out on her maiden voyage across the Atlantic and when 'Korky the Cat' starred on the front page of the new *Dandy* comic. Thousands of people worshipped in local churches and chapels.

A circular issued on 9 July 1935 had urged local authorities to prepare plans for Air Raid Precautions and in 1937 they had to submit them for government approval. The ARP Act of 1 January 1938 raised little interest locally or nationally; but its powers enabled the Home Office and local authorities to enforce the introduction of an air raid precaution system. Later in the year, the first voluntary wardens and helpers started digging trenches and filling sandbags. In January 1939 the Air Ministry appealed to employers to release pilots in RAF Reserve and Volunteer Reserve for continuous training with RAF units for up to six months as this would be important to the air defence of Britain. The Midland Bank in Pontypridd were obviously listening out, for they had already agreed to give leave to their employees to take up training. Also in January, ARP units were set up locally; such as the squads at Brown Lenox chainworks; and at the Albion Colliery in Cilfynydd where Ambulance Superintendent E. John Edwards was appointed ARP Officer with Cadet Officer Fred Wells as deputy. Sergeant Evans was the Chief ARP Officer for the Pontypridd Police Division. A new Civil Defence Act in July 1939 required any employer with more than 30 workers to effect ARP training schemes.

In July 1939 the government told the general public to be prepared for the possibility of war. If air raids threatened, warning would be given by sirens which would sound an undulating note. Hooters would give short blasts. Sirens and hooters would not be used for any other purpose. Warning might also be given by the police or air raid wardens blowing short blasts on whistles. You had to stay under cover until you heard the sirens or hooters sounding continuously for two minutes on the same note, which would be the signal for 'All Clear'. You had to make sure that the gas mask issued to you was kept safely and was carried at all times for immediate use. If poison gas was used, loud hand rattles would give warning. You should put on your gas mask and keep off the streets until the poison had cleared. The ringing of hand bells would indicate that the danger was over. Special anti-gas helmets for babies and respirators for small children would not be distributed before an emergency arose.

All windows, skylights, glazed doors, or other openings which would show a light had to be screened in wartime with dark blinds or blankets, or brown paper pasted on to the glass, so that no light was visible from outside. All street lighting would be put out and instructions would be issued about the dimming of lights on vehicles. An air attack could start so many fires from incendiary bombs that the fire brigades could not deal with them all. Everyone should be prepared to tackle a fire started at home. Attics and upstairs rooms should be cleared of inflammable materials to lessen the danger of fire spreading. Buckets of water and buckets of sand should be kept ready.

The government had made detailed arrangements for the voluntary evacuation from certain parts of the London area and some other large towns of schoolchildren, children below school age if accompanied by their mothers or other responsible persons, expectant mothers, and adult blind persons. (Thousands of evacuees came to all parts of Pontypridd and the valleys in May 1940 and again in the summer of 1944.) Everyone should carry identification. For children a label should be sewn on to their clothes in such a way that it would not become detached.

The government would ensure that there would be sufficient supplies of food, and that every person would be able to obtain regularly a fair share. Steps would be taken to prevent any sudden rise in prices. But if people bought excessive quantities before the full scheme of control was working, such 'panic buying' would be taking food which should be there for others. It was announced on 1 August 1939 that petrol would be rationed immediately if war broke out.

National Service Weeks for recruitment started in Pontypridd on Monday 8 May 1939 and coincided with the opening of the town's National Service Bureau. On the Wednesday, a grand procession through the town included military servicemen, police, special constables, fire brigade, ARP wardens and workers, ambulance services, the Red Cross and the Women's Voluntary Services (WVS). Loudspeakers pressed local people to join the Civil Defence services or enlist in the Forces. Sergt-Major Phelps enrolled recruits for the army at Seccombe's old shop (now jewellers Walker & Hall) on the corner of Mill Street. At the time, Aneurin Bevan MP told a public meeting at Pontypridd Town Hall that no-one knew what day war would break out and that everyone was living permanently under its shadow.

The 5th Welch Regiment of the Territorial Army gave a display in Ynysangharad Park: No 1 Platoon under Lieutenant H. Probert gave an exhibition of signalling and No 2 Platoon gave an exhibition of

anti-aircraft defences. The Pontypridd Fire Brigade and Auxiliary Fire
Service under Chief Officer David Muir and Deputy Officer D. Lewis
gave a display at the Orchard Field in the park. An air raid siren (dubbed
'Wailing Willy') sounded the approach of aircraft which circled overhead
and created a realistic mock air attack. There was a demonstration
showing how to deal with magnesium incendiary bombs (they each
weighed one kilogramme) with stirrup pumps and buckets of water and
buckets of sand. The stirrup pump was a hand-operated pump with a
foot-rest and a nozzle for producing either a jet or a spray. If you threw
a bucket of water on a burning incendiary bomb it would explode and
throw burning fragments in all directions. You could smother it with
sand or dry earth. Fire-watching duties were introduced from late 1940
when it was compulsory for factories and offices to have staff on night
duty to deal with incendiary bombs. Later, all men between 16 and 60
were liable for 48 hours of fire-watching duty every month. By 1943 an
estimated six million men registered as Fire Guards. They had no
uniforms but wore armlets. A National Fire Service was formed in May
1941 and replaced the hundreds of independent brigades that existed
previously.

Firemen staged an air raid exercise at Nantgarw in early August 1939
and an ARP evacuation exercise of 3,000 employees on the Treforest
Trading Estate took place later that month. The ARP first mobilised on
1 September. The Chief Warden for Pontypridd from the outbreak of war
was D. Milton Jones JP of Tyfica Crescent with J.P. Humphries as Head
Warden. The Principal Wardens for the districts included: W. Edryd
Lewis, Cilfynydd; the Revd J. Ifor Jones, Graig; Ivor Phillips, Hopkinstown; W.W. James, Lan Park; D. Haydn Jones, Rhydyfelin; James
Hastings and Frederick Smith, Trallwn; J.T. Jones, Treforest.

Full time wardens were paid £3 a week. Their huge annual wage bill
nationally shocked many ratepayers and local councillors. ARP centres
and sector posts were set up locally in halls and public houses. Cilfynydd
ARP had their centre at the Commercial Hotel (the Spite) and used the
large room, now part of a restaurant, with access from Cross Street
opposite the old snooker hut by the Workmen's Hall. In Treforest the
ARP Centre and St John Ambulance First Aid Post was near Taff House,
in the old Reading Rooms at Taff Meadow across from St Dyfrig's
Roman Catholic Church. Local Civil Defence organisations made use of
every available hall or room elsewhere in the area. 'ARP' plates were
fixed on the houses of many of those who had qualified as wardens.
Under the Emergency Powers (Defence Regulations) of 1939, persons
were forbidden, within general hearing of the public, to sound any siren,
hooter, whistle, bell, horn, gong or any other instrument. The ringing of

church bells would indicate an invasion. It was in order to sound a bicycle bell or motor horn if the use was proper. ARP wardens strictly enforced the rules. A local man was fined £5 (nearly two weeks' wages) for blowing a whistle in the street.

Men and women ARP volunteers were wanted to form decontamination squads in readiness for possible gas attacks, to fill sandbags, and for fire-watching duties. Later, local residents were asked to oblige the air raid wardens by leaving buckets of water outside their houses. This would save the wardens 'a great deal of time and inconvenience' in case of fire. Local police officers and special constables were lectured about the dangers of incendiary bombs and the Ministry of Home Security urged that industrial buildings should emit as much black smoke as possible to act as a screen during air raids. Boys aged from 14 to 18 were wanted to help with first aid, blackout arrangements and to become messengers and dispatch riders. All cyclists were asked to report to the local Medical Officer, Dr Severn, for duties. Messages were also carried by the Pontypridd Boys Civil Defence Pathfinders in the charge of Captain J. Glynn Jones OBE MC. Most usherettes at cinemas in Pontypridd became qualified in ARP work.

ARP wardens in blue battledress and steel helmets patrolled the Pontypridd streets and co-ordinated their activities with the police, fire and ambulance services. They trained for gas attacks and sternly warned people who did not carry their gas masks. A publicity poster issued in 1939 told that 'Hitler will send no warning—so always carry your gas mask'. About 40 million masks were distributed in cardboard boxes to British civilians. There were 'Mickey Mouse' masks for children. Masks were intended to be carried everywhere after the outbreak of war but people soon relegated them to cupboards and attics. 70,000 gas masks arrived in Pontypridd in late April 1939 for early distribution and the WVS, ARP workers and other volunteers helped to assemble them. The masks were issued throughout the district from 9 May 1939 in the evenings at the nearest school. They were free of charge but any damage or misuse was penalised by a £5 fine. The volunteers and school staff helped to fit the masks and give out the small cardboard boxes in which to carry them. In the classroom, children often sat at their desks wearing their gas masks for inspection by the teacher. One blackboard in a Cilfynydd Junior School classroom chalked the warning, 'Silence! I can still hear you talking'. People were advised to wear their gas masks for ten minutes every week, just to get used to them.

The ordinary gas mask, or properly the civilian-type respirator, consisted of a metal container or filter filled with material to absorb the gas and a rubber face-piece with a rectangular window of mica. It would give adequate protection against breathing any of the known war gases but would not protect against the gas burnt in cookers and gas fires. You held the mask in front of your face, thrust your chin well in and pulled tight on the adjustable straps, held together with a buckle, over your head. A piece of cardboard was held under the filter to prevent air intake while you breathed in to check that the seal round the face was airtight. You were told to keep the gas mask in its box and away from heat and strong light which would spoil the material of the mask. There were no masks available in the first consignment for children under four years old. In May 1940, came the threat of a new gas capable of penetrating the existing gas mask with lethal arsenic gas. To safeguard against this danger, every mask was fitted with an additional filter—a cylinder like a small furniture polish tin which was fastened to the gas mask container with adhesive tape.

Only the ordinary adult style masks were available at first for toddlers; but supplies of new Mickey Mouse masks arrived later for children aged from about two to four years. Painted in red and blue and with large ears, the masks resembled very much the Walt Disney character. Children had great fun trying them on in front of a mirror. For babies, gas helmets were issued. They were built round a metal framework and had a large mica window. The baby was strapped in and air was supplied through a rubber tube connected to a small bellows which the mother had to pump up and down continuously. Civil Defence workers, such as police officers, firefighters and ARP wardens were issued with a 'civilian duty' mask which had separate eye-pieces, a large can-shaped filter at the front and a rubber ear-piece to enable the wearer to use the telephone. It was carried in a haversack.

Brick-built surface air raid shelters were erected on local factory sites and in parks and school playgrounds. On the Treforest Trading Estate one block of shelters, recently demolished, stood by the river bridge near the Maesmawr cottages and railway halt. Five air raid shelters were built at Mill Street school soon after the start of the war. The Hawthorn School air raid shelter with capacity for 700–800 children was completed in February 1940. Shelters were built in Ynysangharad Park—those near the new cable-stay river bridge by Marks & Spencer were demolished in recent years. Surveyor W. Cecil Evans of the Pontypridd UDC received permission from Glamorgan County Council to create trench shelters near the pavilion end of the cricket field in the park. The children conducted to the five shelters at Mill Street school (and, no doubt, at other local schools) found the frequent air raid alerts gave them great chances to read and swap their comics like the *Dandy*, *Beano*, *Jester*, *Wizard*, and *Hotspur*. In September 1939 the air raid precautions in schools scheme required that children who could get home within seven minutes should go from class as quickly as possible. They were to attend the school nearest their homes. Gas masks must be kept with them until hooks were provided. And the milk in schools scheme for certified under nourished children would continue.

Anderson shelters, 6 ft high, about 5 ft wide, and 6 ft long or more, constructed from curved metal sheets bolted together on a base frame were sunk in 3–4 ft deep pits in back gardens and banked with earth. Many Pontypridd residents created colourful flower beds on them. A few shelters had electric light fitted but the light from a candle in a jam pot was more general. The shelters were considered to be safe except from suffering a direct hit. They were named after Sir John Anderson, then Minister of Home Security, early in 1939. They were free for anyone who earned less than £5 a week (which meant most workers) but cost £7 for those who earned more. Some 2¼ million were made. Some owners installed bunk beds in the shelters and kept ready there a supply of food, water, first aid kit and perhaps an emergency suitcase of spare clothing, personal belongings and valuables. Despite all efforts to make the shelters comfortable, they always seemed to be damp and draughty and smelly. Some of their occupants had to fight a fear of spiders and creepy-crawlies. Many shelters became waterlogged.

Over a million Morrison shelters were made. Named after Herbert Morrison (later, Lord Morrison of Lambeth) the shelter resembled a long, oblong box with strong steel sections and wire mesh sides. It was set up indoors and could be used as a table during the day. People without private shelters were advised to seek protection under the stairs during air raids and many families in Pontypridd well remember their being squeezed up for hours under the stairs or under the flat stone in the pantry.

Speakers toured Pontypridd and the Rhondda warning people to be on their guard against enemy spies—Fifth Columnists—who may be operating in the area. There was a proposal to camouflage public buildings in Pontypridd as there were several that would 'provide splendid targets for the enemy'. Cardboard coffins, collapsible for easy storage, were stockpiled in 1939 and a million burial forms were issued to local authorities by the Ministry of Health in case of massive casualties. A Treforest man, Leading Signalman Francis Brinley Batten, aged 28, was among the 99 men who died when the submarine *Thetis* sank in Liverpool Bay on her trial run on 1 June 1939. She was beached on the Anglesey coast a month after the war started and recommissioned as *Thunderbolt*, but lost with all hands off Sicily in March 1943.

In 1936 Hitler sent troops into the Rhineland in violation of the

Locarno pact. In Spain, General Franco started the civil war by landing his nationalist troops, the fascists, at Cadiz to engage republican forces. Hitler occupied Austria in March 1938. The *South Wales Echo* carried a picture in March 1939 of a barrage balloon at Cathays Park in Cardiff and in May a photograph of anti-aircraft guns practising there. On Friday 1 September 1939 Hitler invaded Poland.

War declared

At 11.15 a.m. on Sunday 3 September 1939 thousands of people in Pontypridd and its villages sat by their wireless sets to listen to the broadcast from the Cabinet Room of 10 Downing Street by the Prime Minister, Neville Chamberlain. He announced:

> This morning the British Ambassador in Berlin handed the German Government a final Note stating that unless we heard from them by eleven o'clock that they were prepared at once to withdraw their troops from Poland a state of war would exist between us.
>
> I have to tell you now that no such undertaking has been received, and that, consequently, this country is at war with Germany ... You may be taking part in the fighting services or as a volunteer in one of the branches of the civil defence. If so, you will report for duty in accordance with the instructions you have received.
>
> You may be engaged in work essential to the prosecution of the war, for the maintenance of the life of the people—in factories, in transport, in public utility concerns, or in the supply of other necessaries of life.
>
> If so, it is of vital importance that you should carry on with your jobs.
>
> Now God Bless you all. May He defend the Right. It is the evil things that we shall be fighting against—brute force, bad faith, injustice, oppression and persecution—and against them I am certain that the Right will prevail.

CHAPTER TWO

Into Battle

In late August 1939, telegrams went out calling up the Royal Navy, Army and Royal Air Force reservists and the Territorial Army. All Civil Defence units were mobilised on 1 September 1939. On the first day of the war, Parliament passed the National Service (Armed Forces) Act which made all fit men aged from 18 to 41 liable for call-up to the Forces. This was later extended to include men up to 51 and unmarried women between 20 and 30. Conscripts would be paid a shilling a day and their wives at home would get 15s. a week. The rates immediately went up to 1s. 6d. a day and payment to wives increased by 2s. a week as long as the husband allocated 3s. 6d. a week out of his own money. The Schedule of Reserved Occupations issued in 1939 exempted many men from military service, but gradually various trades or professions were removed from the list or the age of reservation was raised. The individual deferment or postponement of service of key workers replaced the block group system. Exemption could be claimed on grounds of religious or other beliefs. About 3,500 conscientious objectors were given unconditional exemption, 15,000 were allowed to perform duties of a non-combatant nature with the Army and 29,000 were exempted provided they worked in agriculture.

It was decided that it would not be appropriate to hold the annual Armistice Festival of Remembrance that year. The first casualties of war among local men in the fighting services were announced in December 1939 when Petty Officer Albert Jones of Garth Hill, Gwaelod-y-Garth, and Marine Gunner Aegean Stubbs of Stow Hill, Treforest, were killed in HMS *Exeter*, one of the three cruisers engaged in the Battle of the River Plate against the German pocket battleship *Admiral Graf Spee*.

Many other local servicemen were killed in action through the long years of war and their names are remembered on war memorials in Pontypridd and the district. Many others were wounded or taken prisoners of war by the Germans and by the Japanese to languish for years in brutal prison camps. A number of local soldiers imprisoned by the Japanese were members of Cardiff's own 77th Heavy Ack-Ack Regiment, Royal Artillery. Some of the men, including Bombardier Haydn Jenkins of Greenfield Cottages in Church Village, did not survive their captivity. Those who did could speak of cruelty and privation. One prisoner who survived his captivity in Japan was RAF airman R.W. (Bill) Thomas of Howell Street, Cilfynydd, who spent time in a camp situated between Hiroshima and Nagasaki, the cities destroyed by atomic bombs in August 1945.

The families of many local servicemen (including the family of Gunner Thomas Powell, 239 Battery of the 77th HAA, of Oakland Crescent, Cilfynydd, who was a prisoner of the Japanese) have much cause to thank and remember Miss Daisy Colnett Spickett, then of Merthyr Road, for her help in arranging American and British Red Cross parcels for them during the war. She was highly respected in Pontypridd, the town of her birth, for her caring during the depression years of the 1920s and 1930s and she founded the Old Bridge Community Centre in 1926 to help the unemployed. Miss Spickett was later an Old Bailey barrister and lived in Kensington Gardens in London; but she always kept in contact with her many friends in Pontypridd. She died in June 1978, aged 85. Her parents were James E. Spickett, solicitor and clerk to the Pontypridd Burial Board, and Mrs Sarah Louisa Spickett who was a former president of the Pontypridd Women's Liberal Association.

Winston Churchill became Prime Minister on 10 May 1940 to lead a National Government and said that he had nothing to offer but blood, toil, tears and sweat. People everywhere worked hard for victory. They toiled in the factories and mines to increase output and were more full of energy and defiance and community spirit than ever before. Undeniably, that was the picture, too, in Pontypridd.

In June, after the evacuation from Dunkirk when more than 335,000 troops escaped from the beaches of France in Royal Navy ships and thousands of small private boats, Churchill vowed in his usual stirring wartime rhetoric that we would defend our island. In the House of Commons on 4 June 1940 he said: 'We cannot flag or fail. We shall go on to the end. We shall fight in France; we shall fight on the seas and oceans; we shall fight with growing confidence and growing strength in the air. We shall defend our island whatever the cost may be. We shall fight on the beaches; we shall fight on the landing grounds; we shall fight in the fields and in the streets; we shall fight in the hills. We shall never surrender ...'.

In the House of Commons on 18 June 1940 Churchill reviewed the question of the imminent invasion of Britain and said:

> I expect that the Battle of Britain is about to begin. The whole fury and might of the enemy must very soon be turned on us. Hitler knows that he will have to break us in this island or lose the war. If we can stand up to him all Europe may be free and the life

of the world may move forward into broad, sunlit uplands. But if we fail then the whole world, including the United States, including all that we have known and cared for, will sink into the abyss of a new dark age ... Let us, therefore, brace ourselves to our duty, so bear ourselves that if the British Empire and its Common-wealth last for a thousand years men will still say, 'This was their finest hour'.

The battle intensified through August and September 1940 as the German Luftwaffe tried to gain mastery of the air over Britain as a prelude to invasion. Rumours spread throughout the country that the invasion had started. The pilots of RAF Fighter Command strained and died to prevent the reality and prompted another memorable Battle of Britain speech from Churchill on 20 August 1940:

The gratitude of every home in our island ... goes out to the British airmen who, undaunted by odds, unwearied in their constant challenge and mortal danger, are turning the tide of world war by their prowess and by their devotion ... Never in the field of human conflict was so much owed by so many to so few.

The blitz of London and provincial towns and cities began. The air raid sirens sounded often here in Pontypridd, and members of civil defence organisations and the public watched and waited and expected destruction and devastation from the air.

Invasion looms

Signposts and street names in Britain disappeared in June 1940 to frustrate an invading army. But servicemen and women and civilians soon wanted the restoration of some of them and they began to reappear a year later. (By June 1944 most were restored.) By July 1943, with very little private motoring possible because of petrol rationing, taking the train was the only way to travel any distance. But the call-up of 100,000 railwaymen had left the railways seriously undermanned and the Ministry of Labour directed men and women into working on the railways. The shortage of good quality fuel reduced the efficiency of steam locomotives. Trains became dirtier because of inadequate maintenance. Rail travel was made very difficult by the absence of many name signs on stations. And journeys in the darkness of the blackout sometimes frustrated passengers. One railway poster advised, 'If you can't see the [station] name and can't hear the porter's voice, ask another traveller. If you know where you are by local signs and sounds, please tell others in the carriage.' In the booking hall at Pontypridd GWR station a large publicity poster depicted a soldier pointing at you and asking, 'Is your journey really necessary?'

Civilians became more closely involved in the war on 14 May 1940 when the Secretary of State for War, Anthony Eden, broadcast an appeal for men aged between 17 and 65 to join a new force of Local Defence Volunteers (LDV). He said that large numbers of men were wanted. It would be a part-time job, so there would be no need for any volunteer to abandon his present occupation. When on duty he would form part of the armed forces. He would not be paid but would receive a uniform and would be armed. A notice in the *Pontypridd Observer* on 25 May 1940 signed by Captain E.B. Beech MC of 67 Taff Street asked that all persons owning motor lorries or motor cars who would be prepared to lend them for the purpose of transporting members of the Local Defence Volunteer Force in the event of emergency, and all owners of motor-cycles who would be prepared to act as despatch riders, be good enough to send in their names and addresses immediately.

The LDV was renamed the Home Guard in July. By then, more than a million had joined. The LDV and the Home Guard made-do with a forage cap and a khaki armband with black lettering in the early days until uniforms started to trickle in. On 17 February 1942 a new law made Home Guard duty compulsory and men liable to prosecution if they failed to attend for 48 hours of training a month. Men who worked all day in factories, mines, shops and offices changed into their uniforms in the evenings and gathered at parades and trained in serious Dad's Army readiness for the awaited 'Eagle Day' German attacks (the day of the enemy 'maximum effort' came on 13 August 1940) which the enemy had planned to lead up to their operation 'Sea Lion' invasion of Britain. (The day it was due to start was later revealed as 15 September 1940.)

In June 1940 a Ministry of Information leaflet, 'If the Invader Comes', warned that the Germans threatened to invade. Ordinary men and women would have their part to play and must not be taken by surprise. When Holland and Belgium were invaded, civilians fled from their homes. They crowded on to the roads, in cars and carts, on bicycles and on foot, and this helped the enemy by preventing counter-attacks. If the Germans came, by parachute, aeroplane or ship, people should remain where they are. If it is decided that the place where you lived must be evacuated, you would be told when and how to leave. If you ran away, you would be exposed to far greater danger because you would be machine-gunned from the air. You would also block the roads.

The code word 'Cromwell' would be flashed to military commanders if an invasion was imminent or happening. In their invasion, the Germans would create confusion and panic by spreading rumours and issuing false instructions. People should not believe the rumours or spread them. When you received an order, you should make quite sure that it was a true order. Most people knew their policeman and ARP warden by sight and could trust them. They could also tell whether a military officer was really British or only pretending to be so. If in doubt ask the policeman or the ARP warden. (On a calming note, an advertisement advised that 'in these times of extra tension, build up your nerve reserves with Ovaltine'.)

The leaflet warned that our troops and the Local Defence Volunteers could not be everywhere at once. Ordinary men and women must be on the watch. If you saw anything suspicious, go at once to the nearest policeman, police station, or military officer and tell them exactly what you saw. Be calm and try to give exact information about the time and place. If parachutists came down near your home, they would want you to give them food, means of transport and maps. They would want you to tell them where they have landed, where their comrades were, and where our own soldiers were. Do not give any German anything. Do not tell him anything. Hide your food and your bicycles. Hide your maps. See that the enemy gets no petrol. If you had a car or motor bicycle, you were to put it out of action when not in use. It was not enough to remove the ignition key—you must make it useless to anyone except yourself. It was said that any Nazis who landed on Welsh shores would be dealt with 'as the occasion demanded' for the country was at war and the kid glove method was a thing of the past.

People might be asked by military officers or LDV authorities to help in many ways: for instance, to block roads or streets in order to prevent the enemy from advancing. Road blocks usually consisted of oil drums filled with concrete. But never block a road unless you are told which one you must block. Then you can help by felling trees, wiring them together or blocking the roads with cars. If you were in charge of a factory, store or other works, you should organise its defence at once against sudden attack. If you were a worker, you should know in advance who is in command and make sure you understand the system of defence organised and know what part you have to play in it. Make certain that no suspicious strangers enter your premises. Remember always that the best defence of Great Britain is the courage of her men and women. Think before you act. But think always of your country before you think of yourself.

Ready with his gun

Some of the important purposes of the Home Guard were to observe, report and slow down any airborne attack by erecting road blocks to prevent parachute troops from linking up. Parachutists and invasion from the sea were genuinely expected. The Home Guard was important, too, for the sense of involvement in the war effort that it gave to its members. They had few firearms at first and armed themselves with broomsticks and wooden rifles and pick axe handles—some fitted with old First World War bayonets. Gun owners were asked for their help. Owners of lorries, vans and cars were again urged to lend their vehicles to Home Guard units. Several small concrete and steel forts known as pill boxes were constructed at strategic points in the district. One pill box guarded the Cilfynydd to Abercynon road near the Albion Colliery; one in Mill Street, near the Merlin Bridge, covered the road to the Rhondda; and one was sited at Llantwit Road in Treforest, on the hill by the School of Mines (now the University of Glamorgan).

Home Guards set up nearby road blocks made from round concrete blocks. They stopped buses and checked passengers for identity cards. If these were not offered, the Home Guard issued notes for offenders to produce them at a police station. Bryn Roberts (Market) of Merthyr Road recalls that people travelling, say, to the Rhondda from Cardiff could be asked what they were doing in the area. If anything seemed suspicious, arrests could be made. At the road blocks the emphatic 'Halt, who goes there? Friend or Foe?' startled the night at times. If the guard's next words were not 'Advance friend and be recognised' there could be a shot from one of the First World War Canadian .303 rifles issued to the Home Guard in Pontypridd and to many battalions of men throughout the country. The men of Pontypridd had bayonets for their rifles but did not possess any of the significant Lewis machine-guns.

Jim Rees of Ynysybwl tells that morse code was practised between Home Guard signallers on the colliery tips of the Albion in Cilfynydd and the Lady Windsor in Ynysybwl. The Cilfynydd Home Guard was once signalled that a parachutist was seen descending above Eglwysilan Mountain at Cilfynydd:

> The very young members of the Cilfynydd guard on duty that night made full haste in that direction. The blackout needs to be experienced to fully appreciate its effectiveness, but the young lads on their first 'active' mission exhibited little fear. After a mile or so travelling over rough and muddy terrain one of the youngest members of the guard, Joe Male, was confronted by an approach-

ing bulky figure. He had no live ammunition, but bravely he challenged: Who goes there! He had no reply; but as instructed Joe challenged three times. His challenges were ignored, and in a confident but staggering gait the figure lurched out of the darkness towards him. When almost on top of him Joe lunged with his bayonet stabbing the advancing man in the arm—the only occasion blood was drawn by a member of the local Home Guards. The victim turned out to be a local who was 'drunk as a coot'. The signal transmitted to Lady Windsor guard was 'Mission accomplished, thanks!' Joe's act was highly commended by his commanding officer. The guards were informed later that the parachutist seen and reported by Ynysybwl guard was a British airman who had been obliged to eject and had landed safely.

There were reports that the airman, Pilot Officer Ralph Havercroft, had baled out over Maerdy. His Spitfire crashed near Llanwonno. He came to earth on the Cilfynydd mountainside in the direction of Llanfabon.

When an air raid warning siren sounded, Home Guards in the town reported to their headquarters at the sandbagged White Hart Hotel (now Silks Nightclub) on the Tumble. Stores for the town battalion were issued from the White Hart. Bryn Roberts was one of the men engaged on such duties and for the administrative work of attending to daily Standing Orders and the issuing of instructions. Volunteer cyclists enrolled here to carry urgent messages. Men of the town were seen many times marching four abreast on parades through the town and on their way for practice at the rifle shooting range sited just behind the School of Mines. Sandbagged machine-gun emplacements dotted the area villages at vantage points. Army lorries, armoured cars and bren gun carriers were familiar sights on local roads at times during the war.

Pontypridd Home Guard (2nd Glamorgan Battalion) had two full-time officers: Captain Ernest B. Beech MC, Adjutant, and Captain W.A. Jacob (a stockbroker). The Sector Commander was Colonel W. Lester Lewis, magistrates' clerk. The third anniversary of the founding of the Home Guard was celebrated with a parade and drumhead service. More than 1,200 men of the 2nd Glamorgan Battalion paraded through Pontypridd. Representatives accompanying some of the Civil Defence services included Superintendent Howell Rees and Inspector W.E. Jones, police; Column Officer John, National Fire Service; Dr Tudor Williams of Cilfynydd and Superintendent Clift, St John Ambulance; Major S.B. Watkins, Army Cadets; D. Milton Jones JP, ARP Services Wardens; Chief Inspector Evan John, Special Police; and Mrs R. Stanley Evans and Mrs Godfrey Thomas, Civil Defence Ambulance Drivers. The nationally renowned ATS band headed the procession and the Ynysybwl Silver Band and the St John Ambulance Band also attended.

The parade numbered more than 2,000 and marshalled on the Broadway with Lt-Col. T.A. Cousins, Officer Commanding the battalion, in charge. It headed for Ynysangharad Park and marched past Col. Lester Lewis who took the salute outside the swimming baths. He was accompanied by a number of officers, Cllr C. James (chairman of the council) and other civic dignitaries. The parade, which included Lt-Col. W.H. Edwards MC, the second in command of Pontypridd Sector, and many platoon officers and headquarters staff, assembled on the rugby field for a service conducted by the Revd T.E. Rogers (chaplain) of St John's, Graig. The officer commanding congratulated the battalion, urged continued devotion to duty and read an Order of the Day before the parade reformed and marched back to the Broadway for dismissal.

Col. Lester Lewis congratulated the battalion on their smartness and bearing, and all the officers, NCOs and men for their consistent devotion to duty over the past three years with the result that they had reached their present standards of efficiency. This was an occasion for looking back and realising how different their position now was from the dark and perilous times of mid 1940:

> The nations for whom we fought were crushed and broken by the might of Germany and we said as we faced what appeared to be a hopeless prospect: 'Very well, alone!' And we prepared our meagre resources to meet the onslaught that appeared certain and imminent. And then overnight, almost, you came into being. I remember how you came in your hundreds to answer the call and with next to nothing except that stoutness of heart you always had and that always will be yours, prepared to meet an enemy armed with all the weapons of modern warfare ... Whether victory be around the corner or whether the road be long we will stick together to the end. I would like you all to think when the horrors of war are over and you walk in peace again that you as Home Guards did your duty as strong men armed and helped in no small measure to keep our house in peace and our country inviolate.

By the summer of 1943, nearly two million Home Guards served in more than 1,000 battalions. During the war, 1,206 members of the Home Guard were killed.

There was a Home Guard unit at Ynysybwl commanded by Major Gwilym Gower, and the Brown Lenox Chainworks had its own platoon.

A unit was organised at the Albion Colliery in Cilfynydd for weekly drills under former army Sgt J. Jackles. The Cilfynydd Home Guard, under Lt-Col. W.H. Edwards of Richard Street and Lt Jack Howells of Oakland Terrace, could often be seen on route marches from the village to Fiddlers Elbow, near Quakers Yard, and back to their drill hall in the red brick building in Richard Street (at the rear of the old Richards Arms) or to their guard room at the Cilfynydd Inn. Lt Charles Burgess was also in the Cilfynydd unit in 1941. Many exercises took place near the old Cilfynydd GWR station which had been demolished in January 1940.

The Cilfynydd Home Guard held periodic dances at the village social (or unemployment) club in Park Place and at the Workmen's Hall in Howell Street to support fund raising events, as did other local Home Guard units in their villages, and these social get-togethers created a feeling of great comradeship in the Pontypridd area. The Cilfynydd Home Guard held their first dance at the local Workmen's Hall in November 1940. Their dance in February 1941 at the local social club was in aid of the Cilfynydd Home Guard Rugby Club. On Christmas Day in 1941 the team played Cilfynydd RFC at the Welfare Grounds in aid of the local Prisoner of War Fund. A lemon sent by a serviceman in North Africa was raffled in aid of the fund when Cilfynydd RFC played a select Cardiff XV in April 1943.

Locally, there was probably the only Mounted Home Guard unit in the country, formed by farmers from Eglwysilan and the surrounding area.

The real Dad's Army

D-Day veteran Harry Hartill of Elm Street, Rhydyfelin, tells that he wrote a letter to the *Pontypridd Observer* in September 1989:

> To many, *Dad's Army* (the television series) is a huge joke, a half hour of laughs and spills. Yet, in the spring of 1940, the Duke of Lancaster's Own Yeomanry, a cavalry regiment, was being transformed into an artillery unit and moved into Pembroke Castle and Llanion Barracks at nearby Pembroke Docks.
>
> I'm not sure of our total strength, but when the air raid sirens sounded we could all crowd into the boiler house under one of the barrack buildings. We had a mixture of uniforms, some in battle dress, a few in cavalry breeches, some in old style tunics with brass buttons and caps. A member of the regiment was Arthur

Lowe, later to become Captain Mainwaring of *Dad's Army* fame.

We arrived in the barracks in an assortment of civilian vehicles, two Morris Minors, a Standard 12, and a military Humber Snipe. We also had a furniture van with the name W.E. Evans on the side and a flat-backed fruiterer's lorry which had a huge board behind the driver's cab saying 'Persil' in huge letters. Our armaments were half a dozen rifles without firing pins, one Lewis gun which only two of us were permitted to fire, and a six-inch Howitzer which had probably seen service in the Boer War and bore a brass plaque on the barrel saying 'property of Birmingham Parks Committee'. This was what we had to defend Pembroke Dock with.

When German parachutists were reported landing in the vicinity we piled into the furniture van armed with sticks to go and round them up. We had no contact with the Air Force but when an enemy plane passed over the town we placed white canvas strips like an arrow pointing the direction taken. This was to help our own planes if one happened to pass. Our Lewis gun was mounted on a tripod and surrounded by sandbags, being manned twenty-four hours a day, though we were not allowed to fire during the hours of darkness.

The CO did receive a letter from a nearby Air Force station. The pilot was congratulating us on our aiming but added would we please confine our shooting to enemy planes only, as his plane had several holes in it. On August 19 I watched a German plane drop a stick of bombs on nearby oil tanks. The fire was to last three weeks and claim the lives of five Cardiff firemen. We went on our flat-backed lorry to dig slit trenches in which the firemen might shelter from machine-gunning planes. When we left Pembroke for the quiet of Pontypridd, the fires were still burning.

Our furniture van came to grief when we descended the Graig Hill and took the top off as we passed under the railway bridge on the Tumble. Arthur Lowe, who must have gathered valuable knowledge at this time for the *Dad's Army* series which followed, was billeted at Treforest, probably in the Boys' Club or Roman Catholic Church Hall until 1941. Looking back, we must have been the original *Dad's Army*.

6. *Left:* Ministry of Health warning, spreading the word to the factory. *Right:* Poster recruiting for one of the toughest wartime jobs. (*Crown Copyright*).

7. 'A' Company, 2nd Battalion (Pontypridd) Home Guard, 17 May 1941.

8. *Above:* Cilfynydd Home Guard had their guardroom in the top room of the Cilfynydd Inn (photo 1957). *Below:* Bottom of Richard Street, Cilfynydd, looking towards Cilfynydd Inn and road to Abercynon. A large high explosive bomb fell (middle distance) on the Common in 1940, near to the tip landslide of 1939 (photo 1957).

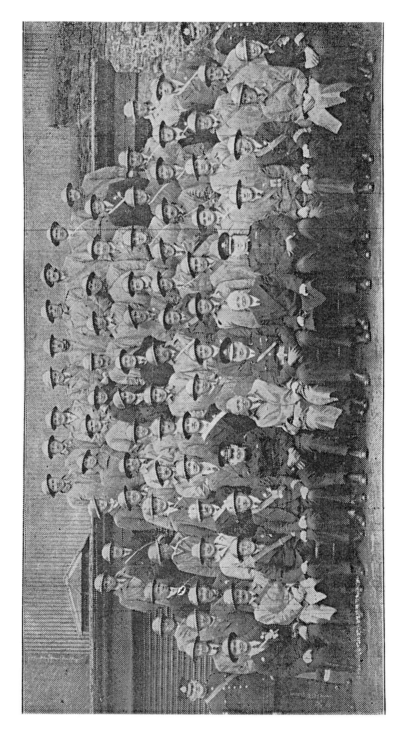

9. Pontypridd and Treforest Special Constables. spring 1940.

10. *Left*: Special Constable Albert Hogarth, based at Treforest police station, and his wife Nurse Hilda Hogarth, who helped nurse some of the Dunkirk wounded treated at Pontypridd Cottage Hospital in 1940. *Right*: Rose Mantle, one of the many wartime PUDC bus conductresses, pictured in the 1940s. She then lived on the Broadway.

Beating the invader

In May 1941, when Britain was still threatened with invasion, the Ministry of Information issued a leaflet on 'Beating the Invader'. It contained some rules for civilians and a message from the Prime Minister, Winston Churchill, who said that if invasion comes men and women of all ages would be eager to play their part worthily. Along our coasts where the enemy lands there would be most violent fighting and, apart from essential workers who must remain, the fewer civilians in these areas the better. If the authorities advised you to leave the place where you live, it was your duty to go. Otherwise it would be your duty to stay where you were and get into the safest place you could find until the battle was over. This would also apply to the people inland if parachutists landed in their neighbourhood. Above all, roads must be kept clear. There was no doubt that the Home Guard, supported by strong mobile columns where required, would soon destroy the invaders. In the rest of the country where there was no fighting going on or no close firing was heard everyone had a duty to 'carry on'. It could easily be some weeks before the invader was totally destroyed, that is to say, killed or captured to the last man.

The leaflet also told you what to do if fighting broke out in your neighbourhood: stay indoors or in your shelter until the battle was over. So much the better if you could have a trench ready in your garden: you might want to use it for protection if your house was damaged. But if you were at work, or if you had special orders, carry on as long as possible and only take cover when danger approaches. If you were on your way to work, finish your journey if you can. If you were in areas away from the fighting, stay in your district and carry on. Go to work, whether in shop, field, factory or office. Do your shopping, send your children to school until you are told not to. Do not try to go and live somewhere else. Do not use the roads for any unnecessary journey. Take orders from the police and ARP wardens. There might be times when you will have to take orders from the military and the Home Guard in uniform.

The ringing of church bells was banned in September 1940 except on orders of local military commanders to signify invasion. Ringing of bells would give warning to the local garrison that troops had been seen landing from the air near the church in question. Bells would not be rung all over the country as a general warning that invasion has taken place. The ringing of bells in one place would not be taken up by other nearby churches.

So far as was possible, instructions would be given over the wireless.

They would also be given in newspapers, by loudspeaker vans and perhaps by leaflets and posters. Genuine government leaflets would be given out only by a policeman, ARP warden or postman. Genuine posters and instructions would be put up only on notice boards at official sites, such as police stations, post offices, ARP posts, town halls and schools. During any temporary breakdown to news supply, people should not listen to rumours nor pass them on. They should not use telephones or send telegrams. If small parties of the enemy threatened you or your property in an area not under general enemy control, you have the right of every man and woman to do what you can to protect yourself, your family and your home. People should help our troops and not tell the enemy anything or help him in any way.

The Royal Observer Corps, a uniformed but voluntary civilian organisation, was formed in 1942 when there was no radar. Men watched for aircraft through binoculars, identified and tracked them, and reported their details to air controllers so that our fighter planes could be directed to the right place. The unit in Pontypridd was sited in Penycoedcae. D.G. Ball was Head Observer and Corps members included Matthew Cohen, Enos Ford (secretary of Pontypridd Chamber of Trade), Frederick Jones, and Trevor Jones of the water board. Many special constables enrolled in the Pontypridd area and often their wives enrolled for war work in one of the voluntary civil defence units to play a part if they were able. Some were in the Women's Auxiliary Police Corps, the National Fire Service, and the Nursing Reserve. One special constable was Albert Hogarth, at one time of Dyffryn Crescent in Rhydyfelin. His wife, Mrs Hilda Hogarth, worked in the Red Cross. She helped to nurse wounded servicemen admitted to the Cottage Hospital on the Common on their return from Dunkirk. Miss Thelma Hogarth, their daughter, now Mrs Thelma Jones of Llanover Road, still has preserved her mother's Red Cross uniform, white with its significant emblem, and a dark blue hat with a thin white band. Thelma, a pupil of Pontypridd Girls' Grammar School, recalls helping out in her parents' shop in Princess Street, Treforest, during the war, counting out the thousands of tiny coupons cut from ration books, and later attending an agricultural camp run at Fontygary, near Rhoose, where many young people worked and helped to 'Dig for Victory'.

The St John Ambulance was very active in Pontypridd. The Brigade was inspected on a glorious Sunday, 22 June 1941, at Ynysangharad Park by the Duchess of Kent who met many dignitaries and ambulance personnel and presented long service awards. The St John Ambulance band helped to make the day memorable. Firewatching was on the agenda of a Pontypridd Chamber of Trade meeting convened at the New

Inn Hotel in February 1941 to consider the steps to be taken to protect their premises under the new Fire Prevention (Business Premises) Order 1941. W. Harold Jones, president of the chamber, presided and H. Leonard Porcher, clerk to the council, explained in detail the statutory obligations. He gave his private opinion that in view of the proximity of Pontypridd to the coast it was likely that the order would be applied to the town shortly. Under the order, the first duty of every person responsible for business premises was to his place of business or employment rather than to his private residence. On the motion of William Berriman a resolution pledged businessmen present to prepare adequate schemes immediately—Pontypridd had already seen an air attack and was in the flight path of intruding enemy bombers raiding Cardiff and Swansea.

Men born in 1900, the first of the 41 to 45 age group, registered on 21 June 1941 in readiness for military service. In the House of Commons on 2 December 1941 Winston Churchill announced that men up to the age of 51 would be liable to call up. All men up to the age of 64 could be directed into essential employment. Boys and girls aged from 16 to 18 would be registered and encouraged to join one of the several organisations in which they could obtain training for national service. Two Pontypridd pensioners, both aged 70, were inadvertently called up for the Welch Regiment. In September 1942 the RAF wanted men up to the age of 55 as clerks, barbers and cooks; and others aged between 42 and 50 for training as armourers, flight mechanics and motor mechanics. Women drivers aged between 30 and 45 were wanted in the ATS and the WAAF.

Bevin Boys

The mining industry suffered a depleted workforce and in July 1943 Ernest Bevin, Minister of Labour, dropped a bombshell on delegates at the Miners Conference when he proposed calling up boys over the age of 16 to work down the mines. The announcement was received in silence and miners were opposed to the proposal. Bevin directed that one in ten of all 18-year-old youths registering for national service should go into the mines. In November 1943, Bevin announced that the compulsory conscription of boy miners was to be effected by impartial ballot. Previously, young conscripts had been able to state a preference for one of the armed forces. Many of the boys brought in were unwilling recruits and Bevin quickly realised that compulsion was bound to produce a discontented workforce. Every young man on registering for National

Service at the age of 17½ was given a number that ended with a digit from 0 to 9. A number was then drawn out of a hat and all those whose registration ended with that number had no alternative but to go down the mines. This was a method which ignored all experience, education and physical abilities. Some 45,000 Bevin Boys went to the mines, though only about a third of them worked at the coal face.

In March 1944, a Bevin Boy refused to accept training for the mines and came before a court. He was sent to prison for three months. During March, 50,000 miners were on unofficial strike. One issue was over the 3s. 6d. a week deducted from their wages to cover the value of coal supplied for their own domestic use. Eventually mining peace was assured for the next four years. Wages were frozen until 1948 but the rates were consolidated and guaranteed. The agreement provided for an extra shilling a day for skilled craftsmen and for an increase in piece rates. Strikes were illegal in Britain from 1940 though there were some 2,000 a year. The biggest was at the Betteshanger Colliery in Kent where 1,000 underground workers went on strike in 1942 in a wages dispute. Three were jailed but soon released.

Women take arms

Women rarely saw their servicemen husbands or sweethearts unless the men managed to get leave passes of perhaps 36 or 48 hours. The women at home watched out anxiously for the postman and hoped he would not pass by without bringing longed-for letters from their loved ones. But the approach of a telegram boy charged one with rising horror: the telegram often brought news that a husband or son was reported missing or killed in action. Men in the lowest ranks of the services received pay of only 2s. (later, 3s.) a day. A wife with two children received only 25s. a week plus a compulsory 7s. deducted from her husband's pay. Many families in hardship sold their clothes ration coupons or took lowly paid work to survive. It was not until 1944 that an increase in allowances gave servicemen's families a reasonable standard of living.

At the beginning of the war, women were told to stay at home. They still had to fight long-standing prejudices against working alongside men or taking their jobs, but in 1940 Ernest Bevin, as the new Minister of Labour, urged them to find work in factories. He said that 'women had made a tremendous contribution to winning the last war and will be equally effective in this struggle'. Many Pontypridd women had volunteered for the Forces by April 1941 when those aged 20–21 and unmarried were ordered to register for war work. All unmarried women

and childless widows aged between 19 and 30 were brought in before the
end of the year and became compulsorily liable to call up to the Forces
or civil defence services or for work in factories. Women born in 1917
registered in June 1941. Married women were invited to join the services
and were liable to be directed into industry. By October 1942 all women
aged up to 45 were called for interview but no mother with children
under 14 was compelled to go to work. In February 1943 women made
up 40 per cent of all employees in engineering. In chemicals and
explosives, the most dangerous of all wartime jobs, 52 per cent were
women. One of the problems for them was the danger of their hair being
caught up in overhead machinery. The wearing of turbans became
general practice.

Pontypridd women, too, worked in munitions factories and local
engineering works; on the manufacture and assembly of aircraft parts and
machine-guns; and as welders, sewing machinists and in many other
essential wartime occupations at the Treforest Trading Estate and
elsewhere. Many people worked at the chemical works in the old
Treforest Tinplate buildings. Exposure to the chemicals used made the
skins of the workers become yellow. The *Pontypridd Observer* in its
issue of 25 October 1941 carried a front page official notice that 6,000
jobs were available for women in South Wales for munitions work. They
would be paid £3 a week for average 8½-hour days.

The war years gave women their first real opportunity to gain
independence. Many women war workers, now earning good money,
started going to public houses. They were not able to buy more clothes
because of rationing, and cosmetics were in short supply. So some spent
it on drink. The Chief Constable of Cardiff noted: 'Compared with
pre-war days, the women who frequent public houses exhibit a provoca-
tive spirit of independence in their spending.' The search for women
workers intensified. There was a shortage of domestic servants as they
had been directed to war work; and many previous employers found that
they now had to cook for themselves. In July 1943 all women aged 46
to 50 had to register for war work but they were promised that no young
families would be neglected as a result of any conscription order.

By July 1943 the problem of a woman's pay compared with that of
a man's had still not been settled. Trade unions objected strongly to a
semi-skilled woman already doing a man's job getting less per hour (1*s.*
3*d.*) than an unskilled man who swept the floor and earned 1*s.* 7*d.* The
aim was equal pay for equal work and the rate for the job. The unions
secured a basic minimum wage for women engineers so that their true
value was acknowledged. They also wanted better pay for part-time
workers who worked as much as six hours, five days a week for just 30*s.*

The unions advocated that if two women worked part-time six hours each, covering a full 12-hour day, their two pay packets should equal that of one full-time worker.

Under the National Service Act, many Pontypridd women served in the Forces and performed such vital duties as cooks, typists, clerks, chauffeurs, storekeepers, telephonists, teleprinter operators, dental and sick quarters attendants, and drivers of ambulances and heavy lorries. In the ATS (Women's Auxiliary Territorial Service) they also worked at searchlight batteries or at ack-ack units, locating targets for the anti-aircraft guns. In March 1942 the first women to be called up joined the ATS. The Queen, then Princess Elizabeth, served in the ATS in the last months of the war. In the WAAF (Women's Auxiliary Air Force) the recruits worked at balloon barrage units and as photographers, parachute packers, aircraft fabric workers, or plotted the movements of German raiders for interception by RAF fighter squadrons. They worked as aircraft hands in workshops, wireless operators and instrument mechanics. Many local WAAFs were trained at the RAF station at St Athan. In the WRNS (Women's Royal Naval Service) the women's tasks included maintenance work on naval aircraft, transporting buoys and other equipment, victualling or providing ships' stores and acting as stewards and signallers; and as writers and wireless telegraphists.

Posters urged volunteers to join the Women's Land Army, one of the toughest jobs undertaken by women in the war. They were not made welcome on most farms at first, but it was not long before farmers were crying out for them. The women worked on farms all over Britain and undertook everything from dairy work like milking and making butter and cheese to the heavy work of digging, planting, lifting potatoes and many other crops, threshing, ploughing and harvesting. And rat-catching when the bottom sheaves of corn were thrown up for threshing. They cut and pointed stakes for fencing and made hedges. Formed in June 1939, the WLA had 1,000 volunteers by the outbreak of war and 20,000 by 1941 when conscripts were added. The uniform was a felt hat, green sweater and brown corduroy breeches, but dungarees and wellington boots were worn most often. The girls were not paid as highly as the women in the services, and had no privileges such as free travel vouchers. For a 50-hour week, and even longer at harvest time, they earned about 28*s.* which increased by 20*s.* in 1944. A recruiting drive from February 1944 called for more land girls, who were needed as tractor drivers, milkmaids and for work in pest control. Girls had to be aged between 17 and 35. Their minimum wage was now £2 8*s.* a week, with extra food and lodging when billeted away from home. Many women also enrolled in the Women's Timber Corps.

In later years German and Italian prisoners of war worked on farms throughout Britain. Some Italian PoWs were housed in the old British Legion Club on Cardiff Road near the Dyffryn in Rhydyfelin. Schoolchildren also helped bring in the harvest and with other work. A number of Pontypridd girls spent some the summer of 1945 at an agricultural camp at Rhoose.

In August 1943 almost everyone who was not physically unfit or wholly taken up with household duties had a job of some kind. Then Ernest Bevin announced his 'grannies call-up'—the registration of women aged 46 to 50. Two hundred MPs signed a motion of protest and speakers of both sexes and parties in the House attacked it as a disaster. This was the first public sign of unwillingness to make more sacrifices. 'There is no intention of sending these women all over the country', Bevin said. He promised that no woman in this age group would be forced to neglect her family, and of 750,000 signing on, he expected to get no more than 75,000. He closed entry into the women's services, and the grannies were expected to take over the jobs of younger women.

'Ask the WVS!' was the cry when problems arose in Pontypridd or if help was needed anywhere. The local Women's Voluntary Services, under the direction of Mrs Hilda Porcher JP, had many volunteer workers. They could be seen all over Pontypridd in their green-grey uniforms, red jumpers, greatcoats, and felt hats with red trimmings as they busily helped in the organisation of local affairs. They collected salvage, recruited blood donors, sewed and knitted many clothes for the services, arranged street collections, acted as escorts to evacuees, ran a volunteer car pool. Two or three volunteers helped every day at the British Restaurant at Tabernacle Chapel in town. They helped in the domestic work at the Royal Air Force hospital at Church Village (later, East Glamorgan Hospital) and at other local hospitals and care centres, in collecting war savings contributions, transport duties, ARP services, evacuees reception, and distributing food parcels with the local Red Cross. The WVS was so efficient that by March 1943 plans were already being prepared to continue the work after the war. Now having 'Royal' in its title, the WRVS continues its work today and has its local office in Morgan Street.

The Red Cross organised a national 'Penny a Week Fund' of regular donations to buy comforts for servicemen and women and, like the WVS, had many people of Pontypridd knitting socks, sweaters, scarves and gloves for members of the Forces. Its wartime vice-president in Pontypridd was Mrs Holmes Watkins. The Red Cross served hospitals at Pontypridd (the Cottage on the Common), RAF Church Village, and Whitchurch. They visited the next of kin of mounting casualties to offer comfort and understanding and practical help, if possible; and with the St John Ambulance Brigade they acted as drivers and staffed blood transfusion centres. Their local headquarters moved in recent years from Morgan Street to Pentrebach Road.

CHAPTER THREE

Bombs and Blackout

Raiders overhead

The people of Pontypridd and surrounding villages often saw flames and searchlight beams light the skies towards Cardiff during the Second World War. They felt the thump of exploding bombs and the retaliatory anti-aircraft gunfire amid the throbbing engine drone of enemy bombers.

A single high explosive bomb fell on Cilfynydd Common (Craig Evan Leyshon Common) and blew a large crater near the right hand side of the road from the village to Abercynon. Thomas Hughes of Cilfynydd, working a night shift at the Albion Colliery, was in charge of First Aid and also the air raid siren which alerted the village at 1.30 a.m. He recalls hearing the thud of the bomb coming from the direction of the pithead baths. He said that about 1,300 men were working underground at the time. A direct hit by the bomb on the pithead windings could have caused a dangerous situation for the miners. More than a hundred surface workers took refuge in the colliery lamp room and sought some protection under heavy metal tables. He recorded that it was the night of 12 July 1940 and that the 'All Clear' was sounded at 1.50 a.m. In that July, during which a large crowd gathered one evening at the Workmen's Hall to get advice on what to do in an air raid, Tom Hughes received 38 early warning calls of the imminent arrival of raiders overhead. The number increased to 91 in August and 138 in September.

But if any German parachutists had landed, Tom Hughes was ready for them: all men holding a position of responsibility at the Albion Colliery were given a solid, carved truncheon to protect themselves from the might of the enemy. He told the *Pontypridd Observer*, 'I've never had to use my truncheon but it was always there as a standby. It's still as sturdy now as it ever was and you could have given someone a hefty clout with that.' He said that hundreds more evacuees had arrived in Cilfynydd during the previous weekend and that after the incident many wrote home to their families to tell them bombs had started falling. Many mothers then travelled from London to take their children home. At that time, he had two young girl evacuees staying at his home in Cilfynydd Road who were very frightened by the raid and hid under the stairs for safety. But they soon came to really like Cilfynydd and stayed in the village until the end of the war.

The first air raid siren sounded its alert over Cardiff at 11.55 p.m. on 19 June 1940. Within a month it wailed another 50 times there and locally and many bombs dropped on the city. Nearly 900 high explosive bombs and 2,400 incendiaries fell on the county outside Cardiff before the end of the year. Although Pontypridd lay in the path or turning circle of raiders attacking Swansea and Cardiff, it escaped the devastation and slaughter of such raids on its neighbours. It shared their grief. An air-raid siren was usually mounted on the roof of a high building or tower, and had two vanes of different pitch. A penetrating rising and falling chord sounded the 'alert'; and when regulated a sustained note gave the 'all clear'.

In July 1940 the *Pontypridd Observer* reported that the lady who was in the habit of cleaning her windows during air raid alerts should listen to the advice of the ARP wardens and take shelter at these times. Unlike the people of many British towns and cities, Pontypriddians did not have to emerge from their air raid shelters to find their houses were no longer standing and to face fire-gutted or demolished buildings in streets strewn with shattered glass. But the threat of imminent destruction was implicit in every warning air raid siren. Pontypridd town knew the wrath of German bombs on the night of Thursday 29 August 1940 at the height of the Battle of Britain. During raids lasting more than five hours when bombs fell over a large area of South Wales, Pontypridd was hit by a large number of incendiary bombs and 13 high explosive bombs which dropped near the Lan Wood reservoir and along Lan Park and Tyfica Road. One exploded at McVicar's quarry (named from Hubert McVicar of Quarry Bank Manor) near 'Jacobsdal' just off Pencerrig Street in Graigwen. Several houses and villas suffered slight damage and some boundary walls collapsed. One high wall blew down beside the crater close to 'The Grange' in Tyfica Road. Flying glass splinters caused a few minor injuries.

Incendiary bombs fell on the village of Hopkinstown where local ARP (Air Raid Precautions) wardens and the police quickly put out the fires which threatened to reach a nearby oil-storage depot. D.J. (Jim) Rees of Ynysybwl remembers the incendiaries that fell on Crockett Place dwellings in Hopkinstown, and the efforts of the ARP to contain them. He is one of the pupils of Pontypridd Grammar School who recall that it was school the next morning, and many of them had to pass the home of E.R. Thomas, the headmaster, where they saw the shattered windows of his home and the other homes in and near Tyfica Road. They had to crawl around or over the crater in the road and also be careful of the collapsed walls close by. The headmaster's opening words at Assembly were: 'Well I'm sure you are all pleased to see that I have survived.' They brought a crescendo of booing from the pupils, that emphasised the respect and esteem in which they held him.

It was considered at first that the bombs had been jettisoned by returning aircraft, but later thought to be unlikely. Hugh Trivett of Porth, from his research and records of German night raids and daylight raids over South Wales, notes there much overhead activity in the Pontypridd area on those late August nights of the Battle of Britain. Apart from the bombing of Welsh targets by large and concentrated bomber forces, there were many intrusions of single aircraft, or twos or threes. These were known as 'nuisance' raids by night and 'pirate' raids by day. The object was to cause as much interruption to normal life as possible: one aircraft could bring many stoppages of production, disturb sleep, undermine morale through a constant need to take cover, and put the civil defence units and air defence services under strain. The aircraft also sought targets to emphasise their cat and mouse game while feeling that they were relatively safe. Records show that most of the German raiders that operated over the valleys here were Heinkel 111 heavy bombers from Group KG 27 based in Northern France. The group carried out hundreds of missions—especially on the Eastern front after Germany attacked Russia on 21 June 1941. One pilot had made more than 80 missions over Britain, including 50 over South Wales.

The night skies of Pontypridd filled with constant engine noise of the raiders—especially on 10 July and 1 September 1940 when waves of bombers dropped thousands of incendiaries and then high explosives in attacks on Swansea. The skies to the west glowed red from the fires; they did so again on three successive nights in late February 1941 as Swansea was ravaged by more than 800 heavy bombs and an incalculable number of incendiaries which killed 227 people, destroyed hundreds of houses, shops, offices and factories, and damaged 12,000 houses. Treforest Industrial Estate, with its factories busy on wartime production, escaped attack throughout the war; although its potential as a target is clear from two aerial photographs taken by the German Luftwaffe in February 1941 and now lodged in the offices of the Welsh Development Agency. One indicates the Upper Boat power station as a target. A large parachute mine was aimed at the target one night but blew a significant hole on nearby Mynydd Mayo. The huge explosion was heard in shelters all over Pontypridd and district. A Corona advertisement by Thomas & Evans of Porth told that 'when you are in an air raid shelter, Corona lemon barley or apple crush will keep you cheerful'.

Pontypridd was kept awake and alert by the sounds of raiders and the loud explosions of bombs and mines throughout the bitterly cold night of 2–3 January 1941 when Cardiff was blitzed. The warning sirens sounded at 6.37 p.m. By 7 p.m., fifteen great fires raged in the city. Bright parachute flares pierced the red dome of the sky. 165 men, women and children were killed and 427 were injured that night. Nearly 350 houses were destroyed and 7,000 damaged. Parachute land mines drifted down in and around the city and one shattered the roof and tip of the spire of Llandaff Cathedral. Debris badly damaged the interior of the cathedral. There were other air raids on the city in the following months and on a night in March 1941 more than a hundred high explosive bombs fell on Penarth. Another fierce raid on Cardiff on 18 May 1943 killed 45 people and injured 128. More than 4,400 houses and shops were damaged. The attack was considered to have been a revenge raid for the great RAF 'dambuster' raids on targets in Germany the previous night: Wing-Commander Guy Gibson VC, the leader of the raid on the Ruhr dams, was known to have relatives living at Penarth.

In his speech broadcast on 27 April 1941 Winston Churchill, the Prime Minister, referred to the ordeals that enemy bombing caused the people of Britain and he paid tribute to the courage and fortitude of the civilian population:

> And I went to some of our great cities and seaports which had been most heavily bombed. I have come back not only reassured but refreshed. To leave the offices of Whitehall, with their ceaseless hum of activity and stress, and go out to the front, by which I mean the streets and wharves of London or Liverpool, Manchester, Cardiff, Swansea or Bristol, is like going out of a hothouse on to the bridge of a fighting ship. It is a tonic which I should recommend any who are suffering from fretfulness to take in strong doses when they have need of it.
>
> It is quite true that I have seen many painful scenes of havoc and of fine buildings and acres of cottage homes blasted into rubble heaps of ruins; but it is just in those very places where the malice of the savage enemy has done its worst and where the ordeal of men, women and children has been most severe that I found their morale most high and splendid.

There were many daytime sightings of friendly and enemy aircraft in Pontypridd skies: British Spitfires and perhaps, too, Hurricane fighters were often seen flying up the valley below the height of Coed Craig-yr-Hesg from north of Pontypridd to Abercynon. One Spitfire crashed just beyond Ynysybwl towards Llanwonno but the pilot survived. Near Porth Square, the Free French pilot of a Spitfire based at RAF

Llandow in the Vale flew very low and crashed to his death into the hillside about 200 yards from the road to Trebanog. Some recent excavations there by Colin Gibbon of Graigwen and Hugh Trivett of Porth found evidence of the crash when they unearthed some camshafts and other engine and fuselage parts.

One morning at Pontypridd Golf Club in 1941, two golfers walked along the second fairway to where they had driven their tee shots when a German Junkers 88 appeared out of the patchy low cloud. The bomber was flying so low that some crew members could be seen in the aircraft. It flew westward after it seemed to have just cleared the top of Eglwys-ilan mountain near Paddy's Well, beside the old Roman Road above the fields of Bodwenarth Farm. The sound of machine-gun fire (or perhaps the engines missed) made the two men drop their golf bags and dive for cover in the rough. Frustratingly for them, nothing more was known—except that both missed their putts on the second green.

In the direction of Cilfynydd the fairway overlooked the fields above Coed Bodwenarth, known locally as 'Egan's mountain'. At the junction of some stone walls was an old barn which was the haunt of many youngsters from Cilfynydd, Pontshonnorton (Pontsionnorton) and Coedpenmaen. One resident who often played there had special memories of the place:

> Looking back, I suppose I must have seen one hundred and one of them. Yet when the fete started there was only one dalmatian. Now, more than 50 years after the end of the war, I still recall and cherish my bond with the dog that had a battle to survive.
>
> The fete was held in a field at Bodwenarth Farm in Cilfynydd in the long hot summer of 1940. Money was needed for the Spitfire Fund launched after a string of bombs had fallen on Pontypridd during the Battle of Britain. Generous hands clapped the sheepdogs showing their craft. Pennies tumbled on to the stalls of jumble. Jingling harness added its music as the tradesmen's decorated carts lined up in the adjoining lane for judging. The sun shone. Everything was going beautifully—until a cloudburst of flying ants swarmed on to half-crunched toffee apples and over people's faces and hair and clothes. Everybody scattered. We boys and girls bolted over the stile and along the path to an old barn where our own band of Just William outlaws often played. Looking out from the barn roof, we saw someone crouching in the double-terrace of drystone wall enclosures crumbling on a nearby rise. He turned to reveal the shiny buttons of a local special constable.

We thought he must be tracking the local rabbit poacher or maybe some of those German parachutists we were warned about. All we spotted were grazing sheep and a dalmatian. We realised that the policeman was trying to coax the dog from an adjacent sty where it stood panting and in distress. The dalmatian padded away from him painfully and came slowly into the barn. I was still up in the rafters when the policeman came into view below. He smoothed the dalmatian gently and lovingly and told the wary trespassing onlookers that the dog had stowed away on one of the low-slung carts from the village. Such a bumpy journey was extremely dangerous for her in her condition.

He explained to everyone simply and patiently that the dalmatian was almost nine weeks into pregnancy which was the reason for her enlarged belly. One moment the bitch was being watched over very carefully at home in the seclusion she'd sought on two old blankets in a corner and the next moment she'd vanished. Perhaps she'd been frightened by something and had bolted. Nobody knew. The dalmatian was of proud pedigree and the puppies could be born at any time. The animal needed to calm down. She needed quiet.

I shouted haughtily that of course I knew all about whelping and things like that, for my dog Flint had reared puppies. And that the dalmatian would be thirsty. There was an old bucket in the stream down by the big black pipe and our barrel 'searchlight'. There was some sacking here in the barn to place over the hay.

The copper ordered me down and to be quick about it. But I clambered along a beam, intending to crawl to a lower roof before scampering away. I didn't make it. But the loft ladder broke my fall into the laughing group below. I hoped the copper wasn't going to handcuff me but he was intent on cleaning a badly cut paw. What about me? I needed to support my collar bone and could have done with some sympathy. But everyone was only concerned with the dalmatian. Then we watched in wonder as the first beautiful puppy was born and cared for.

'Why ain't it got any spots?' someone asked. The answer that these would appear after a few days was barely heard above the sudden roar and whine of aircraft overhead. Everyone ran to the barn door at what sounded like the rattle of gunfire to see what was happening, except for the copper and the dalmatian and me. Suddenly, there was a loud bang and the barn seemed to vibrate madly as the plane screamed low over us. 'It was a Spitfire chasing a Heinkel!' shouted an evacuee from the blitz, as an air raid siren wailed belatedly along with the pit hooters down in the valley.

The last of the puppies was born during the 'All Clear' and everything was peaceful and quiet for the new family after the havoc and disturbance of war. I cried out as pain seared through my shoulder. But nobody took any notice—except for the friendly dalmatian who looked up at me for long moments with sympathy and understanding. Her eyes looked blurred with tears like mine as I whispered to her of my distress. A large sheet of polka dots dilated before my eyes and as I swayed and pitched forward I could see a large pack of dalmatians running round and round the barn. I learned later that puppy number one had been named 'Spitfire Pursuit'. It was a pedigree name for the first of the few.

The rumbling engine noises of enemy bombers in the night skies created unforgettable memories for Pontypriddians. Listening closely, they also picked up mysterious sounds at times: whistles, whines, crackles. A young man from Oakland Crescent leaving the Workmen's Hall in Cilfynydd one evening stood on the steps for a moment to accustom his eyes to the blackout when he heard a strange, quickly moving 'shushing' sound pass low overhead and arc down to the nearby meadows of the River Taff. He searched a wide area the following morning, looking for perhaps a crater made by an unexploded bomb or some shrapnel for his collection, but found nothing.

Children were frequently warned not to pick up any suspicious-looking objects. Three boys from Treherbert in the Rhondda were killed and two injured in July 1943 when an object they were playing with exploded on the mountainside. It was believed to have been a bomb or one of the anti-personnel devices thought to be dropped in many areas by enemy bombers. High explosive and incendiary bombs were dropped on the Rhondda and in a raid in 1941 the people killed included three evacuee children from the London blitz.

In September 1940 a man who pleaded guilty to using an indecent expression was fined £3. He told Pontypridd Police Court magistrates that he was sorry, but there had been an air raid on at the time and his nerves were on edge.

Look out in the blackout!

After sunset, the streets of Pontypridd settled into pitch darkness. 'Look out in the blackout' warned the publicity posters issued in the first months of the war. Posters appeared all over Pontypridd—in factories, shops and offices, banks, the market, foyers of cinemas; in dance halls, schools, railway stations, post offices and public buildings. A poster of safety rules advised that 'when you first come out into the blackout you should stand still for a few moments to get your eyes used to the darkness'. But people took chances. They played a deadly game of roulette. It wasn't far—just a few yards across the road and perhaps their bus was coming. So they gambled and ran for it. Hundreds of people in Britain were killed or injured every week in the blackout. In the first week of the war, Jack Fry of Jones Street, Cilfynydd, suffered severe leg injuries when he was knocked down by a car with its lights greatly dimmed. Road accident deaths doubled in the first weeks of war and Pontypridd did not escape. In October, Coroner David Rees gave a warning to motorists to go slowly in blackout conditions when he conducted an inquest on an Upper Boat pensioner who died following a road accident. And in that month, eight-year-old William Raymond (Billy) Powell of Oakland Crescent, Cilfynydd, was killed instantly by a van close to blackout time as he crossed the road near the trolley bus stop at King's Garage or Quarry Siding on Cilfynydd Road. Through the first few months of the war, the blackout was a greater menace to civilians than any action by the enemy.

During the early wartime blackout years, road deaths nationally increased by a thousand or more each year. In 1941, the number of deaths passed 9,000. A new speed limit of 20 mph after dark in built-up areas was introduced from February 1940. From the summer of 1940 and for the rest of the war, learner drivers could drive alone and without displaying 'L' plates.

There were other casualties of the blackout: when Pontrypridd Urban District Council bus driver Stanley Barnes walked to work from his home in Middle Street in Trallwn to the depot at Glyntaff at about 4.30 a.m. in one of the earliest blackouts of the war, he stumbled over a body in Pentrebach Road. He and depot employee David Evans braced themselves for whatever scary bundle would be revealed in the dim torchlight. They found the victim to be one of the marauding sheep which soon became menaces in most local villages after dark.

For fear of air raids, the blackout began on Friday 1 September 1939, two days before war was declared. Small white posters headed 'Lighting Restrictions' were stuck on boardings and telegraph poles and lamp posts. The blackout enforcement lasted from half an hour after sunset to half an hour before sunrise. All street lighting was extinguished. Houses and shops and other buildings in Pontypridd and the villages had their windows heavily curtained. Compartments were darkened in trains. You could shine a torch only if the light was thrown down to the ground so that drivers would not be dazzled; but the torch glass had to be masked by two thicknesses of tissue paper to reduce the beam to a diffused glow so as not to attract enemy airmen. There were several prosecutions for breaking this law. And in March 1942 the guilty person who had bought a torch, with its precious battery, for 2*s*. 11*d*. had used celluloid. The magistrate pointed out that anyone selling a torch had a duty to tell buyers that they could only be used with a paper covering.

Car drivers and the urban district council bus drivers could hardly see you even if you wore a white coat or wore a white armband and carried a newspaper as the authorities advised: the headlamps of road vehicles, masked with black shields, allowed only a small amount of light to show through three small slits. Side lights and rear lights were dimmed, usually with newspaper. From the beginning of the war, motorists painted their car bumpers and running boards white, as ordered. White lines appeared down the middle of the road for the first time in general. Roadside tree trunks had rings of white paint. So did lamp posts and traffic bollards. Pedestrians were asked not to walk on the white-painted curb edges in the town as these were very important for the guidance of night traffic. Cyclists suffered from the shortage of batteries as rear lamps were compulsory in addition to the usual red reflectors on mudguards. A curved mask on bicycle front lamps gave only a small glow to light the road ahead. An order made it obligatory for prams to have rear lights fitted and, in May 1940, four rather bewildered Pontypridd women were summonsed for not complying.

Local bus drivers coped well with the difficulties and hazards of driving in the blackout and keeping to their time schedules and were praised by their employers and the public. To ensure the prompt departure times of all local single- and double-decker trolley buses and motor buses, the crews synchronised their watches with the official Transport Department clock known as 'The Bundy', set in its green case on a shop wall in the Ynysangharad Park entrance opposite Mill Street. The clock governed the whole UDC transport system and the working lives of local bus crews. One driver, David J. (Dai) Morgan of Dyffryn Avenue in Rhydyfelin, started work as a conductor on the local electric trams in 1926. On his first day, he bought a watch in Pontypridd Market for 1*s*. 11*d*. which kept strict time with the Bundy until he retired. The clock appeared in recent years at the front of the Municipal Hall. The Pontypridd UDC Transport and Rhondda Transport shared the Pontypridd to Porth route and the crews often had a quick cup of tea in a little cafe next to Garfield's Army Stores, now part of the Woolworth store.

Life was not easy on the Pontypridd buses. The *Pontypridd Observer* reported that some bus passengers were taking advantage of the blackout by passing dud coins to the conductor when paying their fares, an act the newspaper described as 'mean and despicable'. Interior light bulbs in some buses were removed from alternate sockets and those remaining were sometimes painted blue, so that a bus packed with coal-dust blackened miners sitting on the wooden-slatted seats of the wartime 'utility' buses gave an unreal or a surrealistic scene. Mrs Rose Mantle, a wartime bus conductress who then lived on the Broadway, remembered buses with only one dimmed interior light—which had to be put out if an air raid warning siren sounded. Like others, she had a small torch fastened to her tunic to throw light on her ticket rack and money satchel. Rose, latterly of Dynea Close, Rhydyfelin, was known by her many friends to have a fond love of wild birds and wild flowers throughout her long life.

The men and women bus conductors rigorously enforced the new national regulation of April 1942 which, following complaints that people were not able to get on buses without a struggle, made it compulsory that 'when six or more people are waiting they shall form and keep a queue, not more than two abreast'. The old free-for-all scramble to get on at crowded bus stops ended in the war. Chaos sometimes alighted on the Treforest to Cilfynydd trolley bus route when the trolley power booms or poles came off the overhead wires and shot up into the night—all askew. The conductor probed the darkness with a long bamboo in a hit or miss affair to hook the trolley heads of the poles back on the wires. One notorious spot for trolley buses to be stranded in the darkness was at the foot of Fothergill Street in Treforest where buses turning towards the Machine Bridge for the depot had to make a wide and exact sweep until a manual switchover device operated nearby in later times. A certain law ensured that if the trolley bus poles came off the wires in daytime they would choose to do so in the narrowness of Taff Street on a busy market day. To back up the trolley bus fleet, two double-decker trolley buses on loan from Hull entered service in August 1941. Flashes from trolley bus wires sometimes frightened you in the blackness of the night.

Passengers on the 'Ponty buses' easily found a rapport with the crews; and regular travellers had their favourite conductors or drivers and liked to see them on the journeys. Busmen and women during or just after the war included: Bill Banwell, Arthur Barnes, Stanley Barnes, Charles Beer, Ernie Bull, Roy Bull, Eddie Cummings, Ruby David, Les Davies, Rees Davies, Tudor Dorke, Mal Edwards, George Emery, Beryl Evans, Gwilym Evans, Jack Evans, Tom Evans, Eddie Harrigan, Olive Hunt, Harry Jacobs, Hector Jacobs, Phyllis James, Bryn Jones, Mel Jones,

Ernie Kerslake, Horace Lambert, Jack Lambert, Charles Lethbridge, Tudor Lewis, Wyndam Lewis, Dick Lucas, Kate Mahoney, Rose Mantle, Bill Masson, Fred Masson, George Minty, Dai Morgan, Haydn Morgan, Tom Murphy, Albert Nicholls, Harry Nicholls, Bill Owen, Ray Passmore, Reg Perrott, Glyn Pritchard, Ivor Pugh, Archie Purnell, Charles Purnell, Jack Rowsell, Ernie Scaplehorn, Alf Smith, Griff Stephens, Bill Thomas (two), Phyllis Trembath, Jack Trevor, Phyllis Voicey, Cliff Walker, Ernie Webb, Alf Workman. For a long period the Transport Manager was John Powell and his deputy was George Ludlow.

The Pontypridd UDC Transport Department had a fleet of 58 buses at the end of the war and employed 60 conductresses among their staff. Their number decreased as men returned from the Forces. PUDC buses daily transported many of the 10,000 workers employed in the 100 factories on the Treforest Trading Estate.

Passengers on local trains faced many wartime difficulties and changes. Carriages were not lit for the first few months of the war, though conditions improved from 1940 when dim lighting was allowed. Window blinds drawn as an extra blackout precaution also gave some little protection against possible flying glass during air raids. On the Pontypridd GWR station platforms, porters carrying shrouded lanterns loomed out of the darkness to escort the many passengers between stacks of milk churns and piles of mail bags. Women worked along with men at local stations as porters, ticket collectors and train guards. In the booking halls, servicemen returning to camp after being home on leave and workmen off to the local mines and factories were still confronted in 1943 with those large posters telling them to search their consciences and consider 'Is your journey really necessary?' Crisp graffiti replied to one such poster displayed at the new station halt (which opened in January 1942) at the Treforest Trading Estate. The cosy platform refreshment rooms at Pontypridd were lit cheerfully with the help of reflecting mirrors. The windows were heavily blacked out and the doors covered to form a 'light trap' like an airlock.

One bonus from the blackout was a more widely realised beauty of the sky at night. Because of the virtual absence of street lighting many Pontypriddians rediscovered that the heavens were hung out brightly with a myriad of stars and planets and constellations. On clear, moonless nights the great belt of the Milky Way was often dimmed by a lesser galaxy of searchlight beams from batteries sited on Mynydd Mayo (Meio) near Eglwysilan and towards Cardiff and the west. There were searchlight batteries, too, behind Glyncoch towards Ynysybwl and Llanwonno. Moonlight was welcomed to light the way down on earth but it was often a bomber's moon and a threat of danger from the skies.

11. *Above:* Spitfire fighter. One of various types of aircraft seen in the skies of wartime Pontypridd. *(Imperial War Museum, CH 2930). Below:* Hurricane fighter. Another Battle of Britain winner. *(Imperial War Museum, MH 3186).*

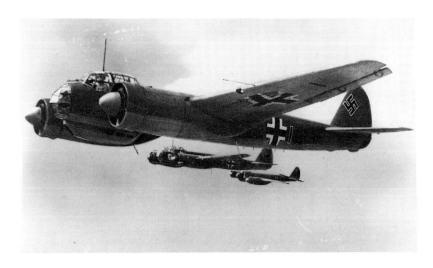

12. *Above:* German Junkers 88 fighter-bomber. (Imperial War Museum, MH 6115). *Below:* German Heinkel 111 bomber. *(Imperial War Museum, GER 1427).*

Taff Valley at Pontypridd.

13. Looking towards Pontypridd in the 1950s. Centre is Lewis Terrace fronting the Victoria Recreation Grounds off Berw Road. In 1940 high explosive and incendiary bombs fell above the railway line and along Lan Park and Tyfica Road.

14. General view of Pontypridd, probably in the 1930s, showing parts of Graig, Graigwen, Pwllgwaun and the town.

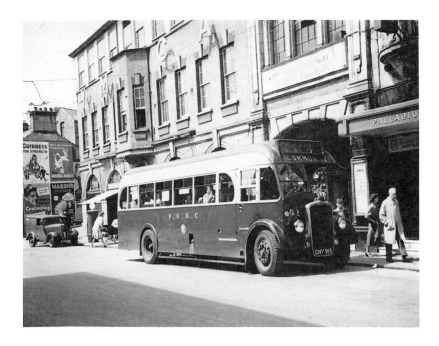

15. *Above:* One of the top class six-cylinder PUDC petrol buses outside the very popular Palladium cinema, now the site of a supermarket, *c.* 1948. *Below:* Motor bus in front of Tredegar Arms and J. Eason's shop just across the road from the YMCA in Taff Street. Crosswell's wine shop and off-licence seen on corner of a road to the one-time cattle market (*c.* 1948).

Danger lurked in the dark streets of Pontypridd. People tripped over dogs and cats and kerbs, toppled over low walls and railings, and bumped into letter boxes and lamp posts. They got lost in the blackness and often had to peer at the numbers on the doors of terraced houses throughout the district to determine which door was their own. Mischievous children played at being ghosts or skeletons or knocked on a succession of doors as they scampered along a terrace and escaped retribution into the night—unless they ran into a burly policeman at the corner. A judicious swipe from his cape deterred the wrongdoers from offending on his patch again. To recall a local limerick:

> Beware the big copper in Trallwn
> Who uses his cape for a baton
> Knock doors on his patch
> And you'll certainly catch
> A bump you won't get a hat on.

You always had to look out in the blackout! Pontypridd's stipendiary magistrate warned that hooliganism in the blackout would not be tolerated and he would impose maximum sentences on offenders.

A lady living in Pontshonnorton Road found it easy and quite pleasant to walk about the blacked-out village on moonlit evenings; but on starry nights with no moon she could merely make out the silhouette of a person approaching. Arriving at her house on one such night, she looked towards the Thomas & Evans shop knowing that her husband would be among the passengers getting off the trolley bus after work. As the silhouette loomed up close to her she put her hands out together and over the man's face while letting out a ghostly shriek which had the desired reaction. She took him by the hand and led the way up the front steps and into the dark passage. She opened the door to the living room, and they walked in to find her husband reading a newspaper in the candlelight.

Windows in shops, offices and homes were blacked-out with shutters or curtains of dark cloth or paper in accordance with advice given in a leaflet issued from the Lord Privy Seal's Office in July 1939 and distributed to every household. It included details on how to mask windows and said, in effect, that one of the great protections against the dangers of air attack after nightfall would be the blackout. On the outbreak of hostilities all external lights and street lighting would be totally extinguished so as not to give hostile aircraft any indication of where they were. But this would be fully effective only if everyone played a part, and saw to it that no lighting in the house was visible from the outside. The motto for safety was 'Keep it dark'. Occupiers of rooms, houses or flats would be responsible for darkening their own lights. The most convenient way was the use of close-fitting blinds made of any thick, dark-coloured material. Otherwise, the windows could be obscured by sheets of black paper or thick brown paper mounted on battens. Thick curtains of suitable material would serve if they covered the window frames with a bit to spare all round. If blinds were already fitted they could be painted some dark colour. If the blinds did not fit closely, the edges of the window panes could be painted all round with dark paint. Lights should be shaded to prevent any light falling directly on the window. It might be simpler to make skylights, fanlights, and glazed doors permanently obscure by applying coats of paint, or pasting them over with thick brown paper. Make sure no light showed when the front or back door was open. Fix a curtain in the passage or in the hall to form a 'light lock'. Otherwise, the light must be switched off before the door was opened. Things should not be left until the last minute or it might be difficult to find the materials needed.

Some blackout material made of 44-inch wide black linen was sold in Pontypridd in 1942 at 1*s*. 6*d*. a yard and made effective blackouts. Window panes were criss-crossed with lengths of sticky tape or paper to prevent flying glass splinters. Many shops in Taff Street had small lit signs in their doorways to reveal their identity. Some pubs and hotels had candles or other lights in biscuit tins hanging outside in which the letters O-P-E-N were cut out. The sign 'No Beer' very often greeted patrons on the doorstep. Some concessions for shop window lighting that allowed lamps in containers to direct the light upwards and downwards but would cast no reflections on the street helped to brighten festivities for the first wartime Christmas.

Cracks of light inevitably appeared in blackout screens or people just forgot to draw the blackout. The local ARP warden would soon be on the scene to explain to the offender that, 'Your blackout is showing.' As the zeal of the wardens increased, their more familiar shout of 'Put that b— light out!' echoed in the streets. Smokers in the streets were frequently warned to put their cigarettes out, although the scarcity of cigarettes and matches soon made more effective 'wardens'. A Home Guard officer was fined 10*s*. 6*d*. for allowing the glow of a cigarette to be visible during an air raid warning. The first prosecutions for contravention of the blackout regulations locally were reported in the *Pontypridd Observer* of 23 September 1939. Some offenders were fined 10*s*. and others £1. It was suggested in the town that the council remove both the gas and electricity meters of people found guilty of not obscuring lights during blackout times.

There were many early appearances in Pontypridd courts for a range
of contraventions of the blackout regulations: several factory owners at
the Treforest Trading Estate were summonsed. A Maesycoed woman was
fined 4*s.* for failing to obscure a light in her home and a man was fined
£1 for lighting a match in the street. The actions of ARP wardens
enforcing the blackout regulations were generally supported or accepted
but some people resented them: a Treforest woman in court in August
1940 for not obscuring her lights said that she thought wardens were
dictators and nuisances. A man was fined a total of 20*s.* for 'failing to
obscure an aperture on a motor omnibus and failing to paint side
reflectors with white paint'. Another Pontypridd man was fined £20 for
showing a light during an air raid warning in June 1940. And in January
1942 a man was fined £40 for exceeding the speed limit during the
blackout. Later, a Cilfynydd woman fined 10*s.*—for allowing the light
from a candle to flicker momentarily in the small panes of her front door
as she shepherded her small children back to bed after sheltering under
the stairs—scolded magistrates that they should be with her husband
'missing in the jungle with the Japs'.

The blackout virtually came to an end from dusk on Sunday 17
September 1944 when 'half-lighting' became legal. It was necessary only
to curtain windows so that objects inside a building were not distinguish-
able from outside. Direct lights were still forbidden and it was intended
that a full blackout would be enforced again if air raid sirens sounded.
Regulations were relaxed slightly for car headlights and better street
lighting was permitted. The total abolition of the blackout in Pontypridd
took effect from 24 April 1945 when the lights came on again all over
the town.

CHAPTER FOUR

On the Ration

The leaflet issued in July 1939 said it was very important that at the outset of an emergency people should not buy larger quantities of foodstuffs than they normally bought and required. The government were making arrangements to ensure that there would be sufficient supplies of food, and that every person would be able to obtain regularly his or her fair share; and they would take steps to prevent any sudden rise in prices. If people wished, and were able to lay in a small extra store of non-perishable foodstuffs, there was no reason why they should not do so. They would be an additional insurance. But people should collect them now and not when an emergency arises.

Ration books were issued to all men, women and children in October and November 1939, the commonest ones being a 'General' book for adults and children over six and a 'Child' book for those under six. Books contained pages of coupons for the first five foods likely to be rationed and pages of spare coupons to be used for other foods rationed later on. The holders had to register with their chosen shop or shops for the rationed foods. The retailer detached a counterfoil from the book and this was his warrant to apply to the local food controller to buy supplies for the total amount he was permitted. The urban district council clerk, H. Leonard Porcher, was the Food Controller for Pontypridd and the deputy clerk, Isaac Edwards, was his deputy controller. National Registration Identity Cards, which were to be carried at all times, were also issued. New ration books were available throughout the war from the Food Control offices in Crossbrook Street, and in the building at the foot of Penuel Lane which housed the local board offices and urban district council in Victorian and later times.

When the consumer bought the foods, the shopkeeper cut out (or, later, marked or stamped) a coupon from the book which corresponded to the ration supplied. The task of counting many thousands of tiny coupons soon overwhelmed shop assistants. Rationing during the First World War had not been introduced until half way through the war—allowing supply and demand to regulate prices which resulted in the cost of food in the shops rising by about 60 per cent. In the Second World War the rationing of butter, bacon, ham and sugar began on 8 January 1940. The amounts of most personal ration entitlements fluctuated throughout the war: supplies depended greatly on imports which were affected by shipping losses through U-boat activity, particularly heavy during the fury of the Battle of the Atlantic in 1942 and 1943 before the constant submarine menace was defeated.

Food rations

Initially, the weekly butter-only ration was four ounces. Later, the total weekly fat ration including margarine and cooking fat was eight ounces, maximum. By July, the ration dropped to six ounces. Early in 1941, when food supplies had deteriorated, the eight ounces weekly ration of fats included not more than two ounces of butter. Things eased from 10 March 1941 when four ounces of butter could be included in the fat ration; but it did not last and it was back to two ounces at the end of June. The bacon or ham ration of four ounces weekly seemed adequate at first in many local households, but the lack of rashers to supplement other meals quickly became evident. The bacon ration increased to eight ounces at the end of January 1940.

After the Ministry of Food said that if each consumer restricted purchases of sugar to just one pound a week there would be enough supplies available for months, the weekly ration for sugar proved a disappointing twelve ounces and the use of sugar for icing cakes was prohibited. It was not easy for cooks to come up with alternative ideas. The use of sugar for making marmalade was also banned. In May 1940 the sugar ration was reduced to eight ounces but with some extra sugar allowed in one month for jam making. For four weeks from 30 June 1941 a double ration of sugar encouraged people to make more jam if they wished. In March 1941 jam, marmalade, syrup and treacle were rationed at two ounces for a week.

Meat rationing started on 11 March 1940 with just 1s. 10d. worth for adults and 11d. worth for young children—the weight varying with the consumer's choice of quality. On 6 January 1941 the weekly ration was cut to 1s. 6d. worth, including all offals previously off-ration. The meat in some houses in peace-time would have made a mere single helping, so a small Sunday joint would have taken virtually all a family's meat coupons. Housewives had to ensure they made the most of the joint over several other days. To make things worse, a week later the ration was reduced to 1s. 2d. worth and then, from 31 March, to only 1s. worth—about eight ounces—plus 2d. worth of corned beef, a meagre portion, although things were even tougher seven years later. From 9 June 1941 all offals—hearts, liver, kidneys, tongues, sweetbreads and tripe—were not rationed, nor were sausages, meat pies and pastes, brawn, jellied veal and similar. But sausages and meat pies in particular often stayed concealed 'under the counter' for favoured customers. Rabbit poachers did a brisk trade in local village pubs, where farmers often caught up with them.

Evan Hopkin Smith farmed at Cwrt-y-Celyn on the mountainside overlooking Upper Boat, the woodland of Forestnewydd and the fields of the old Gellihirion Farm where the Tesco superstore is now sited. From time to time he drove his flocks of sheep to the cattle market in Pontypridd. With his faithful dogs guiding the way, Evan's journey took him past the old Rose and Crown Inn on Eglwysilan and along the road to Penheol-Eli Farm close to the clear spring water of Paddy's Well. The road then dropped steeply beside the Pontypridd Golf Club and hugged the foot of Ty Gwyn hillside down to the Common before falling steeply again down to the Corn Stores hill to the Llanover Arms, where there was once a toll gate, before crossing the Old Bridge to the site of another toll house—the Crosswell's wine shop. Gates once stretched across Taff Street from here. Between the shop and the old Tredegar Arms a road named River Street (also called Ford Street and Turnpike Road) led down to the cattle market. This area now forms part of the car park at the rear of the Taff Vale Shopping Precinct. The war years knew little motor traffic in the streets to cause any difficulties for the drover and his animals.

A cheese ration of one ounce a week started in May 1941 but was increased in June and stood at about two ounces for much of the war. From August 1941 an extra eight ounces ration was given to miners and agricultural workers who took their food to work. At one time, the cheese ration increased to three ounces and in July 1942 to eight ounces (one pound for heavy manual workers). In July 1943 it reduced from eight to six ounces a week and by February 1944 it reduced again to only four ounces.

Most people thought the tea ration of a mere two ounces a week was the unkindest cut of all. But in June 1940 the Ministry of Food asked everybody to use less tea, and to avoid waste and so save on shipping space. A packet of one brand of tea called 'Goldbag' from the Meadow Dairy could not have been more aptly named. There was no tea ration at all for children under five from 27 July 1942, and this blow was undoubtedly more of a misery for older members of a family. From 6 April 1942, the office tea ration was cut by half to eight ounces a week for 20 workers.

Chocolates and sweets went on ration from 26 July 1942 at two ounces a week. After nearly a month, it improved to three ounces and stayed at that amount. The 'Personal Ration Books' issued contained pages of E coupons valid for two ounces and D coupons valid for one ounce. A two-ounce bar of chocolate cost 2½*d*. but also two coupons. Milky Ways faded away but a similar type bar called Starry Way was yours for just 1¼*d*. Lord Woolton, the Minister of Food, stopped the manufacture of all ice cream and for most of the war years children put up with a strange substitute made mainly from arrowroot, condensed milk and water. For many youngsters, condensed milk just spooned from the tin was a treat. All schools were brought into the School Milk Scheme on 1 August 1942.

Rationing of chocolates and sweets made children almost forget what big bars of chocolate used to look like—but not quite: Mrs Florence Baker who lived in Oakland Crescent in Cilfynydd ran a Samuel Driver mail order catalogue from before the war and a couple of friends of her two sons Douglas and Ronald could watch together the opening of the big Christmas parcels that arrived. They sat expectantly at the round table with its chenille tablecloth while the contents were unwrapped, and the boys well remember the mouth-watering delight of seeing their own orders of huge blocks of Cadbury's chocolate, which cost 1*s*. 6*d*. worth of saved-up pocket money. It seemed though that things down in the sweetshop would never be the same again, but at least it would be Christmas Day in the morning.

Because of the shortages of full cream milk, manufacturers used separated milk and called the product 'blended chocolate'. At times a chocolate wrapper was merely a single sheet of grease-proof paper. Some milk chocolate labels were overprinted in black to indicate the correct contents. Red Kit Kat wrappers changed to a wartime blue, showing that it was made with plain chocolate. Many Pontypridd people recalled their (childhood or adult) wartime likings. Some were: Barker & Dobson; Barratt's Paradise Fruits, triangular Ration Bag of sweets and nuts and popcorn, and Snooker Balls; Batger's Vanilla Fudge; Cadbury's Blended, Coffee Creme, Milk, Fruit & Nut, Whole Nut, Milk Tray, and Ration; Duncan's Hazelnut; Fry's Crunchie, and Milk Sandwich; Hitler's Match—mint rock in a likeness of an elongated Swan match box but depicting a soldier, sailor and airman; Mackay's ARP Toffee; Mackintosh's Quality Streeet, and Rolo; Mars; Nestlé's Blended, Plain, and Superfine; Pascall Saturday Assortment; Rowntree's Dairy Box, Kit Kat, Smarties, and York; Terry's Empire, and Oliver Twist; Tobler National Service dessert chocolate. And lots of penny bars of toffee, chocolate, liquorice and nougat.

Food rations varied throughout the war. A general summary of the amount for an adult for a week in about 1942 was as follows: butter 2 oz (57 grams), which could never be spread thickly on toast; margarine 4 oz (114 g), usual for sandwiches, unless for cooking; cooking fat 4 oz (114 g), but the ration was often cut by half; cheese 4 oz (114 g), plus extra 8 oz for heavy manual workers; bacon 4 oz (114 g) or ham, which looked skimpy in the frying pan; meat 8 oz (227 g), an average 1*s*. worth, depending on cut; plus corned beef, 2 oz (57 g) value about 2*d*.; sugar 8 oz (114 g), plus occasional extra for jam-making; jam 2 oz (57 g), part of 8 oz weekly preserves ration; tea 2 oz (57 g), with coupons often traded to make another cup; sweets 3 oz (85 g) or chocolate (and no ice cream); milk, two or three pints (946 g or 1,420 g) as available; eggs, one a week or more likely one a fortnight.

Demands on shipping space prevented imports of poultry feed and so there were fewer eggs in the shops and hence you were lucky to get one egg a fortnight. Tins and packets of 'Dried Egg' powder appeared in the summer of 1942. Milk supplies were reduced, partly because of transport problems, and 8 oz tins of dried skimmed milk powder known as 'Household Milk' were distributed on ration as a welcome supplement from November 1941. The precious tins had labels with blue stars and red and white stripes of the USA flag. You sprinkled four level tablespoons of the powder slowly into a pint of lukewarm water while beating with a whisk or wooden spoon to make the equivalent of fresh milk. It was illegal to give fresh milk to pets.

You also committed an offence if you gave bread to wild birds. Bread was not rationed until after the war but a standard, beige-coloured loaf was introduced in February 1941 and price controlled at 8*d*. a quartern loaf, or four-pounder. The Ministry of Food tried to make popular the 'National Wheatmeal Loaf' made from flour of 85 per cent extraction—compared with 73 per cent extraction for ordinary white flour—but the bread was greatly disliked. An advertisement in the *Pontypridd Observer* urged shoppers to go to Hopkin Morgan's to buy national wheatmeal bread for 'vitamins and victory'. By 1942 white bread was a rare luxury.

The destruction of many catering houses during severe air raids early in the war prompted the nationwide establishment of British Restaurants. Their purpose was to provide quickly served and nutritious meals for workers who lacked the time or immediate public transport to get home at midday. They also helped workers to avoid the belt-tightening effects of rationing and gave them a welcome supplement to their food rations. Another purpose they would fill was any need for the emergency feeding of communities in heavily bombed towns and cities. Winston Churchill objected to their proposed name of 'communal feeding centres' as he thought it smacked of old soup kitchens and defeat.

Fifteen hundred of the restaurants were operating throughout Britain when, in May 1942, local MP Arthur Pearson opened the 47th British Restaurant in South Wales. It was in the vestry of Tabernacle Welsh Baptist Chapel (now the Pontypridd Historical and Cultural Centre) adjacent to the Old Bridge. The Pontypridd British Restaurant proved an instant success and served more than 200,000 meals before the war ended. Its standards earned a high reputation with customers and the Ministry of Food. Meals were available for several hours from midday and consisted of meat and two vegetables, hot pudding and a cup of tea for the charge of 10*d*. With soup served on certain days the total cost was a shilling. Along with the actions to provide such meals, the Ministry of Food made an order on 10 May 1941 with restrictions against extravagance: it was an offence to serve or eat in a restaurant or hotel a meal having more than one of five main foods—meat, poultry or game, fish, eggs, and cheese. From 15 June 1942 the price of restaurant meals was limited to 5*s*.

Ten mobile canteens donated to Wales by people of Welsh ancestry living in the United States operated in towns which had suffered air attack. Pontypridd Women's Voluntary Services staffed one vehicle presented to the town.

Vegetables were not rationed but imported fruit became scarce or unobtainable, especially in 1940. It became more scarce in the following year—some oranges, for example, had to come to the shops through the sea battles in the Mediterranean. At the outbreak of war, leaflets in a 'Dig for Victory' campaign urged everyone to cultivate allotments for growing vegetables or there would not be any potatoes or greens for Sunday's tiny joint. The number of allotments had doubled by 1943. Householders were urged from the beginning of the war to 'Grow More Food' and to help the country's food supplies by keeping pigs and chickens. Smallholdings and garden lawns throughout Pontypridd were dug up for growing some of the three million tons of of food that came from allotments and private gardens in Britain during the war. Pesticide cartons carried swastikas and the slogan 'Tackle the Pest, Tackle him Early'. Government inspectors checked that professional nurseries grew not more than ten per cent of flowers, which were considered a luxury. 'Dig for Victory' posters and leaflets were reissued.

People grew vegetables on the banks of earth covering Anderson shelters and many felt guilty about brightening up the scene with more than the odd clump of flowers. A Ministry of Food notice in September 1941 said that 'food is part of the fight—food must be conserved as ammunition is conserved in a beleaguered city. If you were neglecting to produce all the food you could or were not preserving foods while they were in plentiful supply, then you were playing Hitler's game'.

Stanley Wells of Middle Street recalls an area of the cricket field in Ynysangharad Park given up for the campaign, from which the vegetables were in the main supplied to the British Restaurant in Tabernacle. Historically, there were allotments nearby on the site of today's tennis courts before Ynysangharad Fields became the park in 1923. (The courts in Victorian times were up by a road leading from Bridge Street to Brown Lenox chainworks.) During the winter of 1942 a glut of carrots prompted the Ministry of Food to launch a campaign claiming that eating carrots improved your night vision. It was widely believed. The idea, apparently developed as a cover story for Britain's airborne radar system, claimed that night fighter successes over the country were due to pilots eating lots of carrots and greatly improving their eyesight.

In September 1941 the Ministry of Food asked mothers to give their children sweetened swede and turnip juice as a substitute for orange juice. The Vitamin Welfare Scheme was launched throughout the country in December to guard against deficiencies in the wartime diet. It started with free supplies of blackcurrant juice and cod liver oil for children under two years old. Older children read in horror the newspaper advertisement of April 1943 that 'At this time of the year every child needs a spring clean with California Syrup of Figs'; the very sight of which made them want to run a mile. Rose hip syrup was on sale in March 1942 after a national collection of 134 million rose hips in 1941 yielded 200 tons of the syrup. Volunteer pickers earned 3*d.* a pound, paid on delivery of the produce to branches of the WVS and the Women's Institute. In September 1942 rose hip syrup replaced orange juice for babies after the Ministry of Health announced that rose hips were 20 times as rich in vitamin C as oranges.

The 'points rationing scheme' was introduced on 1 December 1941 and proved very popular. In addition to normal food rations, every ration book holder received 16 points a month, later raised to 20, to spend at any food shop. On their way to a big welcome from shopping queues were 30,000 tons of tinned meats, beans and fish. Fresh fish was not rationed but it was hard to find. A bigger selection of foods of varying points values was gradually added to a long list of supplies of tinned meats and fish and fruits which came under points rationing for several years during and after the war. The points system made it possible for Food Control authorities to include or exclude certain foods depending on what supplies the convoys of ships brought in. As the goods had set 'prices' in both money and points needed, the controllers could steer public demand in the direction required.

Much sought after was the large tin of American sausage meat which cost 16 points. Another favourite was American spiced ham or spam, the proper name being Supply Pressed American Meat. Cooks used it inventively for meals and sandwiches. In a ration book, A and B coupons were worth one point each, C coupons were worth two points—and shrewd housewives spent them with the greatest care while closely watching updated official lists of 'Changes in Points Values' in newspapers and many magazines to find bargains. At one time the total points in a rationing period increased to 24 but when new and simplified ration books appeared at the end of July 1942 the total had dropped to a disappointing 20 again, and syrup and treacle which were once on the jam and preserve ration now cost precious points. Biscuits were on points from 23 August 1942. There was a restriction on the range of fancy cakes available, and making chocolate éclairs was forbidden.

Spam with everything

Housewives made the most of spam. They cut spam sandwiches by the million every day during the war. Spam served as the meat in main meals instead of roast beef and lamb; and the pork in pork pies. The large tin of American sausage meat was one of the best buys: although the slab weighed a couple of pounds or so and took the whole monthly monthly ration of 16 points it was used ingeniously in most of the family's main meals. The thick layer of nearly 8 oz of fat in the tin was greatly welcomed for general cooking purposes.

The Ministry of Food's plump, potato-shaped character Potato Pete claimed 'I'll put pep in your step'. And when a glut of potatoes appeared in 1942 his message in the advertisements in newspapers and magazines was that 'potatoes when boiled are not fattening and are a rich store of all round nourishment'. Before the war, it was often said that potatoes were not very good for you. There was a Potato Pete Nursery Rhymes card illustrated with line drawings, no doubt designed to have a great effect on mother and child.

> Little Jack Horner
> Sat in a corner
> Eating potato pie.
> He took a large bite,
> And said with delight
> Oh, what a strong boy am I.
>
> Jack Sprat could eat no fat
> His wife could eat no lean;

So they both ate potatoes
And scraped their platters clean.

There was an old woman who lived in a shoe.
She had so many children she didn't know what to do.
She gave them potatoes instead of some bread,
And the children were happy and very well fed.

Potato and grated carrot could improve Christmas puddings, and you could save on eggs by mixing the puddings with bicarbonate of soda and milk. In 1943, potato powder, to just mix with water, was introduced to the Forces but none was allocated for home consumption. The Ministry of Food advertised the price of potatoes to wholesalers at £1 a ton.

Stocks were made from vegetables and bits of meat kept by, and thickened with oatmeal or beans. That stock-pot over the coal fire in Pontypridd homes was always ready for a hungry family when those dumplings, or perhaps croûtons baked from wheatmeal bread, were added. Watercress was collected from local woodlands to chop up and add to a saucepan of mashy, bland and—usually reheated—potato soup; though most housewives ensured that their family enjoyed soups that were nourishing and filling. Potatoes and greens were called 'home guards of health'. And you were constantly told: 'Keep them on duty in your diet'. Salad bases were created from young dandelion leaves, hearts of cabbage, shredded cabbage, and carrots tops along with those of radish, turnip, and beetroot if you had no young leaves to chop.

In the summer of 1942, the *South Wales Echo* reported Lord Woolton as saying that, to supplement the egg ration, millions of imported tins of the new egg powder—from a process developed in the USA—were to be distributed. The tins would be 'off ration' at a cost of 1*s*. 9*d*. for a 5 oz tin, equal to twelve eggs. Within a month 19 million tins had been distributed to shops and 15 million more would be available in the next three weeks. The coming of dried eggs meant at least the frying pan had something new to offer. As well as the scrambled eggs, omelettes were created from bits of meat and cheese saved or scraped from odd meals here and there. The Ministry of Food's War Cookery Leaflet No 11 said:

Dried Eggs are pure eggs with no additions, and nothing but the shell and the water taken away. They are pure eggs, spray dried. They are just as good as fresh eggs and can be used in the same ways. One level tablespoon of dried egg powder and two level tablespoons of water equals one egg. After reconstituting the eggs, they must be used at once.

They were used in recipes exactly as fresh eggs, beating as usual before adding to the ingredients; or they could be added dry and mixed with other dry ingredients. Before Christmas in 1943, the dried egg allowance was doubled but you were asked, instead of making cake, to try bread and jam sandwiches moistened with a dash of fruit juice and cover with custard made from plain flour, milk, water and dried eggs.

Scotch eggs were frequently cooked from sausage meat and dried egg: the reconstituted egg mix was poured into small greased basins. Left to stand in a pan with a little boiling water and cooked until set, out came hardboiled eggs ready to be coated with sausage meat and breadcrumbs. Very few Pontypriddians evaded them in a main meal with chips. But they made a change from potato pancakes with sausage meat, or spam and other variants.

Throughout the war, hedgerow harvests provided many fruits for preserving as jams and jellies to see families through the particular severity of rations on winter days. Much garden produce was dried or salted or used for making pickles and chutneys, and you could pulp and bottle tomatoes. Unless you made the effort of making preserves from all that was available—or hay while the sun was shining—you lacked many vital vitamins, or in bleaker times you just went hungry. When out playing or walking, most children would enjoyed eating the hawthorn leaves which they knew as 'bread and cheese'. In season they gathered bowlfuls of blackberries. And wimberries from the mountain slopes of Eglwysilan and elsewhere: the children returning home with tell-tale tongues showing that they were unable to resist the temptation of eating as they picked.

In the austerity of rationing, the Ministry of Food provided many curious recipes. The best known was Woolton Pie—named after the minister, who was presented to housewives as Uncle Fred. His pie comprised a pound each of diced potato, cauliflower, swede, carrot, turnip, parsnip or the like cooked in a large pie dish with added vegetable extract and oatmeal and chopped spring onions and perhaps a little grated cheese on top. No meat. No doubt the more tempted cook ceremoniously carved a slice of spam to go with it, unless she was lucky enough to have bought a rabbit—which made one of the magnificent gourmet meals of the war. You thrived if you were a vegetarian.

Housewives listened to the programme *Kitchen Front* on the wireless every morning at 8.15 to pick up the latest news and ideas. They were often told that food is a munition of war—don't waste it. And the Radio Doctor said let there be a plan for potatoes and vegetables every day. There seemed to be little option and you were advised to listen, read and watch all cookery demonstrations for tips on using food wisely. If the oven was on then always pop in some potatoes to bake in their jackets for all the family.

The Miss Switch Management Centre in Taff Street said that wasting food was sabotage and the only way to redeem yourself was to help the war effort by saving food instead. The Ministry of Food said that you should remember for the sake of your health and your country that 'enough is better than a feast'. There was a recommendation from someone that the remains of yesterday's rice pudding should be used to thicken the soup of today. In these Battle of Britain days, Pontypridd UDC were still providing emergency food supplies of biscuits and Bovril for people taking cover in the town's air raid shelters after the recent bombings of the town.

Fish was not rationed but unlikely to be found until supplies of a new kind of fish called fresh-salted cod came to the shops. We were promised we would like it—and the price, too, of 9*d*. a pound. The fishmonger had to soak the cod in water for at least 48 hours until you bought it for cooking that day. But de-salting still left the taste of the sea.

You were told to eat a good cooked breakfast to set you up for the day. Daily 'Food Facts' suggested that you grate raw potato and a batter mixture into the bacon fat left over. If you had bacon why not fry it with slices of carrot for a delicious flavour. Or fried bread and spam. Or cutlets of potato and carrot and spam dipped in some breadcrumbs. For a change from spam perhaps an omelette made from dried eggs, potato and chopped spring onions with shredded mixed vegetables. Another idea was to bake cubes of stale bread and use as a breakfast cereal. Pea pod soup (pods nicely sieved) made a good and nourishing start to your lunch. Ovaltine tablets were advertised at this time for 'strength, staying power and good health'. You always seemed to be hungry and ready for the next spam and spud sandwich.

Half and half mixes of national flour and mashed potato were used for ordinary shortcrust pastry to help it go further. Cadbury's issued a leaflet of recipes for chocolate cakes. It sold at a penny in aid of the Red Cross. The Ministry of Food wanted your cooking secrets and received a huge range of recipes right up to the (potato) Victory Sponge which you could enjoy with a nice hot cup of tea made from blackberry leaves.

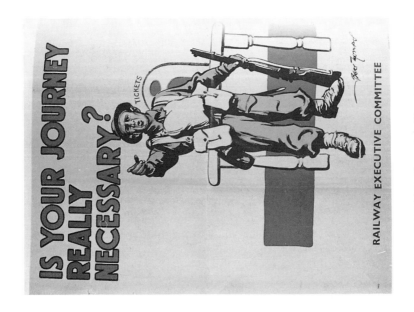

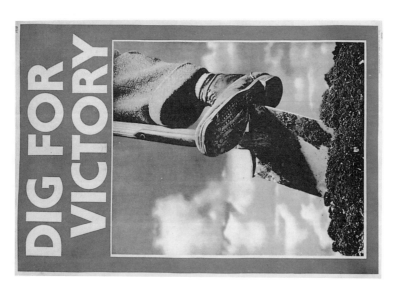

16. *Left:* Famous wartime poster urging everyone to grow more vegetables *(Imperial War Museum, MH 13261). Right:* This poster greeted you at all railway station booking halls and platforms *(Crown Copyright)*.

General View, Pontypridd, showing Graig-Wen Lanwood.

17. General view of the town about 1939, showing the Ynysangharad Park tennis courts and swimming pools, Lanwood schools, and the new block of the Boys' Grammar School classrooms under construction.

Tumble showing G.P.O., Pontypridd.

18. The Tumble in the 1940s: White Hart Hotel left, the Greyhound next door, and former main post office of 1930. The wall on the right has been replaced and all the buildings right, and the Half Moon hotel just off the picture, demolished.

19. Golden Wedding photograph (1945) of George and Edith Francis who lived on the Broadway, both staunch members of St Catherine's Church. He was a compositor for 52 years, 39 of them with the *Pontypridd Observer* at their Broadway offices.

Last mile home

Petrol rationing started at midnight on 22 September 1939. Branded
petrol ceased on the day after war was declared and there was only one
grade of petrol, which was known as 'Pool'. The Motor Spirit Ration
Book stated that the petrol 'must only be supplied into the tank of the
vehicle bearing the number shown on the front of this book and must not
be supplied into any other container'. Some supplies were coloured to
prevent use on the 'black market' and offenders faced severe penalties.
The ration for the private motorist meant only about 150 miles or so of
motoring a month. Petrol coupons, which were issued in readiness from
the very outbreak of the war, varied according to the horsepower of the
car. Cars up to seven horsepower were allowed four gallons, those of
eight and nine horsepower had five gallons, with gradually rising
amounts for larger cars. By mid December about half a million cars
throughout Britain were laid up because of the stringent rationing and the
new heavier taxes. The petrol allowance was reduced to 125 miles a
month by August 1941 and to 50 miles a month by May 1942. From 1
July 1942 the allowance was totally abolished and private motoring was
doomed for the rest of the war.

The exceptions granted for cases of proved necessity were subject to
road checks to confirm that the particular journey was essential and the
route taken was the shortest. The *Pontypridd Observer* reported in 1943
that a Mountain Ash man was charged with unlawful use of petrol. The
court heard the defendant had been granted a petrol allowance to go to
work, but it was clear that on one occasion he had used petrol to visit a
pub. He was fined £10—a significant sum. A trip to the cinema cost a
Cilfynydd man £15 in fines for the unauthorised use of petrol. And a
Treorchy garage owner was fined £30 for the 'grave offence' of mixing
kerosene with petrol. The case came to light after a motorist claimed that
'my car lost power on the hills, and the roads had to be closed because
of the clouds of white smoke coming from the exhaust'.

Shortly before these incidents, the long-serving and patriotic editor of
the *Pontypridd Observer*, Percy S. Phillips, died in hospital a few days
after he was knocked down by a bus in Cardiff Road near his Dynea
Farm home. The next editor was D.C. Lewis and then John Lewis
through the war and for many years after. George J. Francis who lived
on the Broadway with his wife Edith worked for 39 years as a compositor with the newspaper, then printed at its works on the Broadway. A
trolley-bus stop just outside was called the Observer. Edith Francis was
a member of the Mothers' Union at St Catherine's Church in Pontypridd
whose ladies helped the war effort by knitting articles for the Forces.

From August 1942 petrol for all commercial vehicles was dyed red and a private motorist faced prosecution if red petrol was found in his tank. But the black market crooks soon found a way to bleach out the colour by filtering the petrol through a gas mask; and sold it, along with supplies of ordinary petrol they had acquired, at anything from 6*s*. 6*d*. to a £1 a gallon. Pool petrol cost 1*s*. 6*d*. a gallon at the time rationing was introduced and rose to a wartime high of just a halfpenny short of three shillings, double the price, in 1942.

There were severe constraints on petrol for vans and lorries. The government curtailed deliveries from retail shops to save on petrol, rubber and manpower. Grocers, for example, had to place their orders one week in advance so that full loads to an area could be coordinated; butchers could not deliver anywhere within a mile of their shops; furniture vans could be used only when they packed full loads. Several Pontypridd shopkeepers and market traders shared space on vehicles making local collections and deliveries. At dusk, some cars resembled elephants in a jungle darkness: these cars ran on gas from a large bag—shaped like a small barrage balloon—in a wooden crate strapped to the roof. The gas gave mileage equal to about a gallon of petrol and the bag soon sagged and deflated. The UDC abandoned its experiment in November 1939 with a gas-driven lorry which had the gas bag slung underneath the lorry. The Transport Committee introduced large reductions in bus services to meet fuel economy restrictions. They investigated the possibilities of using gas-powered buses and extending the trolley bus service but they did not come about.

More horses and carts appeared in Pontypridd streets. Sometimes their vague shapes could just be made out as they plodded and creaked their way in the blackout. Well known to householders in Pontypridd and probably in all the villages was their very own Co-op horse: the Co-op 'vanner' type horses were part of the everyday scene in Pontypridd for many years of peace and war as they drew the camel-top vans used by bread roundsmen and the floats used by milkmen. Many customers, whose house numbers were well marked by the horses, knew their roundsman's horse by name (and fed it daily with bread crusts in less self-hungry times). They gave the animal a friendly and encouraging pat as it steamed in relentless rain lashing the village streets; or when it stood quietly in the hot sunshine—wearing an old fringed straw hat, with holes cut out for the horse's ears, to keep off the flies. The Co-operative Carriage Works, situated near the riverside at the Glyncoch end of Berw Road, made many carts and carriages and coffins before it closed in the early 1950s. Stanley G. Davies was the manager there.

His son, Peter G. Davies, is treasurer and has been a member for 50 years of the Gelliwastad Club and Institute, a private members' club of ease, courtesy and charm in Gelliwastad Road. He can relate many stories about the interesting pictures of the club and the town that hang on the clubroom walls. Peter Davies lived at one time in Treworgan House on the Gelliwastad Grove hill at the rear of the club. The house looked down over the old Co-operative Society bakery where bare-fist fights were often staged when such shows were in fashion in the early twentieth century. The Gelliwastad Institute, founded in Victorian times by Miss Clara Thomas of Llwynmadoc, Breconshire, was used as a hospital in the First World War to supplement a military hospital in nearby Lan Wood. The old Co-op dairy was also in Library Road at the rear of the club. The dairy buildings were once stables and some of the Co-op's great shire horses were stabled there until after the Second World War. The new housing development of Gelliwastad Court now occupies the site.

Nothing to wear

Clothes were rationed from 2 June 1941: the points system meant everyone having 66 points, or coupons, to last a year. This number was severely cut as the war went on. A man's overcoat required 16 coupons and a suit 26 coupons; and 11 or more were needed for a woman's dress. In effect, people were rationed to one complete outfit for the year. Many of the poor in Pontypridd could not afford to buy new clothes anyway, and sold their coupons to friends or to black market buyers for a little extra cash. For the immediate introduction of rationing, the 26 'margarine' coupons in ration books were utilised until proper clothing cards were issued from post offices in August. The new books of 1 June 1942 had 60 coupons to last until 31 July 1943, later extended to 31 August. Ration books for the next year included a clothing card cut to only 48 coupons. You could buy coupons on the black market for 2*s.* each; or a 'spiv' could let you have a whole book but it would cost you £5 or more. In 1943 the police were concerned about the number of forged clothing coupons that were circulating in Pontypridd; and also concerned that new coupons, which the government claimed could not be forged, were being handed in to shopkeepers. Later, the local police broke up a ring of crooks. The new food ration books also contained a new identity card if you were over 16.

The President of the Board of Trade, Oliver Lyttelton (later Lord Chandos), broadcast an appeal to the nation to show its patriotism by becoming ill-dressed. 'I know all women will look smart, but we men may look shabby. If we do we must not be ashamed. In war the term "battle stained" is an honourable one,' he said. Many battle stained people were seen in Pontypridd and the villages and the valleys in those years, for they were encouraged: 'We must learn as civilians to be seen in clothes that are not so smart. When you feel tired of your old clothes remember that by making them do you are contributing some part of an aeroplane, a gun, or a tank.' The introduction of clothes rationing meant that many small firms closed down, as was aimed, to release factory space and nearly half a million workers for making munitions.

Second-hand clothes were in much demand at Pontypridd Market and attracted buyers from the town and the valleys, many searching for clothes for miners and workmen in heavy industries whose clothes quickly wore out. Second-hand clothes for sale filled the Lesser Hall, once a Victorian theatre, at the market. And whenever surplus army blankets were available they were snapped up and skillfully made into winter coats. The hall was occupied by Leslie's Stores after the war to supplement their Taff Street shops. It later became the Pontypridd Salesroom and was renovated in 1988 as the new Clothes Market.

There were no extra clothing coupons for expectant mothers. The Board of Trade told them to try to avoid spending coupons on special maternity clothes as almost all their existing clothes could be altered easily. They could be worn comfortably until the baby was born, and then altered back again. Mothers received 50 extra coupons for a baby's layette. A nappy needed one coupon, so if you bought two or three dozen there were precious few coupons left over for any other clothes. But not to worry: a Board of trade leaflet enlightened mothers that 'babies don't need nearly as many clothes as people used to think' and suggested a layette of four or five gowns, four vests, three matinée coats, three pairs of bootees and two medium sized shawls. 'Rubber knickers are not necessary and, quite apart from scarcity of rubber, are very uncomfortable for the baby. A laundry basket or even a suitably lined deep drawer could be easily adapted to make a very useful cot for the first few months.'

'Utility' clothes were manufactured from 1942 after government sponsorship of textile materials that could be made into serviceable clothes. Every 'Utility' garment bore an official label: two black circles with a segment cut out on the right of each, beside the figure 41. Manufacture was assigned to a number of firms and followed strict regulations designed to save materials and labour: no double-breasted style jackets and the single-breasted jackets restricted to not more than three pockets; three buttons on the front and none on cuffs; waistcoats with two pockets instead of the usual four; trouser-leg widths restricted to 19 inches. Trouser turn-ups were banned, although some men tried to specify a longer inside leg measurement and have their turn-ups made at home. Shirts were cut shorter and there were no pockets on pyjamas. Growing boys had to wait longer for their first pair of long trousers: from May 1942, only shorts were to be manufactured for boys up to the age of eleven or twelve in order to save cloth.

Men's shoes in 1942 were price controlled at £2 7*s*. 8*d*. and Utility suits at £4 9*s*. Fifty Shilling Tailors in Taff Street advertised their men's cheapest suits in 1943 at £4 15*s*. Elastic was of poor quality: complaints by MPs about the price of braces prompted one to say 'At present it costs as much to keep one's trousers up for six weeks as it formerly did for six years'. To save wool, the length of men's socks was reduced from the normal 14 inches from top to heel to nine inches, but they still needed three precious clothing coupons. One coupon was required for two handkerchiefs or a tie.

Women's Utility garments were to be simple in design but also generally attractive, hard-wearing and good value for money. A two-piece suit would need 18 coupons. No extra clothing coupons were allowed for that dreamed-of wedding dress: most brides wore their 'best' clothes. After visiting Britain in 1944 and seeing for herself the general austerity of wartime weddings, Mrs Eleanor Roosevelt, the First Lady of the United States, returned to obtain the co-operation of American ex-brides in collecting and sending wedding dresses complete with veils to Britain for hire to servicewomen for their special day. Fewer pleats were allowed for skirts. The government controlled prices: top price for women's Utility footwear (about five coupons) was £2 1*s*. Some Utility clothes cost as little as £1 1*s*. for a blouse, 17*s*. 10*d*. for a cotton dress, and 13*s*. 7*d*. for a rayon dress. The cost of a women's coat could not exceed £4. Winter coats were about that price in the autumn of 1943 and needed 18 coupons. Fur coats needed the same number and cost £25.

In the following January sales, skirts were going at 16*s*. 5*d*.—if you could find the four coupons. And two coupons for stockings. Leather shoes were virtually unobtainable locally; but work shoes with soles of beechwood could be found at 13*s*. or so. Later on, the heels of women's shoes were restricted to $2^{1}/_{8}$ inches. A women's simple sailor style felt hat cost about £1. The Board of Trade authorised two designs of utility hat after long refusal to recognise such a 'luxury' but hats were scarce throughout the war. A head scarf tied under the chin, or worn as a turban, was a widely accepted alternative. Elastic sold at 1*d*. or 2*d*. a yard.

Wool was on ration and so knitting was curtailed. The *Pontypridd Observer* 'up-to-data' column for the modern woman carried hints on the re-use of wool. Knitted garments such as jumpers were unravelled and the wool steamed and then wound into new balls. Knitting wool for Forces comforts were obtainable without coupons from the WVS and other channels.

Make do and mend

Stockings were very scarce and before going out, perhaps, to a dance some girls used a leg make-up of sun tan lotion (or even gravy browning) with the seam drawn in with an eyebrow pencil, which often prompted the taunt of 'Oxo legs!' There was also a commercial product called 'Silktona' liquid silk stockings which claimed 'gives bare legs the elegance of sheer silk'. In October 1942 the *South Wales Echo* told women that three million pairs of silk and silk mixture stockings were due in the shops within the following three months, but would be the last British ones to be made until after the war. They would have to put up with very inferior lisle or rayon stockings. In those times of make do and mend, stockings could be invisibly mended at the 'Replacement Cleaners' shop at 35 Taff Street (just opposite today's precinct) and a woman repairer sat in the window where her skill could be seen. Replacement Cleaners also had a factory on the Treforest Trading Estate. Later in the war, American troops billeted all over Pontypridd brought in the first nylons to fascinate their many girl friends. Afterwards, nylons became available in local shops for the pleasure of all.

Women's magazines gave many hints for making clothes: dresses were turned out from bright curtains; and skirts from blackout material. Old silk stockings and odd pieces of silk could be folded and tacked into garments as shoulder pads. One Graig housewife managed to find some of the coupon-free parachute silk which a magazine suggested would make new underwear. (Towards the end of the war, parachutes were made from nylon.) And she said, 'I'm rightly proud of a dress nicely dyed blue that I made from two tablecloths long ago tucked away in a drawer.' A Treforest lady made slippers for herself and her husband from a discarded felt hat and a couple of 'Dai' caps. Cosmetics were rationed and you were told to take your old lipsticks from their cases and melt them down to make new ones. Add a little cold cream and they would make do as rouge.

Two elderly ladies making do at a cottage in Oaklands, Cilfynydd, made small or nettle beer which was superior to pop. John Evans, an evacuee from Kent living in Oakland Crescent, knew well that children were often welcome to a Welshcake made with little fat. And to see a pig's head occasionally being prepared in the cottage meant a brawn sandwich was on the menu as a reward for chopping some sticks of firewood or maybe moulding a little stack of briquettes for the fire by packing old baked bean tins tightly with small coal and wet tea leaves. A tin glowed red hot on the fire and gave out a lot of heat. Potato peelings were used on the fire, too, unless collected for pig swill. Crushed eggshells made a useful scouring powder for cleaning many surfaces. The crust of the many rabbit pies they cooked was made with mashed potato with only a little fat in the flour. As in most households, rabbit made do very well as the meat used for stews and casseroles. And for roasts, too, as a change from the seemingly only choice of stuffed breast of lamb.

Join the queue

Queues were not elusive in wartime Pontypridd. There were long queues and very long queues, and all-of-a-sudden short queues forming more long queues: hence the saying: 'You see them here, you see them there, you see them b— everywhere.' It was certainly true that if you saw a queue forming in town or at the village shop you hurriedly joined it in the hope of finding something to feed your family with, or rescue you from whatever shortage it could. Some local shopkeepers were not averse to leaking the news that some commodity or other would be offered and then wait for a while until a conveniently long queue had formed before opening up. After selling the proportion of stock they wanted to for that day, they kept the rest hidden 'under the counter' or pulled down the shutters abruptly until another time. The culprits were not forgotten by the long-suffering housewives when things changed in more plentiful years.

The list of wartime shortages was endless, and even manufacture of poppies for Remembrance Day in 1942 was curtailed owing to so many difficulties. Paper replaced the wire used for the stems and metal centres. When you bought your poppy, you were asked to hand it back at the end of the day to one of the local centres to be repaired for use the following year, or salvaged. In September 1939 a Controller of Paper was appointed and many national newspapers and magazines had fewer pages. The *Pontypridd Observer* was reduced from eight pages to four but said 'still we endeavour to give you all the news'. Most other newspapers were of the same size and sold at halfpenny or a penny.

Under the Control of Paper Order in 1940 it was on offence to wrap 'any article which does not reasonably require such wrapping or packing for its protection'. The small square of grease-proof paper placed on the piece of newspaper in your local fish and chip shop became smaller and smaller; and soon your chips were often garnished with the print of headlines or stories from your local paper. Later in the war, when paper shortages grew far worse, housewives were asked to always take a sheet or two of newspaper or perhaps a dish along to the butcher or the fishmonger and a cloth to the baker when they joined the queue.

Fuel was always in short supply from the start of the war and, in the first few weeks, bus services in Pontypridd were much reduced to meet stringent fuel economy measures. Schools in Pontypridd closed now and then for short periods from January 1940 because of shortages of coal and electricity. In July 1942 each household was told in a large advertising campaign to set a low consumption target. You could consume up to this target amount with good conscience but you were held on your honour as a patriot not to exceed it. Coal was the base used: one hundredweight (112 lb or 50.8 kg) was deemed to be the equivalent of two gallons of paraffin, or five therms of gas, or 100 units of electricity. A court fined a man £2 for wasting fuel when he left his electric fire switched on for 24 hours. The South Wales Electric Power Company asked householders to sift their cinders when clearing the grate and to use them again in an effort to help save more than two million tons of coal a year. Anything that could be burnt in the grate was collected: from twigs and cones in the woods to rolled newspapers and any unwanted wooden articles around the house.

To conserve fuel, you were asked to be economical in using hot water for bathing and urged to paint or mark a line around the inside of the bath indicating a level of five inches. And not to use any more than this, on your honour. Soap could be bought only against coupons from February 1942 and a week's ration entitled you to three ounces of toilet soap or you could choose from four ounces of hard soap (common household), small amounts of soap flakes or chips, soap powder or soft soap. Shaving soap and cream were not rationed but you were not likely to find any.

In September 1943 many housewives in Britain were concerned at the shortage of dried fruit for making Christmas puddings, although the Ministry of Food promised that extra supplies would be in the shops in good time. Here, the papers advised that if you were feeling low and depressed then go and listen to the happy shouts of all the stallholders at Pontypridd's open-air market on Wednesdays and Saturdays: half an hour there was as good as a bottle of medicine. Several theatre groups in the area performed the pantomime *Mother Goose* and brightened the outlook of many mothers and children as another austerity Christmas approached. A live goose was produced in court as a witness when a Treforest man denied stealing it. A nicely fattened fowl, it apparently stayed perfectly quiet; but magistrates ordered that it must be removed elsewhere for Christmas. Toys were very scarce and the Board of Trade placed a maximum price limit of 24s. 5d. on them. This sum included purchase tax, which was then levied at 100 per cent on all luxuries. Shop-bought Christmas gift-stockings were made from cellophane instead of net or cloth.

You could buy new furniture only if you were setting up home for the first time. So the introduction on New Year's Day in 1943 of the new Utility furniture, well made and generally of smart appearance, was greatly welcomed. At first it was available only to people whose homes had been destroyed by bombs, expectant mothers, or to couples married after January 1941. You applied for a docket that authorised your buying the minimum of furniture needed to start your married life. Scarcity of materials prohibited the manufacture of three-piece upholstered suites. Price controls ensured that the second-hand furniture you sought could not be sold for more than its price when new. There was a waiting list of up to six months for prams (starting after the baby was born) but the government eased problems when they introduced an utility version which cost £10. You would not see any of the large Silver Cross type prams about. For older children, standard bicycles, priced at about £9, were rather easier to obtain.

In May 1943 Thomas & Evans of Porth apologised to customers for delays in house to house deliveries of its famous 'Corona' pop, but most of their delivery vehicles had been transferred to essential war work. The pop could still be obtained from retailers. This increased those collection and 'penny back on the bottle' opportunities for enterprising and cash-strapped boys and girls. There was a great summer drought in August 1944: a beer drought, with most pubs and clubs in the town, villages and valleys displaying 'No Beer' or 'Sold Out' signs on their doors and windows to overwhelm their customers. Relief came with 'unofficial' rationing of one pint of draught beer or one bottle of beer to each customer whenever the watched beer drays came. It was reported that the shortage was due to suppplies being reduced by half to enable servicemen in Normandy to have a share. Beer was flown to France in 90-gallon tanks specially fitted on Spitfire and other aircraft. In the NAAFI, each man was given a weekly ration of two pints at a total cost of 1s. 5d.

At this time a well-known Pontypridd licensee, H.W. Mitchell of the Park Hotel, died after serving there for 28 years. Two other wartime licensees who died (in 1945) were Jehonda Lewis of the New Inn in

Cardiff Road, Rhydyfelin, after serving for 39 years; and David Ebenezer of the Albion Hotel in Cilfynydd who died within a week of his father, Daniel Ebenezer. A bottle of Scotch whisky, which was 12*s*. 6*d*. in 1939, rose to £1 5*s*. 9*d*. by 1942. Beer went from from 6*d*. a pint to 1*s*. 3*d*.

Shortages prompted much wartime graffiti: drawings of a character called Chad, a long-nosed face looking over a wall, appeared just about everywhere in Pontypridd, with inscriptions of 'Wot—no matches?' or 'Wot—no beer?' and hosts more. Another familiar sign from Chad was 'Wot—no fags?' and few cigarette packets were on display in the shops for long. Brands at the time included, from Player's: Navy Cut (Medium, Mild, and Cork Tips), Clipper, Gold Leaf, Virginia, and Weights; from Will's: Capstan, Gold Flake, Passing Clouds, Star, Tank, and Woodbine. Other popular brands of cigarettes included: Army Club, CWS Silk Cut, Churchman's No.1 and Tenner, Craven 'A' Cork Tipped, De Reszke Minors, du Maurier, Greys, Kensitas K4's, Master's V, Morris's Virginia Blend, Pall Mall, Park Drive, Pennants, RAF, Robin, Senior Service, Three Bells, and Viceroy. When the American troops came to Pontypridd they brought a popular range with Camel, Chesterfield, Lucky Strike, and Philip Morris. Matches were scarce and so various patterns of petrol lighter, made in plastic with very little metal, were in the shops at the end of 1941 at a controlled price of 6*s*. 6*d*.

It was illegal to manufacture confetti and also illegal (a waste of food) to throw rice at weddings; so most wedding guests relied on their office or bus conductor friends emptying the coloured paper discs from punches. The Sugar (Restriction of Use) Order of 1940 made it an offence to place sugar on the outside of any cake after baking. That grand three-tiered cake drooled over at a wedding reception was made of cardboard and perhaps all there was to cut was a tasty sponge. Your plate, cup and saucer were not easy to replace. You could be lucky now and then if you turned up at the market at the right time and joined the queue. It was the same for your knife, fork and spoon.

Farmers wanted to see the number of pet dogs greatly reduced and their foods fed to fowls instead. Tinned food for dogs was scarce and many dog owners bought supplies of horsemeat.

From mid 1942 it was hard to find bed linen but you might come across coarse sheets. The manufacture of bedspreads and table cloths was forbidden. Towels were scarce and put on ration some months later. There were shortages of so many things: alarm clocks, buckets, camera film, carpets, combs, crockery, curtains, cutlery, envelopes, fly papers, frying pans, hairclips, hairpins, hot water bottles, linoleum, needles, pens, pencils, pipe tobacco, polishes, razor blades, saucepans, teapots, thermos flasks, toilet rolls, toothbrushes, wallpaper, writing paper.

The 'black market' flourished in wartime. In Pontypridd, as every-where, there were citizens not considered to be patriots who tried to obtain more than their fair share of goods in short supply. Food and many other commodities were rationed to ensure fair shares for all. The term black market referred to the illegal and anti-social trade in goods that were rationed or hard to find—such as luxury foods, whisky, cigarettes, petrol and much more—usually at extortionate prices of perhaps ten times the true value. The price of gin for example was 22s. 6d. a bottle but many people were happy to pay £10 or nearly five times the advertised price, and kept coming back for more. To make life harder for black marketeers, Herbert Morrison, the Home Secretary and Minister of Home Security, announced in May 1942 that under Defence Regula-tions the maximum penalties for black market activities had been raised to twelve months imprisonment on summary conviction and to fourteen years penal servitude (imprisonment with compulsory labour) on indictment.

In Pontypridd, a farmer was fined £8 10s. for selling potatoes to unlicensed buyers. A market stallholder was fined 10s. for not keeping accurate records of all the goods he bought. Another market trader was fined 10s. for selling a lettuce without holding a licence. Three Cilfynydd boys were charged with breaking into the canteen of the Albion Colliery and stealing 100 packets of Franklyn's twist tobacco, which doubtless would have found a place on the black market. And a shopkeeper was fined £1 for not displaying the price on a tin of sardines. In September 1943 Stanley Evans, the stipendiary magistrate for Pontypridd, gave a stern warning to anyone trafficking in illegal clothing coupons. 'The practice of obtaining coupons by fraud is so serious that prison sentences must be imposed in future', he said, after handing out fines to a group of thirteen women for such offences.

CHAPTER FIVE

Cadets on Parade

The Air Training Corps (ATC) was launched by the Air Ministry in February 1941 to provide preliminary training on several evenings a week for boys aged 16 to 18 intending to join the Royal Air Force or the Fleet Air Arm, although the cadets were not necessarily called up to those particular services. A notice in the *Pontypridd Observer* of 22 February 1941 invited applications from boys aged 16 and over to form a Town Air Training Corps Squadron. Forms were available from and returnable to any school. There would be training in (for air crew) maths, navigation, morse code, aircraft recognition, and general administration duties; and (for technicians) training in mechanics, flight engineering, electrics, wireless operating, and MT (motor transport engineering).

The ATC was Britain's first state-sponsored regimented national youth organisation. Within six months 200,000 recruits had enrolled. Early in April 1941 more than 150 boys attended a meeting at Pontypridd Boys' Grammar School to form the Pontypridd No 1004 Town Squadron. Another squadron (No 557) formed from pupils of the school was already in full operation at their headquarters at the school. The commanding officer of both squadrons was Flight-Leutenant E.R. Thomas, the highly respected headmaster of the school. He was the father of Miss Lettice Thomas JP, a leading citizen of the town today.

Among the 1004 Squadron officers at times under command of Flight-Lieutenant Thomas were the Adjutant, Flying Officer T. Glyn Davies; the Equipment Officer, F/O Wilfred Cowdry, the Pontypridd Librarian; Flying Officers T.N. Dowse, E.G. Mort, R.D. Pitman, S. Williams; Pilot Officers F.R. Lamey, G. Lewis, K. Rogers, A.G.Smithson, J. Vickery; Warrant Officers T. Green, F. Payne, F.J. Symons. The Medical Officer was Dr A.G.M. Severn and the Chaplain was the Revd Emrys Jones of St David's.

Squadron officers presented proficiency awards and badges through the years as the cadets passed their examinations. To name a small number of cadets: at a Pontypridd ATC New Year social evening at the Shelley Hall of the YMCA on 22 January 1942 awards were presented to G.W. Broome, D. Chapman, J.N. Cobbledick, H.S. Jones, D.J.D. Latham, E. Lowman, D. Morgan, K. Owen, N. Phillips, W.T. Pike, T. Smith, G. Stallworthy, W.M. Tilling, A.E. West, and S.E. Wells—Flight

Sergeant Stanley Wells, the senior cadet and the leading bugler. When he left the Royal Air Force in 1948 he became a warrant officer in the 1004 ATC squadron. He was keenly interested in amateur drama in those days and joined the Pontypridd Theatre Club who rehearsed at the Community Hall in Sion (Seion) Street and afterwards in the upstairs room of the Queens Hotel. Stanley is now an active member of the Players' Theatre at Gelligaer.

Stanley Wells acted in a sketch included in an evening of entertainment at RAF St Athan during an ATC summer camp there during the war. The other cadet players, decked out with swastika armbands, were the 'Junior Luftwaffe' and Flt-Sgt Wells's parody of Hitler brought tremendous applause from the servicemen and women who packed the NAAFI hall. Stanley Wells attended the first meeting of the formation of 1004 Town Squadron, comprising four flights and later a drum and bugle band. They drilled at the tennis courts above the boys' grammar school. By December 1941 the squadron strength numbered 200 which continually increased. A 'Detached Flight' was formed at Church Village. One interesting acquisition of the squadron was a Pegasus aero engine which allowed opportunities for instruction to potential mechanics among the cadets. The squadron first occupied a headquarters at the old Treseder engineering building alongside the Newbridge Arms in Foundry Place, Coedpenmaen, and from September 1944 at the grammar school.

The building in Foundry Place was originally the infamous Model Lodging House, a Victorian doss-house. In the upstairs room in Victorian times men used to sleep on a line, literally: a taut line of rope stretched from one end of the long room to the other and the men would drape their arms back over it and sleep suspended in a row without any bedclothes. There were some old lath and plaster private cubicles on one wall which the ATC cadets had to demolish before the room could be made more presentable. Several distinguished service personnel visited the headquarters from time to time, including an impressively decorated Russian woman sniper, named as Ludmilla Pavilchenka, who reputedly had killed 300 German soldiers.

The Crown Film Unit and other production companies released a number of propaganda films during the war and the cadet forces were often able to see them at local cinemas as part of their training. One evening in its formative year, Flt-Sgt Stanley Wells recalls that 1004 Town Squadron paraded in front of the grammar school. They did not have a band then but, accompanied by the Pontypridd Transport Band, they marched along Tyfica Road, down past the library and through St Catherine Street and Taff Street to dismiss outside the Market Street entrance to the Town Hall Cinema. The young men knew pride and a self-respect from their accomplished discipline and smartness. They watched on this occasion the London Films production *The Lion has Wings* an inspiring 76-minute documentary drama tracing the steps leading up to the war, a reconstruction of a bombing raid and the actual RAF squadron departure from and return to its base. Watching some of these black and white films with their social history content, when they are resurrected on television today, often brings memories to many boys and girls in Pontypridd in the war years of how the town looked and behaved then.

In the first year of its formation, the 1004 Squadron ATC Rugby Club had played several teams from South Wales squadrons, 25 cadets had passed their proficiency tests and another 30 had joined the RAF. To observe Thanksgiving Sunday, the air cadets paraded through the town on Sunday 5 July 1942. The St John Ambulance Band headed the parade. Group Captain Grenfell DSO, the chairman of the RAF selection board at Penarth, took the salute by the town swimming baths in the park. The vice-chairman of the ATC committee at this time was Hubert McVicar of Quarry Bank in Graigwen. The ATC was the largest of the youth organisations in wartime Pontypridd and all the cadets were active in joining in the spirit of things. A large number went to the County Cinema in the week beginning Monday 16 November 1942 to see the picture *First of the Few*, the story of R.J. Mitchell who designed the Spitfire which played so great a part in winning the Battle of Britain.

In celebration of the first anniversary of the entry of Russia into the war, a parade was held on 22 June 1942 by the Home Guard 2nd Glamorgan Battalion, St John Ambulance Brigade, Air Training Corps and other organisations. They were addressed at Ynysangharad Park by the chairman of the urban district council, Edwin Rowbotham JP, County Councillor Rees Williams and Arthur Pearson MP. Section Commander Colonel W. Lester Lewis took the salute. An Armistice Sunday parade through the town on 8 November 1942 led by the Treforest Salvation Army Band comprised the Home Guard, air cadets, Women's Junior Air Corps, sea cadets and the ambulance cadets. Wreaths were laid at the Garden of Remembrance in Ynysangharad Park. The *Pontypridd Observer* told of the increasing number of local servicemen reported killed, missing, wounded or taken prisoners of war.

In October 1943, F/O Richard Pitman, headmaster at Pontshonnorton school, took to both ATC squadrons the posthumous Distinguished Flying Cross awarded to Pilot Officer (Billy) William Ronald Berriman McCarthy of Castle Street, Treforest, who died in 1942 aged 23. WRB's medal was lent by Mrs McCarthy, the airman's mother, who worked at the Great Western Railway goods station in Gelliwastad Road. Her

colleagues there made evident to the lady and her daughter, Mrs Evelyn
Morgan of Rhydyfelin, their recognition of the pilot's sacrifice.

On the fourth birthday of the Air Training Corps in January 1945
1004 Squadron, still commanded by Flt-Lt E.R. Thomas and now with
F/O Wilfred Cowdry as adjutant and F/O T. Glyn Davies as equipment
officer, had a detached flight at Rhydyfelin under F/O E.G. Mort (and the
other at Church Village under F/O R.D. Pitman). At this time the civilian
committee of the squadron comprised Arthur Pearson MP, president; Cllr
Evan Morgan, chairman; E.L. Evans of the National Provincial Bank,
financial secretary; Tudor Jeremy, treasurer; and Bernard M. Murphy,
secretary. By this time, more than 250 local ATC cadets had joined the
Forces. One of them, Cyril Morgan, wrote to the *Pontypridd Observer*
from his home in Brisbane, Australia. He remembered the good times he
knew as a cadet in 1004 Squadron which put on several revues to raise
money for the war effort. He told that he was still very proud of his time
as a cadet in Pontypridd and that the training and social life served him
well when he joined the RAF, serving as a flight engineer/air gunner. He
flew many missions in Liberator bombers in the Far East.

The WJAC (Women's Junior Air Corps) was formed in Pontypridd
in the summer of 1942. It proved to be very successful and 100 cadets
were on parade in late July at Mill Street School. The WJAC and ATC
jointly arranged a dance at Christmas 1942 in the top room of the
YMCA which attracted over 300 WJAC, ATC, Sea and Army cadets.
The masters of ceremonies were F/O T. Dowse and W/O F. Symons. The
dance was the first of several arranged at local halls by members of the
WJAC. A dance on 1 May 1943, also at the popular YMCA, attracted
many, with tickets priced at 2*s*. 6*d*., reduced by a big one shilling for
cadets and members of the Forces.

WJAC cadets presented with their proficiency awards at a local school
by Dr A.G. Mitchell in August 1943 were B. Austin, D. Brennan, M.
Delbridge, A. Evans, J. Evans, G. Griffiths, M. Harris, S. Harris, T.
Harris (one), T. Harris (two), N. Herbert, M. Howells, T. Howells, M.
Lewis, B. Maton, A. Meats, M. Morgan, B. Mower, J. Parker, C. Rees,
J. Symmons, K. Thomas, M. Webb and E. White.

Observance of Battle of Britain Sunday in 1943 (requested by the
King) was held in Pontypridd with a parade of RAF servicemen, ARP
wardens, B Division of the Glamorgan Constabulary, Pontypridd WJAC,
and Air Training Corps. Headed by the ATC drum and bugle band, the
parade marched from Morgan Street to Bridge Street, Taff Street and
Mill Street for a service in St Catherine's Church conducted by Revd E.
Austin Evans, the vicar of Glyntaff. Afterwards the parade entered the
park at the West Street gate and dismissed at the bandstand.

20. Officers and cadets of 1004 Squadron ATC, pictured at the Municipal Buildings, soon after its formation in April 1941. The Commanding Officer, headmaster Flt-Lt E.R. Thomas, is ninth left in the front row.

21. Officers and cadets of the Women's Junior Air Corps, formed in Pontypridd in the summer of 1942, with headquarters at Mill Street School. Photo *c.* 1942.

22. Pontypridd Sea Cadets, *c.* 1943–4. *Above:* Crew of No 1 Lifeboat aboard their training cutter at Cardiff Docks. *Below:* Nos 2, 3 and 4 boats at Cardiff.

23. *Above:* The Rocking Stone (Y Maen Chwyf) and stone circle on Pontypridd Common; also the Monument, centre right. 1950s. *Below:* Richard Street, Cilfynydd, in 1957. Evans & Tucker and the Meadow Dairy groceries were just on the left. Some shops on the right were the Carini Italian cafe, Meyrick ironmongery, D.C. Evans butchers; and the greengrocery of Charles Seymour, home to evacuees Bill Churchman and Peter Smith.

24. The Monument, photographed in 1994. Erected in memory of men of the 5th Battalion of The Welch Regiment killed in the Great War.

A building known as Corner House was opened as the Air Training Corps Welfare Club on Thursday 11 November 1943 when proficiency certificates were presented to several cadets. It was placed at the disposal of the ATC by the directors of Rediffusion Ltd and local manager D.G. Ball. The building stood just off Taff Street at the top of Gas Lane and the road to Temperance Place, between the Fifty Shillings Tailors (today's Supa Snaps) and the Haines (previously Heath's) shop, across the road from the graveyard of Penuel Chapel. It had a large lecture hall, a games room with a billiards table and a canteen. The ATC and WJAC cadets assembled for the official opening stood in silence as a token of sympathy with the family of Cpl Howard Gardner, an ATC Cadet and Home Guard despatch rider of Church Village who was fatally injured in a motorcycle accident the previous day.

A social evening was held at the Corner House on 2 December 1943 by the WJAC, with Unit Commander Mrs Baldwin-Jones presiding, to make presentations to Adjutant Evelyn Jackson of Penycoedcae who was going into the nursing profession and Sqn Ldr Mavis White of Tonteg who was going into industry. Musical items were given by cadets Joyce Clift, Grace Hunt, Beryl Jones, Joan Matthews and Betty Mower. The Corner House was often a good spot for the boys and girls to meet before going off to a dance or the romance of the 'pictures'.

As its name implies, the building was once the Lyons' Corner House with its white and gold decor. Before the war you could have teas served with a selection of cakes by the 'Nippies', as the waitresses were known, dressed in their black frocks with white aprons, collars and hats. The Lyons' Tea vans were seen in the town delivering supplies there and to their shops in the area, one of which was in Treforest. Corner House was used for Perrins Furniture in the 1950s and was a Conservative Club in the 1970s until it was demolished in recent years.

An Army Cadet Force unit was formed in Pontypridd in February 1942 with its headquarters at the Drill Hall in Taff Vale Park in Treforest. Initially, attendance would be set at a maximum of 50 hours a year and, whenever possible, weekends or longer periods away in camp. The syllabus of instruction would include map-reading, signalling, marksmanship and drill.

A detachment of Sea Cadets was formed in Pontypridd in May 1942 and used the Deaf and Dumb Institute (now replaced by a new building known as the Glamorgan Mission for the Deaf) in Tyfica Road as its headquarters, and also trained at the Shelley Hall. By October 1942, the Sea Cadets had 89 recruits under command of Capt. R.G. Radcliffe RNVR (one of the family of well-known 'pop' manufacturers in South Wales), with Sub-Lt Aneurin Beard as 'Jimmy the One'. They also had a drum and fife band which was always welcomed in the town. One Sea Cadet, Jim Rees, recorded that many cadets would remember the times of sea and boat drill at Cardiff Docks where they had the use of training cutters; aboard minesweepers at Port Einon off the Gower when, to board the minesweepers, eight cadets at a time had to wade up to their necks in the sea to reach a lifeboat and then transfer to the ships. The cadets would remember witnessing three ships in collision during a turning manoeuvre off the coast; interesting experiences in HMS *Glendower* at Pwllheli; and aboard a gale-damaged USN cruiser.

Training for the sea cadets included examinations to obtain promotion, first from ordinary seaman to able seaman which would be of value when the time came for the cadets to join the Royal Navy. Some of the many early cadets whose names can be recalled include — Boucher, Gerwyn Davies, Ivor Dodd, Jack Dodd, Alan Evans, Alan Gilbert, John Gittens, Roy Green, Graham Harris, Gordon Hastings, Sid Heal, Billy Hughes, Jacky James, Henry Jones, Alec Kane, Harold Lewis, Dennis Morgan, Jack Morgan, Billy Porter, Jim Rees, M. Riley, Dai Rogers, Tom Rundle, — Scuse, Cliff Thomas, R. Thomas and Tom Williams. During one parade by the Sea Cadets through Taff Street, as Jim Rees remembers, one of their number was to give the order 'Eyes Right' when they reached the saluting platform at the Fountain with its serving officers and many dignitaries. The cadet then saluted the officers with an ordinary salute to the forehead instead of a smart salute to the butt of his rifle, which caused many watchers to cringe at this momentary lapse from a very efficient and disciplined force.

The ATC, ACF and Sea Cadets and their bands often marched through the town and district: particularly in support of the festivities during the special 'Saving for Victory' weeks (see Chapter 7). They attended church parades, thanksgiving services, anniversaries and victory celebrations. The parades were frequently headed by the ATC 1004 Squadron drum and bugle band which made a great impression; and many people still remember the contributions to its success from the flamboyant and daring Drum Major Howard Mitchell (brother of one-time market butcher Gwyn Mitchell), big bass drum stalwart Sergeant Edward Morgan, and its other stars. The bandsmen and instruments were always immaculately turned out. Those who saw the many parades would watch in awe and expectancy as Howard, who joined the Royal Navy in 1945, expertly twirled his mace with appropriate ostentation and hurled it higher and higher into the air. Mostly he caught it; but some of his more daring skyward launchings caused a momentary stir among the drummers and buglers and anyone standing too close for comfort. The bandmaster, latterly, was Warrant Officer

Tommy Green who lived in one of the small cottages at the foot of Graigwen Hill. A single bugler, or sometimes a trio, sounded the *Last Post* and *Reveille* at the Remembrance Sunday services in Ynysangharad Park or at the Monument on the Common.

As part of Salute the Soldier Week in May 1944, the Air Training Corps marched from Cilfynydd, through Ynysangharad Memorial Park to Market Square where the savings indicator was sited and several activities took place. On other days during the week, the Army Cadets with their band marched to the square from Trehafod, and the Sea Cadets and their band (and another daring drum major) marched up from Treforest. The *Pontypridd Observer* reported that each parade was signalled by efficiency and smartness, and the cadets had rousing receptions everywhere. One evening in the week a naval parade from Treforest comprising the Pontypridd, Aberdare, Caerphilly and Merthyr Sea Cadets, headed by the Pontypridd drum and fife band, marched to Ynysangharad Park. At the rear of the procession was a decorated lorry, drawn by two fine horses, which carried the four court ladies of the Savings Queen; and also the five paratroopers dropped over the park earlier in the day. Captain F.G. Glossop RN took the salute at the Fountain in the area of Taff Street then known as Penuel Square which was overlooked by Penuel Chapel, now demolished but once the dominating centrepiece of the town.

Each of the three cadet forces held its own and also inter-cadet forces boxing tournaments in Pontypriddd and the district during the war years. On Wednesday 17 February 1943 the Army Cadets held a boxing tournament at the Central Homes. Some of the contestants were Pte C. Cannard, Pte K. Fry, Cpl Gaze, L/Cpl J. Jones, Pte W. Jones, L/Cpl T. Lewis, Cpl Manning, Pte W.H. Payne, L/Cpl M. Richards, Sgt R. Skuse, and Pte M. White. ATC boxers at this time included Cadets Douglas Jones, G. Bannan, Mervyn Humphries, Malcolm Stewart and Ken Williams. Cadets Douglas Jones boxing at eight stone and Mervyn Humphries at ten stone fought through to represent 1004 Squadron ATC at the Silver Wings Championships held at the Albert Hall in London on Saturday 12 June 1943. Both won their contests and brought their Silver Wings titles home to Pontypridd.

All cadet forces attended annual summer camp for a week. The ATC returned home on Saturday 14 August 1943 after a week in camp at RAF St Athan in the Vale of Glamorgan. The 1004 Squadron drum and bugle band had always been considered locally to be a first class band and on this occasion it proudly led the Aberdare and Pontypridd squadrons into the main gate of the station. On the Wednesday, the band deputised for the RAF band at the passing out parade of some 300 RAF airmen and

WAAFs. Their flawless playing on the square was complimented by the senior RAF officer present; and later the station commander sent a letter of commendation to Flt Lt E.R. Thomas at the Pontypridd headquarters. On the Thursday, three cadet buglers opened the station sports with a fanfare. The bandmaster, Warrant Officer Tom Green, thought the trio were nervous of the occasion but they made no error. The cadets enjoyed spending mornings exercising in the huge gymnasium and swimming in the baths, as well as spending time 'square bashing' under three RAF sergeants. In the afternoons they took part in outdoor sports, including boxing and swimming. They made inspections of aircraft and workshops and took instruction in many subjects of interest including flying simulation with Link trainers. On the Friday, every cadet had a ten-minute flight in a Dragon Rapide or Dominie biplane. Afterwards it was an evening at the station's Astra cinema and comradeship in the NAAFI before lights out and home next morning.

A memorable week was also spent at the Royal Naval Air Station at Dale on the Pembrokeshire coast in August 1944 with flights enjoyed in small Proctor aircraft and trips on speedy air-sea rescue launches. Visits to smaller RAF stations, like Llandow in the Vale, gave some individuals a chance to build up their log of flying hours. The Pontypridd ATC were at RAF St Athan in August 1945 when VJ Day was celebrated. All the station personnel were exuberant at the news of the ending of the war with Japan and large bonfires were built and set alight. The ATC band was called out and, as cadets recall, everyone followed it in Pied Piper fashion through the station to finish by the main gate where they were given loud cheers and greeted by the fire and smoke which engulfed and gutted the nearby Fire Picket (or firewatchers') hut.

The Air Training Corps celebrated its golden jubilee in 1991. It is no longer a recruiting agency for the services, and cadets are given an insight into several aviation and related subjects. The Pontypridd 1004 Squadron joined in the anniversary celebrations and some of its cadets took part in an amateur radio special event.

Escape or cry

The mass escape of 67 German prisoners of war from Island Camp, Bridgend, on the night of 10–11 March 1945 caused a scare in Pontypridd and throughout South Wales. Doors were firmly bolted and windows barred while everyone waited for news. Reports told of escapers being sighted everywhere. One ATC cadet recorded his memories of the escape:

A colleague and I donned our blue Air Training Corps uniforms and joined the search for the enemy. Suitably armed with a stout stick and a broken flare pistol that saw veteran service in the First World War, we scoured the Eglwysilan mountainside before dropping down into woodland near Cilfynydd.

We searched some farm buildings and prodded everything with a handy pitchfork before turning reluctantly homewards. But, as chance would have it, we took a path which passed an old barn. We crawled silently through the rickety doorway, as alert as hunters suspecting big game perhaps. Then above the distant chattering of magpies we heard the significant murmur of voices in a corner of the barn partly screened by some loose bales of straw. We trod softly, listened, and froze. The guttural sounds were obviously German. We had tracked the enemy down.

Tingling with patriotism, we chosen young heroes felt honoured to answer the call of King and Cymru to do our expected manful duty this day. The situation called for careful action on our part to trap the Germans while sending for help from the police and the Home Guard. But, impetuously, our bursting hearts signalled a direct assault straight away to call for unconditional surrender. So we charged in with chilling yells, brandishing stick and pistol, confident of frightening the Messerschmitts out of the escapers. Iron crosses or not.

The first enemy we hurtled upon was a huge man with a torso carved from rippling bronze. He sprawled beside a smashing blonde woman in pink and silk. The man's granite jaw dropped in the warm embrace of the barn before he sprang into life, frenziedly tugging on his boots. We raced off. I led the field well ahead of my poor mate who fell at the brook and was promptly saddled with the toe of the Welsh miner's vengeful boot on his fast-retreating posterior.

Lucky me, I was the one that got away.

CHAPTER SIX

Children at War

Evacuee invasion

On Sunday afternoon 19 May 1940 the peace of Pontypridd town was
shattered by the rousing cheers of thousands of residents who packed the
yard and platforms of the GWR station on the Tumble. The band of the
Salvation Army strived to make its welcome heard as the two special
trains steamed in. Similar scenes overwhelmed many Welsh towns and
villages that day: the evacuees had arrived! Five hundred pupils from
schools in Kent spilled out of the carriages and descended on the
community—and into their hearts. The train arriving at 4.05 p.m. brought
236 children and 21 helpers and teachers from schools that previously
had been evacuated to Canterbury from Rochester and other Medway
towns; and the train at 5.30 p.m. brought 274 children from schools
previously evacuated to Faversham from Chatham, Gillingham, Rochester
and Erith. Two other special trains which carried about 1,200 children
steamed on into the Rhondda. Many excited passengers thrilled to the
new and exciting experience and perhaps touch of mystery of their great
adventure. Safety-pinned or tied to their identity labels, the youngsters
were laden with gas masks, school satchels, suitcases, haversacks, parcels
and carrier bags.

   Each child received two presents, a tin of condensed milk and a tin
of corned beef, which was a Ministry of Food idea intended to safeguard
local food supplies. The children trekked to schools on the Graig for tea.
They were given hot meals served by J.A. Evans, headmaster, and Miss
Mary Morgan, headmistress. J. Harold George and Mrs George, master
and matron of the Central Homes, provided the meals in conjunction
with the Pontypridd Education Committee. The evacuees were medically
examined by Dr A.G.M. Severn, Medical Officer for Pontypridd, and the
Assistant Medical Officer Dr Doris Williams, before being packed into
a fleet of buses and 19 motor cars which took them to the reception
centres in the town and villages. A delighted Miss M. Butterfield, the
headmistress of Rochester Girls' Grammar School, charged with the care
of the first group to the Welsh hillsides, was overcome with tears by the
welcome. She said that they had a very good journey to Wales and
arrived on time. No words could express their appreciation of the

welcome and the arrangements made for the children's tea. Journey's end found the tired army billeted in homes all over the district and faced with their tedious orders to write 'safe arrival' postcards home to worried and tearful mothers or foster mothers which they had last seen on far away railway station platforms. Some cards bore the message, 'Please bring us home, Mum.'

At the time, the *Chatham, Rochester and Gillingham News* reported that local children in a large exodus to Wales had a warm welcome. It said that schoolchildren from the Medway towns who had been evacuated to Sittingbourne and other parts of Kent at the outbreak of war were among several thousand who made the journey to find new homes in Wales. And they had left behind with their foster parents of less than a year cherished memories and a feeling of real loss. They gave the evacuees a rousing send-off, but handkerchiefs were used for more than merely waving goodbye. 'We couldn't feel worse about it if we were parting from our own kiddies,' said one Canterbury foster mother who expressed the inner thoughts of many. All except two of the Rochester teachers who had been with the children in the reception areas had gone with them to their new billets. The newspaper went on:

> The scenes at the departure railway stations were as quaint a mixture of pathos and fun as those scenes at our own local stations nine months ago, when the children first started on their strange journey—but this time there were new and novel differences. The kiddies brought with them gas masks, bags containing a change of clothing, and a day's rations. Each child had an identity card fastened to its clothing. They were seen off, too, by many other children with whom they had made friends during the first long winter of war. Ten thousand children had been expected to travel from the area but over two thousand of these had been taken home by their parents. Wales, they thought, was a little too far away. When the children reached their destination the scenes were strikingly reminiscent of seaside resorts on bank holidays. Many will live in miners' homes in the almost derelict Rhondda Valley. Some children, seeing for the first time the queer aspect of colliery country, stared in amazed silence before starting to talk about it 'nineteen to the dozen'. Will they have something to write home about? The bulk of the evacuees seemed to have had good billets with loving foster parents but, for some, the billets were less than satisfactory. Several personal accounts had given some insight into how these children's lives were changed and how they all had to cope with a different culture.

25. Two posters issued in support of the evcacuation scheme. (*Left: Crown Copyright; Right: Imperial War Museum, MH 6712*).

26. Pontypridd Boys' Grammar School opened in 1896. This photograph of 1996 shows some of the old buildings and the new classroom block, started in 1938 and completed in 1942. Some 150 evacuees from the Sir Joseph Williamson's Mathematical School, Rochester, Kent, stayed at the school from May 1940 to July 1942.

27. The playground at Ynysangharad Park (1950s). The large house immediately left of Lan Wood School is 'Jacobsdal', used as a hostel under the evacuation scheme. Site now occupied by Pontypridd & District Club off Pencerrig Street, Graigwen.

28. Pontypridd Girls' Grammar School, March or April 1941, showing pupils of the evacuated Chatham Girls' Grammar School. Winnie Rolfe (née Bassett) is second left second row from front, nearly in the third row, and with coat collar buttoned up to the neck. Joan Poynter (née Quarrington) is at right end of the second row, half hidden by the girl in front of her.

The evacuees were officially welcomed on the Pontypridd station platforms by Cllr Jesse Powderhill JP, chairman of Pontrypridd Urban District Council, who told the gathering that Pontypridd would give them all the hospitality they would possibly need. The dignitaries accompanying him for the important occasion included Cllr Evan Morgan (vice-chairman) and Councillors Arthur Brown, Percy James, John Jones, H.G. Joshua, George Pugh, Mrs Blodwen Randall and E. Rowbotham. Council officers present were H. Leonard Porcher (town clerk), Raymond Jones (education and billeting officer), John Powell (transport manager), Dr Severn (MOH), and Idris Williams (treasurer). Some of the others present, well known in Pontypridd and remembered over the years, were Arthur Pearson, the local MP, Police Superintendent W. MacDonald, Inspector L. Wilkins, Mrs Hilda Porcher representing the WVS, T. Glyn Davies, D. Milton Jones, E.R. Thomas headmaster of Pontypridd Boys' Grammar School, Miss Mary Jenkins headmistress of the Girls' Grammar School, Arthur Parry the GWR stationmaster; local teachers L.B. Collier and J. Ellis Williams and other representatives of the National Union of Teachers who had done much work in arranging for the reception and billeting of evacuees. After Miss Butterfield had responded, the evacuees gave three cheers for the chairman.

One of the teachers of Erith Technical Institute with the children on the Canterbury train was W.H. Tallis, a native of Pontypridd and an ex-pupil of the grammar school, whose father lived in Graig Street; and one teacher with the Faversham children was W.S. James, a native of Penarth. Extensions and alterations had been made to the Pontypridd Boys' Grammar School from 1938 and included a new and spacious assembly hall and a new block of classrooms (the large white building) which were officially opened on 1 April 1942. Many evacuees remember the school: about 150 pupils from Sir Joseph Williamson's Mathematical School, Rochester, and Erith Technical Institute were educated there until July 1942.

A short history of the Sir Joseph Williamson School in its magazine for the summer term of 1940 told that everyone was recalled from summer holidays and assembled on 26 August 1939. For days they awaited news of final evacuation arrangements. On Friday 1 September, the day when Germany invaded Poland, 163 pupils boarded the 11.15 morning train for the 25-mile journey from Rochester to Canterbury. Everywhere they knew hospitality and sympathy. Until lessons could be arranged they found opportunities for indoor recreation at several halls or spent the time filling sandbags to pile up against the walls of a new hospital; and hop picking which provided a little pocket money. Classes were then arranged in the old hospital for their school, Rochester Girls'

Grammar School, and the few boys from the Erith Technical School who had also come to Canterbury. Kent was rarely disturbed by the screech of an air-raid siren and there was a gradual drift back to the Medway towns.

After the Easter holiday, more pupils returned home to Rochester. But on 10 May 1940 Hitler's forces invaded Holland and Belgium and Kent ceased to be a safe refuge for children. Parents were advised of a possible second evacuation. On Friday 17 May the headmaster told the boys that all whose parents consented were to be sent to South Wales. The magazine said:

> To many the news came like a bombshell, rending ties of friend-ship and scattering hopes and visions; but to others the sudden change brought merely fresh excitement. The next day was filled with hurry and bustle; postcards and labels had to be written, ration cards and library books given in, school books and bags and bicycles collected, lists made, groups arranged, telegrams and telephone calls answered, anxious parents interviewed, and, at the billets, packing and provisioning effected.

At half-past nine on Sunday morning the train carrying one of the first parties of English evacuees to know a second exile pulled out of Canterbury station for its seven-hour journey to South Wales. The passage through the Severn Tunnel caused some mild excitement but by the time train arrived at Pontypridd station most of the boys and girls were weary and hungry and thirsty, for only at a few halts was water available for them. They were glad the journey was over. The generous welcome of the reception roused their flagging spirits. What drew their immediate attention was the great crowd that could be seen from the high platform. And the strains of the Salvation Army Band. At the Graig schools they met the headmaster and headmistress of the boys' and girls' grammar schools, to which the boys of the Mathematical School and the girls of the Rochester Girls' Grammar School and the Chatham Girls' County School were to be attached for an indefinite period.

Gatherings of local people here and there waved to the two packed trains bound for the Rhondda. Nearly 5,000 residents of Tonypandy, Trealaw, Penygraig, and Llwynypia thronged the streets leading to Tonypandy station to meet 500 evacuee children who were loudly cheered into the town on the Sunday evening. Traffic had to be diverted on the Miskin Road. Hundreds of Trealaw children lined the street from the station and cheered the evacuees to the instructional centre where they were entertained and medically examined. Crowds blocked Station

Street and Stag Square in Treorchy when 400 children arrived. They were cheered all along the route to the school where meals were prepared for the evacuees, who were of all ages. And almost all the villagers of Ton Pentre turned out to welcome another 191 children and their 29 teachers and helpers and escorts. Of these evacuees to the Rhondda, 286 were from London's West Ham and had been re-evacuated from the east coast towns of Clacton, Frinton, and Felixstowe. Within six months, nearly 10,000 child and adult evacuees had flocked to the Rhondda.

In a June smiling with Dunkirk spirit, nearly a thousand evacuees came from Acton in London. Shortly after 1.30 p.m. on 17 June 674 children and 56 adults arrived at Pontypridd station to reinforce the first influx. They were welcomed as usual by local dignitaries. Alighting from the train, many of the children immediately made for the boys taking orders for chocolate and swamped them. A large cheering crowd greeted them as they walked down the High Street where local children waved miniature Union Jacks. For some of the evacuees it was the second move from their homes in London's East End, from where they had been evacuated originally to Sittingbourne and other quiet areas of the Kent countryside, and to parts of Sussex. That all changed with the fall of France and the threat of invasion. Later in the evening 169 more children and 13 teachers arrived in town. And at 9.30 p.m. 70 London evacuees from elementary schools in Islington and Shoreditch arrived at Cilfynydd where they were met by the junior school headmaster D.J Griffiths. They were billeted and tucked up in bed by eleven o'clock, most of them exhausted.

Registration for further evacuation from Rochester was undertaken. On 2 June 1940 the 11 a.m. train left Rochester station with 123 boys from the Sir Joseph Williamson School, and with them were 23 younger brothers and sisters and so forth. Also, a number of girls from the grammar school. They were bound for Porthcawl where they arrived at 7.30 p.m. to a great welcome. They were taken to Coney Beach Cafe where they tucked into a huge spread. More boys arrived on 25 June. On 6 July, the Sir Joseph Williamson School's traditional Founder's Day Service was held in both Porthcawl and Pontypridd, the former at ten o'clock conducted by the Revd Fenton Morley. At twelve o'clock the Vicar of Pontypridd, the Revd G. Shilton Evans, conducted the service and gave the address at St Catherine's Church. In late September 1941 some of the evacuees from Rochester were re-evacuated from Porthcawl to Cilfynydd.

More evacuees followed: another batch of 162 children and mothers from bombed areas of London arrived on 30 September 1940, some of them homeless. The reception party at Pontypridd GWR station were Councillors Jesse Powderhill (chairman), George Paget, Percy James, Hopkin Smith, D.T. Jones and H.G. Joshua; the teachers' representative on the Pontypridd Education Committee, Miss D. Dummer, and members Raymond Jones, H.G. Rose, T.J. Gowan. The evacuees were placed in various hospitals in the Rhondda, Caerphilly and Pontypridd until billets were found. At the time there were only 16 offers of accommodation. Raymond Jones, chief billeting officer, appealed for more billets. Most of these evacuees went to Cilfynydd.

In March 1942 Pontypridd Education Committee advertised for a resident maid at 'Jacobsdal' which was an emergency hostel under the Government Evacuation Scheme. Jacobsdal was a large Victorian house which stood at the end of a lane from Pencerrig Street in Graigwen. The house was later demolished and the site used in 1971 for the Pontypridd and District Club and its car park. Until then the club had been situated in Morgan Street, alongside the subway cut in 1898 to remove the danger for pupils crossing the railway tracks to attend the Lan Wood schools.

The evacuees of 1940 formed part of the second government scheme (the first was just before the declaration of war). The phoney war was over and the Blitz and the Battle of Britain were about to begin. Many children longed to be back in their home surroundings but most soon made tracks with their new friends who engaged in exciting woodland adventures and tickled for trout in the brooks. They shared street games, fist fights, and door-knocking larks in the blacked out villages; or joined daring intrusions into billiard halls, reading rooms, farm fields and secluded ready-for-scrumping orchards. But by 1942, many evacuees countrywide had returned home: the worst of the Blitz had passed, though there were still daylight and night raids.

The *Glamorgan County Times* reported on 26 October 1940 that official evacuees to the Rhondda numbered nearly 5,000. Of these, 2,068 children of school age arrived unaccompanied and 1,236 were in parties of mothers and children. On Wednesday of that week 800 more were expected in the valley. On Thursday 800 mothers and children were due to arrive, and a third party of 800 mothers and children was expected in a few days time, making a total of 5,700. Unofficial evacuees in Rhondda homes totalled 1,500. These included parents of official evacuees, exiles returning home, those who had never lived here but had relatives here, those with Rhondda residents in their employ, and strangers to the valley.

With tragic irony, three young evacuee children of the Jameson family (George aged 13, Ernest aged 11, and Edith aged 8) were killed with 27 other villagers when incendiary and high explosive bombs fell on Cwmparc in the Rhondda on the night of 29 April 1941. The children, who were buried in Treorchy cemetery, were remembered in a ceremony in 1989 when youngsters from three Rhondda primary schools went to the graveside. Also visiting were the victims' three sisters from Manor Park in London, one of whom, Vera, had her legs crushed in the raid.

In April 1942 Wendy Williams, a four-year-old evacuee from London, fell into a deep and narrow crevasse on the mountainside above Graigwen. A local man, R.F. Beechey, located her when he was lowered into the crevasse. Les Richards, aged 14, of Hopkinstown was lowered head first during the rescue attempts. After working on the night shift at Lewis Merthyr colliery, 29-year-old Arthur Bengough of Hopkinstown Road went down head first into the crevasse and succeeded in a thrilling rescue of the girl who had been trapped for 16 hours. In February 1944 Arthur Bengough was awarded the Stanhope Gold Medal of the Royal Humane Society for his bravery.

Memories linger on

Some evacuees to wartime Pontypridd have written vividly of their recollections of those times nearly 60 years ago. Beryle Shilling, now Mrs Tofield, of Chatham, who came to Pontypridd in 1940, remembers:

> We assembled at Rochester station early one morning with our attaché cases. Identity labels were pinned securely to our coats and we were each given a carrier bag containing some food rations. We had been well briefed about what was to happen and happily boarded the steam train, waving goodbye to go on this great adventure to Wales. I can't remember much about the journey except that it was very long and I was quite scared in the Severn Tunnel.
>
> When we arrived at Pontypridd my sister Dorothy and I were taken to St Catherine's Church Vicarage. It seemed so large. We were then introduced to the Revd George Shilton Evans, vicar of Pontypridd, and Mrs Evans. They made us very welcome—two very tired, quite shy young girls. I went to the nearby school and Dorothy, who was a pupil at Rochester Girls' Grammar School, had lessons from her own teachers at another local school. I was quite a novelty at school with my English accent but was treated well. The vicar sometimes met me from school. It made me feel very special, for I'd never been met from school before.

I also went to the local Brownies. My main friend was Thelma. I think she was older than me. She lived at the police station and I spent a lot of time there with her. We used to play in an empty cell which was set aside as her family's air raid shelter. The air raid siren was at the police station and we spent a lot of time playing beneath it. It made a lovely place to hang dolls clothes after washing them.

The vicarage garden was a good place—more like a field really. We played 'tennis' over the washing line and had tea out there sometimes. The church had a striking clock which I really missed when we had to move to Porthcawl. The maid at the vicarage was named Doreen and I spent time in the very large kitchen with her. Helping her (her words, not mine). Then there was 'Chips' the dog. He loved it when we picnicked in the garden. The vicar's birthday was the same date as mine and we kept in touch to the end of his life. He came to Rochester to see us after the war. I was able to take my husband and eldest children to see them after they had retired to Weston-super-Mare, and Mrs Evans made Welsh cakes for our tea.

One incident I remember was my introduction to the bathroom. (We didn't have one at home—a tub in the kitchen and a loo in the garden was what I knew about.) This bath was so large I had a job to get in it. And all this hot water out of taps. And a little button on the wall: I pressed it and Doreen the maid turned up to see what I wanted. I didn't know that it rang a bell in her kitchen. I remember we had nettle tea at breakfast. Good for the digestion. My time in Pontypridd was all too short. But the Rochester Mathematical School came and we went to Porthcawl. Pontypridd will always have a place in my heart and maybe I will come and see it again.

Bill Churchman, who has lived in Melbourne, Australia, since 1965, was a pupil at 'Holcombe'—Chatham Technical School for Boys—from 1937 to 1940. The last year at the school was spent in evacuation, with several months of it in Pontypridd. His personal memories of the town and its people are happy ones and he is still in touch with the daughter of his foster parents, though he is well aware that some evacuee children were not so lucky. When war was declared his school was evacuated to Faversham near Canterbury. After the German invasion of Holland, Belgium and France in May 1940 the children were soon re-evacuated to Pontypridd.

The spring and summer of 1940 was blessed with bright, sunny weather [Bill Churchman recalls]. A rail-route had been worked out that took us by train round the city of London and across the southern counties and eventually to Pontypridd. From the GWR station we walked to a school nearby on the Graig from where some of us were sent by coach to the village of Cilfynydd. Mr and Mrs Charles Seymour of Richard Street had agreed to accept evacuated children but I have the firm idea that they anticipated small children. My colleague Peter Smith and I were 15 years old and must have represented quite a challenge to feed on wartime rations. However, neither then nor at any time through the war do I recall being hungry without the means to satisfy hunger.

The greengrocery shop kept by Charles Seymour in Richard Street for many years is well remembered in the village.

Wales is completely different from Kent. There are crags and steep hills where we could walk freely and dispel our energy. The Welsh culture was something new to us: the language, singing, the coal mines, community life. It held a fascination and affection for me which has remained through life. One of our neighbours in Richard Street was a diminutive elderly woman who always wore a man's cap. She was a Welsh speaker with no more than a few words of English—one of the last of a vanished generation.

Our own school teachers from Chatham were with us and, following the same procedures as in Kent, we were taught wherever a vacant schoolroom could be found. On some occasions our energetic chemistry teacher Mr James took us on long walks. War came close when a stick of bombs dropped on the open countryside of the common just north of Cilfynydd. One can only imagine that the target may have been the Albion Colliery. I remember the arrival of the police (one evening in early June 1940) at the shop owned by Frank Carini after the declaration of war between the United Kingdom and Italy. The Carini cafe was only a couple of doors away. Mr Carini was apparently an Italian national. The ship SS *Andorra Star* was used to transport enemy aliens to Canada for internment. It was torpedoed and sunk in the Atlantic and Mr Carini lost his life.

My recollections of Wales are of great kindness. We were received into the homes of strangers with complete openness. It must be remembered that my particular age group, 14 and 15 years old, were on the threshold of adulthood and mature enough to hold our place with people. My sister, about three years my junior, has completely different recollections and, in fact, was so unhappy that our father eventually brought her back to Kent. My stay in Wales was short: while in Kent I had taken the examination for apprenticeship in HM Dockyard and I returned to Chatham to begin a new phase in life.

Mrs Marjorie Drew, now of Tonbridge, Kent, was evacuated from New Malden, Surrey, close to London. She was seven years old when she came to the Cottage Homes for children at Church Village. Today, the 'houses' are known as Garth Olwg. She and her brother and sister were in the Homes because their mother died after they had arrived in Wales. Their father worked at one time for BOAC, then transporting aircraft engines and parts from London to Treforest. Marjorie recalls that:

> I have only good thoughts of my time at the Village Homes: of going back to the house for our milk at mid morning from the school; having an un-spillable inkwell; going on picnics with the house mother; walking to church on Sunday twice and being pleased to be picked to work the bellows for the organ—can't remember the name of the church; it seemed a long way, up a hill I think.
>
> I remember walking to the village with our sixpence pocket money on Saturday—the only time we went out of the grounds usually. The sweet shop made up fizzy drinks with tablets of different flavours in soda water which we loved. I don't remember buying any sweets there. I remember going to the National Museum in Cardiff and seeing barrage balloons around the docks. And a long walk to the Devil's Bridge which stepped down the hillside and led us into Rhydyfelin. I enjoyed the VE Day party held in Nantydall Avenue in Rhydyfelin. All the children were in fancy dress: I was Britannia, my brother was 'the house that Jack built', and my brother was a Russian.
>
> I recall visiting the American forces at the RAF hospital just a short walk from the Homes; receiving new clothes from American families and writing to thank them. And going with my sister to the Pontypridd Cottage Hospital with scabies and having lots of oranges given to us.

Marjorie Drew and her family visit Wales quite often as they have relatives in Merthyr Tydfil. The last time they went for a look around the Homes though she was disappointed to see that the old school (near the main road) with so many memories had been pulled down. There is a new school today at the top end of the area.

Mrs Patricia Kay now lives in Crayford, Kent, and was evacuated to Pontypridd as a pupil of Chatham County School for Girls. Pontypridd was not the first evacuation destination for her: she had previously been sent to Kemsley, a lovely Kent village built by the Bowater Lloyd Paper Company for its employees, near Sittingbourne. Patricia remembers:

> I think I must have been taken to Pontypridd some time in 1940. I can't remember anything about the journey except that we were given cream cotton rucksacks which contained, among other things, a tin of corned beef and a large tin of evaporated milk. I can remember going through a large town and being absolutely horrified at what I thought were very young children smoking.
>
> I was billeted at Wood Road in Treforest with a very nice family, the Johns, Mr and Mrs, and a grown-up daughter, Marjorie. They also had a small, likeable dog; and a small, square, dark green car with the registration number BNY 7. The Johns were a very happy family and Marjorie showed lots of mutual affection— what my mother would have called 'lovey-dovey'. I had no contact with local girls, as far as I can remember, but that was probably because when I and my fellow schoolgirls were at school the indigenous children were at home. I can remember that when I passed a couple of girls in one road, they always called out 'Silly vacooees' and made disparaging remarks about my teeth, though I don't know why!
>
> I was sent to chapel (Calvary) almost every evening and several times in Sundays. The organisations I recall going to were The Speedwells, Christian Endeavour, and Band of Hope. When I got back home I told my father I would never go into a pub again—at twelve! There was also a Forces canteen, run by the ladies of the chapel, and I was allowed to serve. Among the goodies we served were what I believe they called hot dogs at the time, though they were totally unlike today's hot dogs. They consisted of thick slices of potato sandwiched with sausage meat, dipped in flour and water batter and fried. Delicious!
>
> Unfortunately, about six months after I was billeted on the Johns they had to move house. They went up the valley, maybe to Treorchy, and I moved to a family further down the road. I was never happy there, although I wasn't badly treated. They had a teenage son and daughter and there were innumerable family rows and I can remember lying in bed and hearing crying. I seem to

remember having liver for dinner nearly every day and hating it for years after I came home.

I still attended all my chapel organisations and I think I took part with great gusto. I did tests of all kinds and remember singing a solo in chapel on a Sunday evening, to the tune of Dvorak's 'Humoresque'. I witnessed a baptism by full immersion and was quite scared. The preacher was a hell-fire and damnation type: very holy and very miserable. At one New Year's Eve party, he walked diagonally across the hall, carrying a large Bible, silencing all participants and endowing them with a strong feeling of guilt.

Over all, I look back on my stay in Treforest as a happy experience and one I would not have missed. I don't remember being traumatised at leaving home, and this has often worried me, but I have talked with others about this and they say the same. Perhaps, because I came from a very poor, not very happy home, my evacuation period was a boost. I don't know, but I was happy to return home. I was known then as Pat Hughes, nobody called me Patricia; and I remember being extremely interested in a dark, very good-looking boy called Idris who had a friend called Haydn. I wonder how many people still remember the little vacooees?

A letter of memories from Mrs Joan Poynter from near Dursley in Gloucestershire gives a lively and vivid account of her evacuation to Pontypridd. She was then Joan Quarrington and she relates:

Looking back on the golden summer of 1939, I seem to remember endless, carefree days. My world was happy and as the favoured youngest child of a close-knit family, secure. Day trips to the seaside, fairgrounds, picnics, tennis, swimming and much laughter loom large in my memory. School was a joy, as I was relishing being in my final term at primary school and, with six others from my class, eagerly anticipating a new move to the grammar school, to which we had gained scholarships earlier in the year.

Alas, this idyll was soon to be shattered. The outbreak of war during the holidays ensured that our family would be split. I was evacuated and my brother joined the Royal Navy, destined never to return.

I went with my primary school to a village only ten miles from Chatham, and most of us were warmly welcomed into local homes. However, soon we became nuisances as we few, who should have been at other schools, could not be accommodated at the over-crowded village hall. Eventually we were given tuition one morning a fortnight, which left a great deal of time to be bored and into mischief. As the expected bombing didn't transpire, I found myself hopping on a bus and spending long weekends back at my house. Gradually, more evacuees were doing the same and by Christmas most had returned home permanently. The authorities decided to re-open the grammar school, albeit on a part-time basis, in the new year, and thus I joined this group of part-time students.

My education hadn't been completely neglected though as, during the previous idle weeks, local boys had taught me to roller skate, walk on stilts, and introduced me to the noble art of 'scrumping'! None of these accomplishments has proved to be of the slightest use since, but I was proud of them (the first two anyway).

Appreciating mornings only school meant that I was enjoying life, when defeat at Dunkirk and the real fear of invasion closed the school once more, and another mass evacuation took place. The first Sunday in June saw us once more congregating at Chatham station, waving goodbye to families, before boarding a train to an unknown destination.

The journey was long, hot and tedious, no refreshments were to be had, our packed lunches from home were soon consumed; but it was to be 13 hours before we finally drew to a halt at a small station, still not named as all name plates and signs were removed during the war in order to mystify invaders. There was quite a welcoming committee to greet us, including a brass band, which remained silent as it was too dark to read the music. We trudged to a hall where we were selected or rejected by prospective hosts. My friend and I were chosen by a kindly couple, although it wasn't until we reached their house that we learnt we were to stay with them in Crumlin, Mon., as we thought for the hostilities. The following Friday, however, we were ordered to pack our bags, and meet the following morning at the local school.

We boarded the coach and set off on another mystery tour (child psychologists would have a wonderful time today) and, after about an hour, stopped again in a school playground.

I didn't have long to ponder on our surroundings, as I was soon bundled into the back of a car and within a few minutes deposited outside an imposing Edwardian house in a wide, leafy avenue in Maesycoed, Pontypridd. The household consisted of an elderly couple and their school teacher son. The family were quiet, with an ordered routine, rigidly upheld. Into this select group I was catapulted, with disastrous results all round. The family were kind, but not understanding of a child's needs, although I'm sure they did their very best to accommodate me; but I was lonely, being the only one, and bitterly resentful of spending long summer evenings in my bedroom.

My closest friends all seemed to be grouped around the Wood Road area and they urged me to join them, which I did. By standing forlornly on doorsteps, asking to stay, until someone pitied me enough to accept the challenge. The household consisted of a middle aged couple and their 19-year-old daughter Betty (Field). There was also another evacuee from a different school from mine. However, we got on very well and for a few weeks I enjoyed myself within the bustling household. The house was certainly not a middle class one: there was no hot water, bathroom, and the loo was a plank of wood in a hut at the top of the garden, but children are very adaptable.

Things changed, as my bed sharer was transferred to Porthcawl, and a number of my friends returned to Chatham. Homesickness set in. I even contemplated trying to get home on a 1*d.* platform ticket. I had planned this with a friend who was returning with a legitimate ticket. We never discovered whether our ruse would succeed, as a confidante gave us away to our headmistress, and I was in disgrace again!

During the summer holidays we had to report to the school daily, where we played games or idled about within the grounds until we had permission to have outings with hosts or visiting families. When my folks came for a brief visit in August, they duly went to seek permission for my leave of absence and were immediately regaled with the tale of my criminal inclinations, to which my Dad replied, 'At least it shows initiative.' The matter was then closed.

I returned to the usual routine enlivened by another primary school friend who, driven from Chatham by air raids, joined our household. Schooling was rather fragmented as we were allowed to use the Girls' School on a part time basis; the rest of the day being spent in cramped, chilly chapel rooms. Teaching must have been a nightmare under these conditions. Science was taught by theory only—laboratories being unavailable, at least for us juniors.

Winter advanced, but apart from a few isolated air raids we were left undisturbed.

Easter brought some excitement: my eldest sister was to be married and Betty, along with my other sister and myself, was to be a bridesmaid. We travelled to Chatham for the event, which was a triumph in itself considering that the previous week my parents' house had been damaged by the effects of the blast of a bomb which had demolished houses just 50 yards away. Our doors and windows were shattered, plaster from the ceilings added to the disorder, as did the rearranged walls. My mother's main concern, as she surveyed the mess heightened by a thick layer of soot, was for the wedding dress hanging in the wardrobe. Fortunately all was well, and a marathon cleaning and repairing job ensured a happy outcome the following week.

Both Winnie (Bassett), my fellow evacuee, and I had been suffering from an irritating rash on our fingers although it was barely visible. When we reported it on the first day of our summer term, we were immediately despatched to the local hospital, with the diagnosis of scabies. We entered a ward where occupants had the most disfiguring skin conditions I have encountered before or since. We languished in this ward for a few weeks before I complained of feeling unwell and, on being diagnosed as having diphtheria, was swiftly transferred to Tonteg isolation hospital. Winnie, I think, was allowed home; but I was incarcerated until August, as along the way I developed hepatitis. (My 'scabies' completely vanished within a few days of entering Tonteg hospital.) My story in this hospital was quite enjoyable though; as I spent the time, when feeling better, helping with smaller patients, sunbathing, gossiping with the nurses, who seemed to confide in me (after all I wasn't going anywhere, to spread tales), and reading anything that came my way. The food was good, presumably the hospital had extra rations.

One morning, to my delight, I was declared fit, and soon an ambulance deposited me on the doorstep of 132 Wood Road. There I sat for some time as the house was empty and locked. But I must have had some money, because I remember making my way to the Post Office and sending a telegram home announcing my release. Much to my surprise, my mother appeared the next day and late that same evening we were ensconced within the now depleted family circle.

Most of the girls who travelled from Chatham to Wales had returned and by September 1941 all Chatham schools had re-opened, and thus two years later than planned I was attending full time at my intended school.

Winifred Bassett (now Mrs Henry Rolfe), who lives in St Albans, was a pupil at Chatham County School for Girls until she came to Pontypridd in September 1940 when she was just 12. She left her home very early one morning when the Battle of Britain raged and it took nearly four hours for her to go through London to Paddington during an air raid. She and her friend Joan Quarrington stayed at a house in Wood Road next door to Channel swimmer Miss Jenny James. Winnie recalls the vivid scenes of massed yellow daffodils at the Glyntaff Cemetery alongside her school on Palm Sunday. She remembered that the Rochester Mathematical School started up a Scout Group using premises at St Catherine's Church. She had no idea how long it continued but local boys joined, too. She was amused to learn from letters to her from other evacuees that the Girl Guides of Chatham County School practised semaphore from the grounds of her Treforest school across to a point on the Barry Mountain. Several people wrote that children under eleven years of age were expected in the town, and that is why the groups of evacuees were billeted around the primary schools. 'It must have come as quite a shock when teenagers, some very mature, arrived at Pontypridd station', Winnie said. The memories from her pen, too, vividly portray the life and experiences of an evacuee in Pontypridd:

Seven girls from a local Kent primary school passed the scholarship for Chatham County School for Girls in 1939. We were eleven years old. It took me until some time in 1942 to finally arrive at the County School, the last of the seven, all of us with a variety of stories to tell of our adventures on the way. Three of us lived in the same road, all friends together; the others lived not far away within the school catchment area. We lived on the edge of the Medway Towns, woods, orchards and farmland on our doorsteps. Undulating farmland, with quite steep hills, a very pleasant countryside to live in.

In September 1939 we seven began our lives in a secondary school in Sittingbourne, Kent, some miles from our homes and families. The Chatham County School were even nearer to Europe and Germany: they were evacuated to Faversham. Home was a target area for bombing once the war began, Sittingbourne eight miles away was far safer(?). I lived with relatives with whom I happened to be staying at the outbreak of war; the others in billets in a village on the outskirts of the town. Adjacent to the village was the huge paper mills, an enormous factory complex that the enemy would know for sure had no strategic significance. When nothing alarming happened and the rest gradually returned to their families and the Medway Towns schools re-opened, my father deemed it to be safer for me to stay with our relatives.

I knew that most of my friends were evacuated to Pontypridd by the beginning of June 1940, but I still stayed where I was. At the time of Dunkirk we watched the trainloads of troops rescued from the beaches, passing through Sittingbourne. Little did I know at the time that the evacuee trains shared the railway system with the returning troops and as a consequence spent a lot of time being shunted off the main lines while the troop trains went by.

At the end of the school year I returned to my home. If I thought about it at all I presumed that I was home for the school holidays; what was happening around me still seemed to be a long way off. People rarely travelled very far from home in those days, so foreign parts really did not make much impression on my brain. The Battle of Britain, the bombing raids and life spent in and around our Anderson shelter changed all that. On Friday 13 September 1940, with bags packed, my mother set off for Wales with me and two other stragglers to join our school at Pontypridd. Apart from parts of South East London and a couple of long forgotten holidays in Sussex and Essex, my mother had never ventured many miles from home. Now she was undertaking to take charge of three youngsters to deliver far from her home and anticipating, if she could find somewhere to stay for the night, to return to Kent the next day.

We travelled to London by the early morning coach, after a very disturbed night. The air raids were particularly bad the previous day and the night bombing was in full swing. The shrapnel falling fast through the glass roof of Paddington Station was our first idea of what it was like to be in central London.

The journey took hours, we left London at about ten o'clock in the morning and did not arrive at Treforest station until almost 5 p.m. A barrage balloon came down and draped itself on the engine just outside Newport; it really was quite an experience. We were met at Treforest by the mother of one of the evacuees co-opted by the school as the welfare officer. She had rooms in a house near the station so spent a lot of that afternoon walking to and fro to meet each train that arrived from Cardiff. She had almost given us up for lost when we finally arrived, tired, very hungry and thirsty, our sandwiches long gone and no station buffets open or tea trolleys anywhere along the route.

The rest of the day is almost lost in a haze. I joined one of our original seven at 132 Wood Road, Joan Quarrington; two others had billets with families within a few doors of us. Mr and Mrs Field, who became lifelong friends as a result of that meeting,

welcomed us and made us feel at home immediately. The other
two girls left us to go to their billets, strangely I cannot remember
either of their names, although we shared such a terrifying
experience. The calm and normality after the noise and trauma of
the life we had just left was so strange. I can remember most
vividly that the tea table was laid for the family meal and in the
centre was a plate of BANANAS. This was indeed a different
world, such a fruit disappeared from the menu long before. I had
never heard the Welsh way of speaking before and yet when my
evacuee school friend arrived home for her tea she was quite at
home, as if she had lived there for years. When I met Betty Field,
the daughter of the house, I had no idea that she would become a
real friend. It is surprising how events shape themselves.

My mother, after a cup of tea and a meal, asked where the
nearest hotel or guest house was in the hope of finding somewhere
to sleep for the night. Although the head mistress of my school
knew that my mother was undertaking this mission to re-unite
pupils with the school it never crossed her mind what difficulties
might lie ahead. I shall never forget 'Uncle Will' who looked so
astonished that my mother should think of leaving the house. He
told her that of course she would stay with me and if my father
agreed she could make it a respite holiday away from the bombing
until I settled down. Over the next couple of years that home
developed rubber walls to accommodate visitors. I settled into a
very comfortable existence.

Chatham School shared Treforest County School with the local
pupils. We used the facilities in the afternoons and on Saturday
mornings. In the mornings we used a Congregational Chapel in the
centre of Pontypridd. At Treforest I shared a desk with a Buddug
Jones. We each kept our text books in our own piles, and I
suppose made extra efforts to keep the desk tidy. I took ages to
learn how to pronounce this girl's name and we never met or
exchanged notes as many of the girls did. I enjoyed the walk to
and from school; the surrounding mountains intrigued me; the
foaming river Taff so rock-strewn and black, unlike any river I
knew. Then of course there was the canal: we had several different
paths to use. It was all so new to me.

Our headmistress was Miss Marion E. Mitchell a gaunt,
forbidding looking woman, who arrived from Chatham every so
often and hauled us in one by one to question us on our welfare.
I have often wondered how Miss Mitchell co-operated with Miss
Jenkins, the headmistress of Treforest school at that time. She was

a different personality altogether. She sailed along the corridors in her gown, a tall, white-haired, rather distinguished looking person. You watched for her and behaved when she was around but there was a different feeling about her presence.

Christmas 1940 was an occasion. 'Aunt Ada' had parents living in Cardiff, her father worked for the Treseder family who owned nurseries on the outskirts of the city. We were told that a Christmas tree would arrive at Treforest station but we must pay the carriage on it. It was a present from the firm for two evacuees. We duly pushed an old wheelbarrow down to the station to collect the tree, all seven feet or more in height at a cost of 1*s*. 6*d*. The ceilings of the houses in the part of Wood Road where we lived were high, but in its container, when finally dressed, the tree plus star brushed the ceiling. We had a really good Christmas. My mother came down to stay.

The family had many friends so we went out visiting or a lot of people came for the evening and supper parties were lively affairs. If anyone came to see any of the other evacuees and visited to see how I was faring, it was the excuse for more invitations to spend the evening with us. We often went to Cardiff, shopping and a meal at the Kardomah Restaurant before going out to Ely to have tea with Aunt Ada's parents. Sometimes we went by bus to Cardiff, often by train. When we travelled by bus from Ely we changed to a tram at Canton. Back in Cardiff I watched the tram go under the bridge into an area that I knew nothing about. I was told that I would not like it as it was dangerous and rough in the Tiger Bay area.

I loved the main shopping arcades, the big stores. I used to think that I was back in London again. The castle of course was well sandbagged so I had no idea what it really looked like through the gates. In the New Year of 1941 my father arrived for his first visit, a surprise present for me. He came off the overnight train from London and found his way across the city centre stepping on broken glass and miles of hose pipes. His visit coincided with the Blitz on Cardiff.

I remember how one Sunday evening we waited on Cardiff Queen Street Station for the train back to Pontypridd. It was eerie in the light of the blue lamp 'dim out' even if it was preferable to a complete 'black out'. Everyone stood around quietly listening to a group of men singing: we had chanced on a choir returning from some evening engagement. The singing was something that I will never forget. They travelled in the next carriage to us so we were entertained all the way home.

The one thing that has always seemed so odd to me is how easily we slipped into this life. Betty Field met one of the soldiers from the Lancashire Regiment billeted in Pontypridd and he was soon part of the family scene. The mixture of accents in that household must have sounded strange and yet somehow we all fitted in.

About this time both Joan and I developed a rash on our arms that irritated badly when we became warm. After the Easter Holiday we went to the doctor about our rash and, to the consternation of us all, we went to hospital. We had scabies. There was a bad outbreak of it at the time, plus impetigo, an even more unpleasant skin complaint. We caught the scabies from another girl in our year after us all putting our clothes on a chair together when we went for a school medical. She was whipped off to the isolation hospital at the time of the medical; we passed our problem round for a while before we were incarcerated. The isolation hospital was full so we were admitted to the old work-house on the Graig (then called the County Hospital to try to remove some of the stigma of going there), not the ideal place to be at that time. Four of us ended up in a tiny ward away from the younger children all suffering with the same problem. The hospital was packed with patients; the main wards adjacent to us full of elderly women, many from one of the hospitals bombed out in Cardiff.

We spent three weeks in that awful place. The food was terrible, thin clear soup of a strange grey/fawn colour, grease floating on top and minuscule amounts of slivers of vegetables. A hunk of bread accompanied this delicacy. We had salt Icelandic cod smothered in parsley sauce. I have never touched a dish covered in white sauce since. The most memorable meal of all was boiled liver, strong tasting, tough and a strange mauvy grey colour served with watery potatoes. It was years before I ever touched liver again. In the evenings when the Sister in Charge was out of the way we would sneak down to the staff kitchen and help hand out the drinks and assist the patients to sit up in bed. Scabies passing round everywhere, but the nurses had such a job with so many patients. Our treatment consisted of total coverage of sulphur ointment for five minutes and no washing it off. Then a bath followed by another layer of sulphur ointment. Everywhere and everything smelt and tasted of sulphur ointment.

As far as I can remember, none of our school mistresses visited

us while we were in the hospital. It was just as well that we had
such a caring family to bring us parcels of food. In the end my
parents arrived to find out for themselves what was happening to
us, as no one would allow us back to Wood Road. The Medical
Officer saw my parents and explained that we were suspects for
diphtheria; there had been deaths in the hospital. I had been
immunised against the disease and was allowed to go home that
afternoon. Joan was not so fortunate: she caught the disease and
went to the old isolation hospital at Tonteg where luckily she was
more bored than ill. Her next problem was that she caught
hepatitis from one of the nurses, so had a very lengthy stay in the
hospital. Visiting at Tonteg meant standing in the hospital yard and
shouting through the ward windows. Eventually her mother
arrived, Joan was discharged from the hospital and returned to
Chatham.

I spent most of that summer term at home. It was a lovely
summer and I was able to spend hours out in the sun while my
scars faded. I had huge scabby spots by the time I left the hospital
and wore bandages on my arms when I went out. It was several
years before I was able to go out in the summer without a cardigan
or long sleeved clothes. Each week I went to see the Medical
Officer until he passed me free from infection. My mother stayed
for several weeks until I began to recover my normal weight and
looked more normal. Aunt Ada took me to so many places. We
went to Cardiff frequently. On one occasion we visited the
National Museum and also out to St Fagan's Castle to walk in the
grounds. I remember going out on the Barry mountain with dishes
to pick winberries. I think that everyone who went to Wales
remembers winberry pies. What a wonderful discovery those juicy
fruits were. It must have been during that time that Aunt Ada and
I went to Porthcawl for the day. I borrowed a bathing costume and
we walked down through the gap in the barbed wire entanglements
to the sands beyond to swim in the Bristol Channel. It was very
different from the coastal resorts of Kent.

Uncle Will was a roundsman for Morgan Harris bakeries and
his round covered some of the district up as far as Porth. At some
time during the late autumn of 1940 Aunt Ada arranged to meet
Uncle Will outside one of the grocery shops on the mountainside
in Porth. We were all shocked at the conditions in which people
lived in the Rhondda Valley. It was a dark grey afternoon, very
misty and wet. The river looked black and menacing. Women
walked around with their babies swaddled in blankets wrapped

round their mothers' bodies. We had never seen people living like
it before. It was so different from Treforest and Pontypridd. Close
by the grocer's shop stood the baker's van, its horse a large near
black animal with the stable name of Prince. Most of the cart was
on the pavement and the horse had his head inside one of the front
doors waiting for a tit-bit. The grocer wanted to meet 'Billie's'
evacuees, and we had such a warm welcome. We each came away
with a tin of fruit (a luxury at that time) to put away for Christmas.

The market at Pontypridd was a delightful discovery, especially
the undercover section with its mixtures of stalls and smells of
fruit and vegetables, cheeses, Welsh cakes, fish and poultry. I came
to like black pudding, but the first sight of bowls of laver bread
gave me no appetite at all to try the strange delicacy. Saturday
lunchtime we went into town for a cafe meal to eke out the
rations. On the corner of Mill Street and Gelliwastad Road was a
small cafe, Lloyd Loom chairs and glass topped tables. My
favourite meal was Spam, egg and chips. Now I believe that corner
lies under the dual carriageway that cuts the town in two.

At the end of 1941 our school returned to Chatham. My father
was still not entirely happy about the way the war was going. He
coupled that with the upset that I had in the hospital and, as I was
settled and happy, I stayed behind. A number of us stayed and
joined the Treforest School. I soon made friends with some of the
girls and really enjoyed the novelty of being in a school where the
morning assembly was conducted in English one week and in
Welsh the next. We quickly learned to scan the Welsh hymn and
prayer books and could sight read enough to join in, even if we
did not have a clue about the sense of the words.

I left Pontypridd some time in 1942, as far as I can remember,
to join my own school. I was bridesmaid to Betty Field in the May
of that year, when she married her soldier (Harry Throup) who
came to the town about the same time that I did. I was delighted
to be asked. I helped to ice the wedding cake with chocolate icing,
and prepare the other food. It was truly a war-time wedding.

We all remained friends and years later the family came to my
wedding in Kent. I think that although things did not always go
well for evacuees, for many it was a great experience with many
happy endings and lasting friendships. The planning into the first
evacuation was methodical and precise without any real idea of the
feelings of the population of Britain. In the second evacuation,
necessity was the overriding consideration, as many people had to

be moved from the south eastern corner of Britain. The whole thing worked inspite of those in charge, which was just as well.

It was not until the summer of 1995 that I finally realised an ambition to see the church at the summit of Eglwysilan Mountain. I had climbed part of the way up the mountainside several times back in the 1940s, but the higher one climbed there was always another path disappearing into the distance. In the end I reached my goal, by car. The church was boarded up as a deterrent against further acts of vandalism, but the churchyard was well kept and still in use. It was the spectacular views across the mountain tops and valleys that affected me most. I had no idea that it was possible to see across the Bristol Channel into Somerset and Devon. I was so fortunate to have picked such a clear day for my visit.

Chatham County School for Girls was renamed Chatham Girls' Grammar School in 1944. The roll for 1939 should have been a record 490 pupils but 198 were evacuated officially and more than 100 more privately. Most girls returned to Chatham by September 1941 and all by the beginning of 1942 when the worst of the air raids were over. In 1944 came the doodlebugs or flying bombs, which were so unpredictable that there was no time to get to the shelters and the girls had to get under the desks to avoid flying glass. One youngster, Stella Cox (later Mrs Bostock) recalls that Miss Ledingham became a real mother to her group of evacuees to Pontypridd, and each biology lesson for the sixth form began with enquiries about the younger girls' welfare.

When doodlebugs fall

The billeting allowance at the beginning of the war for people taking in evacuees was 10*s*. 6*d*. for one child and 8*s*. 6*d*. each for more than one. The government required a contribution from the parents of evacuees of 6*s*. for each child to help support them. But collecting the contributions proved too troublesome for their worth. The allowances were slightly increased from time to time. For the 1944 evacuees fleeing from the V1 flying bombs and the V2 rockets the allowances were fixed on a scale ranging from 10*s*. 6*d*. for a child under the age of five to 17*s*. 6*d*. for a person aged 17 or over. The allowance for an adult, who would provide her own food, was 5*s*. and another 3*s*. for each accompanying child. Some households living on the breadline found these allowances attractive or even a godsend. But sometimes selfishness prevailed—not everyone opened their hearts with their homes to the evacuees. And there were inevitable tensions between some unsympathetic householders and the uprooted children. A leaflet from the WVS in 1944 advised that 'Some children may try your patience by wetting their beds, but do not scold or punish; as this will only make matters worse'. Evacuees seemed more content in the towns of depressed areas like Pontypridd: the home conditions of many of the children from parts of London were not unlike (or were far worse than) those here. In some rural or more prosperous areas, perhaps, social divisions were often sharply exposed and greater frictions easily arose.

Local organisations were active in making evacuees feel at home. The Trallwn Ward Evacuation Welfare Committee had Cllr Percy James as chairman and Miss R.L. Thomas as secretary in May 1940. A reception for evacuated mothers in Trallwn organised in January 1941 was a typical and happy affair. Present at the reception were Arthur Pearson MP and Raymond Jones, Director of Education. Two sketches were performed by Mr McCarthy's Party of Cilfynydd Ladies. A similar club was formed in Cilfynydd and members gave an evacuee tea at the Unemployment Club in Park Place in the village soon after the New Year in January 1942. The Cilfynydd Evacuation Committee had Cllr Arthur Seymour as chairman, Miss Blodwen Evans as secretary, and Mrs T.J. Burrows (wife of local schoolteacher Tom Burrows) as treasurer. Among other well-known villagers present at the reception were teachers Miss Blodwen Ashton and Miss Clarice Blizzard.

Throughout July 1944 thousands of official and unofficial evacuees of all ages poured into Pontypridd and the Rhondda from the London area in the third evacuation scheme. Lack of volunteers made finding billets for them very difficult. The newcomers had escaped from a new peril: the doodlebugs or buzz bombs, Hitler's V1 flying bombs, the first of which fell on London on the night of 15 June 1944, just a week after the D-Day landings in Normandy. Casualties were high and the V2 rockets were to land with more devastation shortly afterwards. The V1 was a pilotless aircraft with a speed of 370 mph and a range of nearly 200 miles, carrying a one ton warhead. The droning engine noise grew louder as the aircraft approached until its fuel was exhausted, whereupon the jet motors cut out suddenly and the doodlebug plunged to earth. Because most attacks came in daytime many people were not able to take shelter through the long hours of an 'alert'. Despite the terror, death and great destruction, humour was indefatigable: one newspaper cartoon pictured a parrot telling the cat lying beneath its cage, 'Purr if you must, but for heaven's sake don't cut out suddenly.'

The first V1s were launched from sites in the Pas de Calais in France and from sites in Holland. Nearly 10,500 were launched, of which 4,300 were shot down or tipped over and fell to the ground after striking barrage balloons or the cables. They still exploded. By the end of the first month 1,600 people had been killed and 4,500 seriously injured, and 100,000 houses damaged. In all, the V1 missiles killed 6,139 people and seriously injured 17,239.

The V2 was the second of Hitler's V-weapons, his 'vengeance' weapons. The rockets travelled at 3,000 mph. They could not be intercepted and the 2,000 lb warhead exploded without any warning. The first fell in Chiswick, west London, on 8 September 1944 and about another thousand were to come. There was a news blackout of the V2 rocket attacks until 10 November. They killed some 2,800 people and seriously injured more than 6,000. The V2 campaign ended when Allied troops overran the launch sites. The last fell in Kent on 27 March 1945. During the entire war, more than 61,000 British civilians were killed and more than 127,000 were injured.

In September 1989, to commemorate the 50th anniversary of the outbreak of the war, many ceremonies were held in the Rhondda during the 'Rhondda Remembers' evacuee reunion weekend when 500 former evacuees made a nostalgic visit to their second homes. People of the valleys lined the streets to welcome the evacuees as they stepped off the special train, this time for only a short visit.

CHAPTER SEVEN

Saving for Victory

Spitfire targets

Raiders were seen many times in searchlight beams or spotted in daylight hours in Pontypridd skies. But few people had a close look at the enemy aircraft, stamped with their black crosses and swastikas. So a pilot's eye view of a German Messerschmitt Me 109 fighter aircraft displayed in the enclosed swimming pool in Ynysangharad Park in February 1941 created much local curiosity. The display formed part of the local savings programme—countrywide National Savings groups energetically supported the war effort.

Many towns also held their own 'Spitfire Fund' to raise money to buy fighter aircraft. Townspeople decided to launch a Pontypridd Spitfire Fund after their meeting in late August 1940 at the Shelley Hall of the YMCA. 35,000 people visited a Royal Air Force display at Taff Vale Park, Treforest, in October and November 1940 to see a German Heinkel He 111 twin-engined bomber shot down during the Battle of Britain. Admittance charges of 3*d.* for adults and 1*d.* for children raised £300 towards the Pontypridd Spitfire Fund. Crowds of people lined the streets of Treforest to watch RAF transport conveying the bomber to the paddock down by the works of the *Pontypridd Observer*.

Bert Wilcockson of Llanover Road, Pontypridd, recalls that

> The Heinkel bomber had been shot down somewhere, pretty intact. I was a Home Guard at the time and we were posted at night to guard the plane against souvenir hunters. The night that my companion and I were detailed, we hung about until 2 a.m. and then decided to try and have a doze inside the plane. My companion found a spot just inside and I made myself as comfortable as possible in the middle of the plane, underneath what was the mid-gunner's position. I remember lying there in my greatcoat, and watching the moonlit gunner's slung seat above me, and wondering what perhaps had become of the poor German. In the light of dawn I soon found out—the roof of the Heinkel around the slung seat was splashed with dried blood. The blazing eight guns of the Spitfire which shot him down must have blown him to pieces.

The busy organisers of dances, concerts, collections, whist drives, races, parades, football matches, and many other local events worked hard for a year to raise the £5,000 cost of the Pontypridd Spitfire. The aircraft took to the skies with 'Yr Hen Bont' (the Old Bridge) emblazoned near the cockpit and so named after Pontypridd's famous eighteenth century single-span bridge over the River Taff.

Newspaper and poster cartoons urged everyone to 'Squash the Squander Bug'—an evil creature that tempted extravagant spending. Publicity posters played an important part in the war by informing and inspiring the public with patriotic slogans. National Savings posters invited everyone to hit back at the enemy with purchases of 15*s.* National Savings Certificates which would be worth 20*s.* 6*d.* in ten years. Other posters urged the public to save for supremacy and the way to victory. One prompted the public to 'Fight in the Streets – Belong to Your Savings Group'. Pontypridd Local Savings Committee organised street or village groups to sell shilling savings stamps from door to door. Special Savings Weeks were held throughout the country on several occasions: War Weapons Weeks in 1941, Warship Weeks in 1942, Wings for Victory Weeks in 1943, and Salute the Soldier Weeks in 1944. War savings weeks started in Pontypridd with big parades of military, cadet and many civil defence units. Total National Savings throughout the town and district during the war topped £4 million.

Poster publicity became a wartime art on the home front and was used in direct appeals to the general public urging them to increase their savings, and to avoid waste. Many kinds of poster appeared over the years to encourage a fighting spirit and your taking care of yourself and the country. They added colour all over the district. Well-known ones included:

Hit Hitler With Your Savings

Join Your Savings Group Now!

Join Your Factory Savings Group

Join The Crusade – Buy National War Bonds

You Can Help Me Build A Plane

Back Up The Fighting Forces

Three Words to the Whole Nation – GO TO IT!

Freedom is in Peril – Defend It With All Your Might

Put Out Waste Paper

Careless Talk Costs Lives – 'Keep It Under Your Hat'

Look Out In The Black Out!

War Weapons Week

More than £¼ million of savings had been raised in the area in 1940 and at a civic reception at the Municipal Buildings to open the War Weapons Week, held in Pontypridd on 8–15 February 1941, H.H. Davies (treasurer) of Lloyds Bank announced that promises received had already passed the £100,000 target aimed for. W.W. Wakefield, MP for Swindon and Parliamentary Secretary to the Minister for Air, opened the week which he hoped would be the beginning of a continual flow of savings and that people would cut their spending to the bare minimum to help play their part in the war effort. He was welcomed by Jesse Powderhill JP, the chairman of the urban district council, who presided, and by Arthur Pearson, Member of Parliament for Pontypridd. Among those present were Sir Gerald Bruce, Stanley Evans (chairman of the War Weapons Week committee), David Christopher (vice-chairman), E.E. Morris (secretary) and D.G. Ball and Edward C. Lewis (respectively chairman and secretary of the publicity committee).

The Pontypridd Battalion of the Home Guard, commanded by Colonel Lester Lewis and Captain E.B. Beech MC, and detachments of the Royal Navy, Army and Royal Air Force marched past the Municipal Buildings where the salute was taken by the Earl of Plymouth, accompanied by Lady Plymouth. In the afternoon a fire-fighting display was given in Ynysangharad Park by the Pontypridd Fire Brigade and the Auxiliary Fire Service commanded by Captain D. Muir. Mrs Hilda Porcher JP opened a WAAF exhibition and recruiting centre at the Shelley Hall of the YMCA. Also at the YMCA was the busy Selling Centre where savings stamps and certificates could be bought. Arthur Pearson opened a war weapons museum at Hepworth clothier's old premises at 72 Taff Street. A naval officer from the Naval Gunnery Instructional School explained the workings of various naval exhibits and there were contributions from the other services. Included in the exhibits were the winning entries in the slogans, crayon colouring and posters competitions the Education Committee organised in schools throughout the district for children of all ages during the War Weapons Week.

The children played their part with enthusiasm. Idris Newland of Penycoedcae (one of a well-known Cilfynydd family) recalled that a classmate at Cilfynydd Junior School, Gerald Stanfield, was one of the slogan winners. Other winners were Billy Austin, Arthur Bailey, Olwen Bailey, Jack Banfield, Arnold C. Bell, Jack Bennett, Jean Brooks, Peter Brown, Barbara Cook, John Davies, Peter Dickson, Ann Edwards, Ronald Edwards, Mary Gronow, Margaret Jones, Kenneth Kidney, Frank Laming, Hugh Loudon, Jean Morris, Muriel Osman, William Pain, Ronald Prescott, Roy Shears, Norman H.Smith, Gerald Stanfield, Marilyn Sullock, Kenneth M.Thomas, Bernard Vickery, Kenneth H. Watkins, Haydn C.Williams, H.D. Williams and Sylvia Williams.

The crowd-drawing highlight of an exhibition opened on 10 February by Mrs Stanley Evans was the display in the swimming pool at Ynysangharad Park of a German Messerschmitt Me 109 fighter plane shot down, reportedly, by a local boy. Also shown, it was claimed, was the largest bomb to have been dropped on Britain. Jack Jones, the author of *Off to Philadelphia in the Morning* and the play *Rhondda Round-about*, toured the district in a mobile cinema van and addressed several meetings to get the savings message across. The first was near the Tredegar Arms and aimed particularly at the many farmers who came into town on the Wednesday market day. He also presented the competition prizes at the schools. Lady Rhys Williams chaired a special Ladies' Meeting at the Shelley Hall at which Madam Muriel Jones and some members of her Royal Welsh Ladies Choir sang. Ladies' teams entered a skittle competition and played their games at the New Inn Hotel. All the rolls and a dance organised by the Treforest section of the special constabulary aimed to boost savings from all over Pontypridd.

Contributions to the savings target came from many local banks, insurance companies, private firms and small organisations. The public was urged to buy more and more National Savings Certificates, 3 per cent Savings Bonds, 2½ per cent National War Bonds, 3 per cent Defence Bonds, and to make the most of Post Office Savings Banks. Every afternoon at two o'clock the Fire Brigade recorded on the large barometer the total amount invested. By the end of the campaign the town was proud to have more than doubled its target with a magnificent total of £234,699. The campaigns went on: the Rhondda War Weapons Week took place between 22 and 29 March 1941.

Warship Week

Activities held for Warship Week held in Pontypridd from 7 to 14 February 1942 aimed for a target of £150,000, the cost of adopting a corvette, HMS *Tamarisk*, and additional equipment. When Stanley Evans, the Pontypridd stipendiary magistrate, called on H.H. Davies to make the final adjustment of the town barometer, placed on the Town Hall Chambers in Market Street, it indicated that more than £274,000 had been raised, £20,000 of it by the Schools Savings Association. Some had come from the Pontypridd Boys' Grammar School which presented the Ian Hay comedy *Housemaster*, set in a boys' school, on the evenings of 4–5 March with tickets selling fast at 2*s*. and 1*s*. 6*d*.

The events prepared for Warship Week started with a large parade through the town consisting of a naval armed party, a Royal Navy anti-aircraft gun and its crew, searchlight unit and operators, sound location unit and crew, bomb disposal squad and exhibits, a Royal Air Force band and a contingent of airmen, WAAFs, the County School Flight of the Air Training Corps (557 Squadron), the 1004 Town Squadron of the ATC, the Royal Artillery Cadet Corps, the Auxiliary Territorial Services, Royal Observer Corps, Cardiff Sea Cadets with gun and mounting, British Red Cross Society, the Order of St John Ambulance Brigade, a bren gun carrier section, a contingent of the Indian Army, Women's Land Army, National Fire Service, and several bands. During the parade, a RAF flying display took place over the town.

A civic reception in the Council Chamber opened at 3 p.m., at which the speaker was Captain M.R. Bernard RN. The Earl of Plymouth, Lord-Lieutenant of Glamorgan, took the salute at 4.15. Throughout the week there were other events similar to those held for War Weapons Week. A Selling Centre opened in Fountain (or Penuel) Square. Pontypridd Chamber of Trade arranged window displays and competitions with War Savings Certificates as prizes, special badges were on sale, a cinema van toured several factories and villages in the district, and schools held competitions for various age groups in handwriting, painting, and pen and ink sketching, with the winning exhibits displayed in the town. The indomitable Treforest Special Constables organised another dance, at the Shelley Hall. Author Jack Jones, through the Ministry of Information, spoke at the County Cinema and the St Athan Band and Concert Party gave a Sunday concert at the Town Hall theatre.

During the Wings for Victory Week events in Pontypridd in May 1943, Captain F.G. Glossop RN on behalf of the Admiralty presented Councillor Charles H. James JP with a plaque, for the safekeeping of the council, to commemorate the adoption of HMS *Tamarisk*. He could not tell them very much about what the *Tamarisk* was doing except that she was working to a very great extent with the Royal Air Force in escorting convoys. William Berriman presented the captain with a cheque to purchase comforts for the ship's crew. The captain said that the Royal Navy had a very good fling here in Warship Week; and that he, personally, had visited Pontypridd afterwards to receive a handsome plaque the town had given to the ship. In August 1943 Lieut. R. Earlinhead of the *Tamarisk* wrote to the local savings committee. He was not able to give any details of the ship's 'lengthy foreign service' but said, 'As the people of Pontypridd keep striving for victory, so shall the child of your adoption. God Bless you all.'

Wings for Victory Week

Pontypridd Wings for Victory Week was held from 8 to 15 May 1943, although a Royal Air Force display, opened by Group Captain D.J. Thomas, was held at the Shelley Hall for the whole of the previous week. On the Treforest Trading Estate there were daily military parades and other special events such as dances at the Estate Restaurant. On 1 May the beauty queen for the week, Miss Treforest, was selected from 34 competitors. She was Mair Owen of Pencoed Avenue on the Common. A boxing tournament was held at the estate, and a dance for a thousand dancers at the KLG factory canteen on 7 May was followed by a dinner-dance at the Estate Restaurant the next evening.

In his address on 1 May, chairman Stanley Evans of Bronwydd, Tyfica Road, said:

> In May we take our place in the Wings For Victory campaign. The figure we set out to reach this year is £200,000–enough to provide forty fighters. Somewhere in the skies a Spitfire flies, provided by our town and, to our joy, bearing the name 'Yr Hen Bont'. It is not yet given to us to know aught of its doings but we pray its life will be long and its deeds mighty. Now we want to send forty, yea, fifty and even sixty to follow 'Yr Hen Bont' as a worthy memorial to those gallant lads of Pontypridd who have done their work with a selfless devotion that will for ever be a pride to us all. The greater amount we can raise the more satisfied will we feel that we are worthy of those lads who gave their all, and the sooner will come final and complete victory.

At a civic reception in the Council Chamber on 8 May, the chairman,

Councillor Charles H. James, introduced Group Captain G.P. Grenfell DSO, who was to inaugurate Pontypridd Wings For Victory Campaign and invite 'Promises and Investments'. Cllr James welcomed him to the town on behalf of members and officers of the council and the campaign committee who included the clerk to the council, H. Leonard Porcher; E.E. Morris, the campaign secretary; H.H. Davies, treasurer; Stanley Evans, chairman; D.G. Ball, publicity chairman; W. Berriman, secretary of the Troops Comforts Fund; and Police Superintendent Howell Rees.

After the reception, a grand parade of the fighting services and civil defence units headed by the band of the Welch Regiment with their regimental mascot, the white goat, mustered at the Broadway at 4.30 p.m. and paraded through High Street, Mill Street, Gelliwastad Road, Bridge Street and Taff Street before returning to Broadway. The parade included many men and women who had earned distinction during the war. The salute was taken outside the Municipal Buildings by Group Captain Grenfell who was supported by army, navy and air force personnel.

Arthur Pearson MP announced at the target indicator at 5.30 p.m. that the money already received amounted to £82,652. Later in the day, H.H. Davies announced that the sums promised brought the total up to £170,000. A rally of schoolchildren was held in Market Square for community singing and to move the town indicator.

The official Wings for Victory programme for the town told of the special items of interest. These included a 'Bomb for Berlin' on display at the Post Office, on which you could stick a stamp bearing your signature; a Spitfire on view; and a display in Fountain Square by 1004 Town Squadron of the Air Training Corps all week. Special Wings For Victory leave was requested for many Pontypridd servicemen who had been decorated or mentioned; a new Savings Centre in Mill Street opened during the week from 9 a.m. to 6 p.m. for the sale of savings stamps and certificates; and special Wings For Victory films were screened in all cinemas for the two weeks of activities. A window-spotting competition organised by the Pontypridd Chamber of Trade aroused a good deal of activity; a Savings Forecast Competition by post or delivery to the Rediffusion offices in Market Street offered prizes of savings certificates; and special events and competitions taking place in all the local schools caught the interest of the children.

Other events in the Wings For Victory programme for the town included speakers from the RAF touring the district. Crowds gathered to see and wave to a famous and much decorated Czech fighter pilot, Flight Lieutenant Karel Kuttelwascher, known as 'Old Kut' to his comrades. He was credited with shooting down 29 enemy aircraft and reputed to have said, 'But the bravest thing I ever did was to marry a Welsh girl.' Two Sunday Concerts were held at the Town Hall with proceeds in aid of the town's campaign thanks to the efforts of manager Emanuel (Manny) Bloomer. The Pontypridd Skittle League started its special tournament and the Wings For Victory cinema van toured the district. Fighter heroes of the Battle of Britain and the Battle of Malta visited the town to address local organisations. Servicemen visited works and factories and there was the big attraction of a rugby match held at Ynysangharad Park on 15 May with Stanley Evans's XV playing a South Wales XV. The total amount raised in Pontypridd's Wings for Victory Week was £337,140 for 67 fighters.

The finale of the Wings for Victory campaign on 16 May was a grand parade accompanied by bands which included the famous ATS band— often seen in cinema films—which assembled on the Broadway and marched through Taff Street and Bridge Street for a drum head service in Ynysangharad Memorial Park at 3.30 p.m. conducted by the Revd T.E. Rogers, Chaplain of 2nd Battalion Home Guard.

Salute the Soldier Week

Pontypridd Salute the Soldier Week committee were busy in all the wards in April 1944 preparing for the opening of the local campaign in the middle of May. The savings target set was £200,000 but it was hoped to exceed this, for one objective was to equip the town's own 1/5 Battalion of the Welch Regiment and also to supply a base hospital and medical unit. The final figure for the Llantrisant and Llantwit Fardre target of £120,000 for their Week from 15 April was £139,102. Street savings groups, schools, hotels, clubs, and other organisations had fixed their individual targets. There would be a whole week of social events at the Town Hall, organised by E. Manny Bloomer, including boxing matches, with a contest featuring Norman Lewis, the bantamweight champion of Wales. The wards were also choosing their candidates for the savings queen of the week.

A Rhydyfelin man and ex-Pontypridd Grammar School pupil, Graham Hogarth, aged 18 of Dyffryn Crescent, wrote a moving poem which the *Pontypridd Observer* published as a fine incentive to the patriotism of local residents during the run up to Salute the Soldier Week in Ponty-pridd. Graham's sister, Mrs Thelma Jones of Llanover Road, has the poem he created to carve the soldier's name with pride.

Poem for Salute the Soldier Week, Pontypridd, 1944

Salute the Soldier, you who've watched him fight,
You've seen him turned, you've seen him in retreat;
Yet you had faith, somehow you seemed to know,
That from his ashes, more like him would grow,
And strive for victory, knowing no defeat.
You've seen him hit back by superior force,
You've watched him rise like some forgotten star;
To fight on battlefronts flung far and wide,
And fling the fleeing enemy afar,
Across the desert, back to certain doom,
The path of might leads only to the tomb.

Salute the Soldier, you who sit and wait,
Not knowing where he lives, and where he dies;
Yet knowing that his life or death—his fate,
Depends on your support, not tears and sighs.

Salute the Soldier, you who see him die,
For he dies not for one, but for us all;
So should we give our all, a mighty sum,
That men who read of us in time to come,
May say of us who answered every call.

Who faces Britain does not merely face,
Her Army, Navy, Air Force, all her might;
But everyone, down to the merest child,
Who buys a savings stamp to win this fight,

Salute the Soldier, help him on to fame,
He holds the torch, help him to keep the flame.

Graham Hogarth

An announcement that the main banks in town would invest £50,000 in the effort encouraged the organisers and those present at the ceremony which inaugurated the Week at the Municipal Buildings on 13 May 1944. Stanley Evans, chairman of the Week, presided over the meeting, supported by Col. Sir Gerald Bruce, who performed the ceremony, Lady Bruce and Mrs Evans. The chairman of the urban district council, E.

Percy James, extended a civic welcome to the guest of honour and said that the inhabitants of Pontypridd were proud that Sir Gerald Bruce was made Lord-Lieutenant of Glamorgan a little while ago. He had served and still did serve the town so well. Townspeople remembered his efforts to bring hope to the district during the industrial depression in pre-war years: efforts that had helped largely in bringing about the establishment of the Treforest Trading Estate.

Stanley Evans pointed out that Pontypridd's Salute the Soldier Week was dedicated to its own 5th Welch, which had its headquarters in the town. Since its formation forty years ago, thousands of men from Pontypridd had served in the unit. In the last war they had covered it in glory in the Dardanelles, Egypt, Palestine and Jerusalem. In this war again, hundreds of Pontypridd boys were in the 5th Welch and so it was right and proper that the town should be associated with the unit in this great week. Sir Gerald recalled that he was first introduced to Pontypridd at the age of 21 and he had maintained his connection with the town ever since, coming to it practically every day for the past fifty years, as a partner in Morgan Bruce & Nicholas, the solicitors, who then had an office at 49 Mill Street. He thought no appeal could be more appropriate or launched at a more fitting time than the Salute the Soldier Week: we were on the eve of the greatest land invasion ever planned since the world began. He urged the people of Pontypridd to invest all they could and make the week an outstanding success.

Arthur Pearson MP said he hoped Pontypridd would make an extra special effort in the coming week, and added:

> Let it show a degree of resoluteness and faith in the fifth year of this stupendous struggle, so that our own people and the boys who are fighting our battles can receive a measure of encouragement from it. I hope that the week will be an outstanding success and the good name of Pontypridd upheld.

The treasurer of the week, W. Elvet Hughes, said the committee would not be satisfied merely with reaching the target, but were out to smash it and he felt certain they would do so. After referring to the success of the Treforest Trading Estate Salute the Soldier Week, he said, 'I now say to Pontypridd: Go thou and do likewise.' Members of the audience then told of the investments that would be made during the week. H. Leonard Porcher presided over the first ceremony of moving the indicator and there were cheers when Arthur Pearson MP announced that £75,455 had been invested. By 18 May the indicator gave a total of £205,139 and a new target of £300,000 was fixed.

29. The 'Squander Bug', an evil creature that tempted extravagant spending. *(Imperial War Museum, MH 13420).*

30. Graham Hogarth, an ex-Pontypridd Grammar School pupil of Dyffryn Crescent, Rhydyfelin. When aged 18 in 1944, he wrote a moving poem for Salute the Soldier Week, published in the *Pontypridd Observer* as a fine incentive to patriotism.

31. *Above:* Craig Leyshon Cottages on Cilfynydd Common, 1957, showing tipping gantry and overhead lines carrying buckets of spoil from Abercynon Colliery. *Below:* Trolley bus at Cilfynydd terminus at the foot of Cilfynydd Common, across from the Albion Colliery, *c.* 1948.

The *Pontypridd Observer* reported that those stirring spectacles Pontypridd had witnessed in its savings weeks during the war were eclipsed on the opening Saturday of Salute the Soldier Week by an imposing parade of armed forces and civil defence units. Flags and bunting decked every building in the town; the target indicator outside the New Inn Hotel and the platform in Market Square were works of art; thousands of people poured into the town from the valleys. Taff Street, Mill Street, Gelliwastad Road and Broadway filled with seething masses of humanity and all motor traffic was brought to a halt during the parade, though no one seemed to mind.

The parade assembled in Taff Vale Park off Broadway. Despatch riders preceded the procession headed by the goat of the Welch Regiment and by the regimental band, immediately followed by Cymmer Military Band, Ynysybwl Silver Band, Cory Workmen's Silver Band, a WAAF band, and bands of 1004 Squadron Air Training Corps and the Pontypridd Sea Cadets. In the procession, every section was loudly cheered as it marched by: there were detachments of the Royal Navy and the WRNS, the Army and the ATS, the Royal Air Force and the WAAF, American soldiers, American WAAC, Sea Cadets, Sea Rangers, Army cadets, ATC cadets, Pontypridd WJAC, Women's Land Army, Glamorgan Constabulary, ARP wardens, Report Centre personnel, National Fire Service, Decontamination and Rescue squads, First Aid Parties, Red Cross Society, St John Ambulance Brigade, Church Lads Brigade, Boy Scouts, Girl Guides, the 2nd (Pontypridd) Battalion Home Guard; and Old Comrades of the 5th Welch—every veteran with a row of medals—who marched proudly with their standard bearers. In a decorated car was the Savings Queen with her four maids of honour. Last of all came the Royal Artillery with their Bofors guns in a great display. Police arrangements for the control of traffic and the huge crowds in Pontypridd were efficiently supervised by Superintendent Howell Rees and Inspector D.R. Watkins. The salute was taken from the saluting platform at the Municipal Buildings by Colonel J.C.A. Birch DSO, who was accompanied there by Sir Gerald Bruce and other dignitaries.

Salute the Soldier Week was packed with events in Pontypridd. An Army Exhibition at the ATC Corner House headquarters attracted thousands of visitors and many viewed the Ministry of Information exhibition of pictures and documents at the Shelley Hall. At the boxing tournament at the Town Hall, Norman Lewis won the top of the bill ten three-minute rounds contest at 8 stone 4 lb against Johnny Summers on points, and there were good matches at several other weights. On the Thursday, music lovers filled the Town Hall when Pontypridd and District Powell Duffryn Male Choir (musical director Gwilym T. Jones) presented a celebrity concert which included the artistes Miss Joan Hammond (soprano), Gerald Davies (tenor), Tom Williams (baritone), and accompanist Miss Agnes Wilson. During the evening, five paratroopers who were dropped over the town were presented to the audience.

The parachute drop was organised by D.G. Ball, the publicity officer of the campaign. Captain Desmond Brayley MC, a native of Rhydyfelin, commanded the airborne troops who were to drop on to the cricket field in Ynysangharad Park that day. Thousands of people in the park and even more on the Common, Graig and other high vantage points watched as an aircraft circled overhead at about 6 p.m. They cheered as the paratroopers jumped. First man out was Capt. Brayley but a gust of wind carried him into the River Taff for an unexpected wetting; four more men followed, two of whom landed on the cricket field, one in a potato patch and one in some bushes.

The competition to choose the Salute the Soldier Savings Queen was held at a dance organised by D.G. Ball, Tudor Jeremy, Manny Bloomer and others at the Park Hotel (the Butchers Arms of Victorian times) in Taff Street. Twenty finalists, wearing attractive evening gowns, were presented to Ronald Frankau, a stage and radio star, and his wife. The winner, nineteen-year-old, dark haired and blue eyed Eileen Basham lived at Raymond Terrace, Treforest, and was employed as a clerk at the Treforest Trading Estate. She received a letter from Company Sergeant Major J. Cotter of the Welch Regiment congratulating her and saying, 'We are proud of you and the boys have unanimously declared that you are their number one pin-up girl and queen of the regiment.'

The Savings Queen, and her four maids of honour or court ladies, Mrs Valerie Williams of Pontypridd, and the Misses Jean Marshall of Rhydyfelin, Colleen Hicks of Trallwn, and Betty Dally of Graig, attended the County Cinema on Monday evening and received a beautiful bouquet. Schools everywhere celebrated the savings campaign and the children enjoyed many interesting classroom and outdoor projects. On Tuesday afternoon the savings queen and her court visited Treforest Central School (Eileen Basham, Betty Dally and Valerie Williams were former pupils there) and presented gifts of money to the prizewinners in a Salute the Soldier competition held at the school. The work of the boys and girls included woodwork, arts and crafts, masks, poster designs, English essays and original slogans. Salute the Soldier Week was remembered by children and grown-ups for many years as the most thrilling spectacular ever held in wartime Pontypridd. The final savings total achieved was more than £300,000.

Call the WVS

On 16 May 1938 the Home Secretary asked the Dowager Marchioness of Reading to form an organisation to help local authorities with the recruitment of women for the ARP services. Lady Reading was appointed chairman of the organisation known initially as the Women's Voluntary Service for Air Raid Precautions. At the outbreak of war in the following year the WVS had 165,000 volunteers which they could call on for help with many important tasks. The number quickly increased to one million and the name changed to 'WVS for Civil Defence'. In 1966 the Queen added 'Royal' and since then the WRVS has continued to train and equip its members to provide care in the community—Meals on Wheels being one example—and the Pontypridd branch still has its office in Morgan Street.

During the war the WVS helped out by fitting the newly assembled gas masks issued throughout schools in Pontypridd and its villages, acting as billeting offices in finding homes for the many evacuees to the area and escorting them to their new homes whilst giving them comfort, arranging little parties now and then for evacuees and their foster parents (despite the restrictions of food rationing), taking wartime gifts such as 'Bundles for Britain' sent from Canada and the United States to local homes, often meeting up with members of the active British Red Cross Society in Pontypridd who distributed many American Red Cross parcels to those families in great need. The WVS arranged local exchange stalls for children's clothing: no money was needed—the clothes that a mother brought in earned a number of 'points' which she could then spend as she wanted at the stalls.

The Service also operated a mobile canteen presented to Pontypridd, one of ten donated by people of Welsh ancestry living in the United States to towns that had suffered air attacks. Another important WVS activity was taking people to and from the Cottage Hospital on the Common, the hospital in the old Workhouse on the Graig, and perhaps to Llwynypia, as well as to East Glamorgan, the original RAF hospital built during the war, many of whose patients (dressed in a light blue tunic and trousers with a white shirt and red tie) could often be seen waiting at the bus stop on the main road for a bus or a lift into town.

The WVS at Cilfynydd had a duty to assist their head warden Edryd Lewis and other wardens in an emergency. On 15 July 1941 the members had an enjoyable ramble to Llanfabon: walking up the steep Cilfynydd Common and past Craig Leyshon Villas and the quarry near Trefychan Farm and on through the beautiful country lanes to the ancient church; and then home through the hamlet of Cwmheldeg and down into the cwm with its trout stream below the plantation of Coed Pant-du and Albion Villa, known as Jordan's. This WVS branch of the ARP service was organised at Cilfynydd by the Misses Clara and Florence Jones. The ward secretary was Miss Margaret Evans of Cilfynydd Road.

On 10 July 1940 Lady Reading broadcast to housewives telling them that the Ministry of Aircraft Production was asking the women of Great Britain for everything made of aluminium that could be made into fighter and bomber aircraft—Spitfires, Hurricanes, Blenheims, Wellingtons. She said that now they could do something positive that would be of direct and vital help to our airmen. She wanted the things the housewife used every day, anything and everything, new and old, sound and broken, everything made of aluminium—cooking utensils of all kinds, bodies and tubes of vacuum cleaners, coat hangers, shoe trees, bathroom fittings, soap boxes, ornaments and even thimbles. 'Very few of us can be heroines on the battlefront,' she said, 'but we can all have the tiny thrill of thinking as we hear the news of an epic battle in the air: perhaps it was my saucepan that made a part of that Hurricane.' Lady Reading told her audience that 'whoever gives at once gives twice as much' and this brought a flurry of activity in the town.

Salvage drives

Spitfires and savings and salvage were the words of the time and many households in Pontypridd responded to the Women's Voluntary Service national appeal for salvage and gave their unwanted saucepans, pots and pans, and kettles and pegs for recycling. Later in the war, housewives found that their worn-out cooking utensils could not be replaced because of shortages. More than 5,000 pieces were collected from around the town in two weeks, plus several large hampers full of bits. At times, the WVS went from house to house to collect jam jars and bottles, paper and cardboard, unwanted books, and arranged a drive to collect books in good condition in a 'Books for the Forces' campaign that brought in thousands.

Publicity posters urged people to collect many items for salvage and recycling. A cartoon featured Desperate Dan, the character from the *Dandy* comic, who told his army of readers that they could help Britain by collecting waste paper. Children hauling their 'bogies' of orange boxes mounted on old pram or bicycle wheels picked up much waste paper and scrap metal salvage. They trundled their loads to the collection point and left them with the 'salvage stewards' in Seccombe's old shop on the corner of Taff Street and Mill Street. Nationally, a Corps of

Junior Salvage Collectors (Cogs) was set up. By January 1942 the 3rd Pontypridd Group of Scouts had collected 20 tons of waste paper. By the end of the war the local boy scouts under the leadership of scoutmaster W.H. Phillips had collected several hundred tons of salvage and, from its sale, made cash donations to the chapels and churches in the area.

The scouts were always enterprising in their contribution to the local effort of salvage collection and helpful in the preparation of local events. In October 1942 the 1st Cilfynydd Scout Troop organised a dance at the Workmen's Hall in the village with music from Trevor Griffiths and His Majestic Orchestra. The local boy scout (and cub) movement continued to grow from the 1930s. The hut at Cilfynydd was at first in a farm field behind Bryn Road until use was made later of the building in Park Place. The 'be prepared' training of the Boy Scouts reflected the writings of the chief scout, Lord Baden-Powell, in a new foreword to his Scouting for Boys in 1932 that 'A true Scout is looked up to by other boys and by grown-ups as a fellow who can be trusted, a fellow who will not fail to do his duty however risky and dangerous it may be.' In later years the 17th Scout Troop at Cilfynydd brought out a newspaper which they wrote. At this time the scoutmaster was Antonio Carini who owned the popular Italian cafe in Richard Street. He was assisted by patrol leaders Trevor Price and Henry Burrows.

The Treforest troop had its headquarters in a hut at the Dyffryn end of Meadow Street. Alec Kane of Pwllgwaun was a cub and then a scout for ten years and recalls that the 4th Pontypridd Scout Troop thrived at their hut just off Barry Road near the Regent Hall, now the Great Western Workmen's Hall. He joined the Sea Cadets later and a was a kettle drummer in their band. The Girl Guide and Brownie movements in the Pontypridd area were also well attended.

For many children the war brought treasures of shrapnel. They checked ever optimistically over their scrap metal pick-ups for any pieces. They searched along roadways and pavements for souvenirs such as spent cartridge cases from machine guns or even bought the jagged bits of wreckage from bombs and aircraft to build up collections, even though it was an offence to remove any bits from crashed aircraft. They often broke off during their salvage rounds for battles with strings of conkers. The cattie and doggie game grew more popular: for many children, the cattie represented the newest type of enemy bomber they had learned about and the doggie was inevitably the guns of a victorious Spitfire or Hurricane that they piloted in the name of the current popular air-ace in a decisive defeat of the intruder. A spontaneous cartwheel on the pavement was often the counterpart of a pilot's victory roll.

A concerted salvage drive locally from 22 September to 24 October

1941 called for help. Anything would be found useful for the munitions industry. Those iron railings and gates considered not really necessary were requisitioned locally: an obvious target was in Bridge Street by the proposed new entrance to the park (opposite the sub post office on the corner of West Street) where an eyesore row of railings on a low wall stood near the demolished Ivor Court and pub and Llewellyn Court. The substantial river section of the railway viaduct at the Dyffryn in Rhydyfelin was removed for salvage during the war. In October 1942 Mrs Hilda Porcher, Leader of WVS Centre, appealed in the *Pontypridd Observer* for members of the WVS to assist in a 'Non-ferrous Scrap Drive' for all brass, copper, bronze, lead and zinc which were badly needed.

Salvage put out by housewives sometimes stood uncollected; and it was alleged nationally that carefully sorted bundles of waste paper, string, metal and rubber were sometimes seen to be pitched on to a dustcart with the firegrate ashes and rubbish. Historians revealed in post-war years that it was not practicable to make all the pots and pans and other metal collections into armaments. Large dumps of iron railings rusted away over the years. But the personal involvement value of salvage drives boosted the morale of the people who felt that they were doing their bit for the war effort.

CHAPTER EIGHT

Markets and Memories

Pontypridd Market has seen many changes over the past century and its interior today is very different from the market many remember during the Second World War. Entering the market from the Fountain approach in 1939, you walked along a widening roadway with open stalls of fruit and vegetables on either side, some of them built partly over an old pavement. The stalls were protected from the weather by narrow awnings of corrugated iron until the area was roofed-in between 1929 and 1932. In Victorian times horse-drawn hearses creaked their way along the roadway to the graveyard of Penuel Chapel which then dominated the part of Taff Street known as Penuel Square.

The widest part of this section of the market has the frontage of the New Town Hall, built in 1890. To the left of the junction, and actually the ground floor of the Town Hall, were the faggots and peas cafes, as they are today. Beyond was the Provisions Market under its glass roof—today's meat or butchers' market. The Avenue runs to the right of the junction: you walked past the egg stall, Marshman's cockle stall and the rabbit stalls, and then, on your left, the six fish stalls that made up the Fish Market. These stalls, designed by the Pontypridd Markets Company, were the pride of the market and were constructed entirely of marble slabs, each in two stepped-up sloping sections. The last fish stall, considered to be the aristocrat of them all, was enclosed in white-tiled walls with an iron gate and is occupied today by Kerry Greenaway. Branching at a right angle just here is the narrow covered alleyway leading to other parts of the market. Continuing along this side of the Avenue were rows of stalls on which regular tenants stood on raised platforms to offer their wares by dutch auction, a sale in which the price is reduced by the auctioneer till a buyer is found. This was one of the most popular parts of the market, especially on a Saturday night. Opposite were several lock-up stalls where pens for cattle and sheep once stood.

You stepped out into Church Street and took the next entrance which led into the Victorian Market, also known as the Poultry Market and the Butter Market. The long, narrow hall had a row of table stalls on each side and a small cafe at the far end. The walls of the hall were covered with white tiles decorated with green and cream tiles, which are still there. Everything was spotlessly clean and the tables were filled with vegetables, cheeses, cream and dressed poultry. There were three entrances from the hall to the Provisions Market which was filled with food stalls, mainly butchers' stalls. As it is today, the body of the hall was filled with a back-to-back double row of open stalls. These offered a range of goods including cooked meats, sweets, cigarettes and tobacco, bread and cakes, books, bicycle parts and bacon.

There were three entrances (now bricked-up and close to the stalls of John Bevan and Haydn Brunt) into the Lesser Hall which was used wholly for the sale of second-hand clothes. The Lesser Hall, with its wooden floor and lofty roof, was the original Town Hall, built in 1885, and was a small theatre filled with splendour and a rich history in Victorian and later times. It was refurbished in 1988 and became the new Clothes Market. It has since been renamed 'The Arcade'. You retraced your steps or took the rear exit of the Lesser Hall into Church Street and turned left into Market Street, lined on each side with its open-air market of canvas-covered stalls. You could turn into the 'Reserve' entrance to the market, back into the meat market again.

You turned right into the original Fruit and Vegetable Market and perhaps stopped at one of the two wood- and glass-fronted faggots and peas cafes. Near today's Copper Kettle was the Mellor crockery stall with large displays of china set on several rising shelves secured by an arrangement of stout wooden 'keys' or turned spindles. You turned to see a block of four stalls—one tempting you with an array of sweets: trays of home made toffee, striped humbugs, sugared mice, coconut slices and jars of bulls' eyes, gobstoppers, liquorice and pear drops. Stretching for the remainder of the hall (and now an open area with seating) was a row of back-to-back stalls with neat fascia boards and wooden roller shutters, serving frontages to two narrow gangways. On each side was a row of separated fruit and vegetable stalls and along the walls were more stalls selling various goods.

There were 259 regular tenants in the indoor market in 1939. They comprised 61 fruit and vegetable stalls, 49 second-hand clothes (essential in those years of depression in Pontypridd and the valleys), 37 butchers, 32 poultry and cooked foods, 12 cakes and biscuits, nine refreshments, nine new clothes, seven sweets, five fish, four bacon, two grocers, and 32 various classes. Rents varied from 5s. to £2 1s. weekly. There were from 10 to 28 stalls outside on Saturdays and from 10 to 15 on Wednesdays, depending on the season. A small Victorian cattle market, renewed and extended in 1909, was situated by the River Taff and approached down River Street (also known as Ford Street and Turnpike Lane) between the old Tredegar Arms and the one time Crosswell's off-licence building, an old toll house from where gates stretched across Taff Street at one time.

Pontypridd Market is filled with memories for stallholders and shoppers alike. Vivid memories of many people and their descendants over nearly a century of events leading up to the Second World War, the war itself, and the years embracing the aftermath of war; and up to modern times. There is continuity, for many traders associated with the market continued a business from Victorian times down through the generations. Some of today's market traders follow ancestors who were themselves cradled in the trades.

Mrs Frances Roberts opened a stall in 1895 next to the Copper Kettle and specialised in baskets of every type and size. The stall was later run by her son Bryn Roberts, who also took over the adjacent Mellor china stall in 1971. His son, John Roberts, runs both stalls today but baskets are not now in great demand. In a conversation at the end of the war, Frances Roberts explained that the beautiful dolls then on display cost several pounds each compared to a few shillings in the Victorian times she knew. From the 1920s Bryn used to help out on the stall on a Wednesday, during his lunch hour from Lan Wood school and again in the evening. He served on the stall or went off to the GWR station on the Tumble to collect goods packed in large hampers, which he wheeled to the market, unloaded and then returned. Bryn would often have to steer his way among flocks of sheep being driven from the station to the riverside cattle market or to the pens in the market avenue. Sheep and cattle were also driven from local farms. Once sold, some animals grazed in fields off Berw Road until time for killing at the slaughterhouse on the Broadway (on the site of today's Oldway House); or at T. Allan Scudamore's behind Boots, close to the old Captain Williams's brewery off Taff Street, later the Leslie's Stores warehouse; or at the Edwin Phillips slaughterhouse in Morgan Street, behind the Bridge Hotel. The riverside cattle market came to an end during the war.

Bryn was as fascinated as all boys were by the Cilfynydd–Treforest electric trams which used to wait in Market Street, and by the two cannons placed at the Reserve entrance to the market. In later years he enjoyed concerts at the Town Hall and especially the performances of Albert Porter, a famous boy soprano whose family kept the garage in Pentrebach Road for many years. Bryn recalls the yearly Armistice Night Festivals of Remembrance at the hall. Like other stallholders in Pontypridd market, Frances and Bryn Roberts found it difficult to obtain supplies during some of the war years. If a consignment of two dozen Southport egg-baskets arrived at Pontypridd station, desperate customers would follow the delivery cart to the market to make sure of its destination and all the baskets would be sold to the queue at 6s. each. There were no plastic carrier-bags in those days and brown paper carriers remained very scarce.

Stallholders sold virtually anything to supplement their normal goods so that they could make a living. Bryn Roberts bought up surplus newspapers such as the *Daily Herald*, *Daily Graphic*, *News Chronicle*, *Sunday Dispatch*, *Sunday Pictorial*, *Empire News* and other titles of the time. He tied them in rolls for sale to butchers, fishmongers and other traders. There was little else that he could sell except sheets of black paper for making blackout blinds, sticky tape to criss-cross windows as a safeguard against glass splinters should panes be blown in by bombs, or small items like Stotharts Little Liver Pills and twopenny tubes of rubbing oils such as eucalyptus. Another stallholder swore the oil was a cure for all maladies and rubbed it on the noses of her chickens to cure them of colds—and precious eggs kept coming to reward her faith. Because of shortages, the market often closed at 6 o'clock instead of the normal nine or ten.

When his mother retired Bryn and his brother Edward kept the market business as a sideline to their full-time jobs. Then they formed a limited company and opened a shop at Philip Lougher's old shop in Market Street. The men continued to sell shoe leather and leather goods which had been sold on the premises for decades. Other members of the family were well-known traders: uncle David Williams sold fruit on a nearby stall, and a cousin, William Edwards, kept the Hopkinstown Dairy and was a familiar figure with his horse and cart loaded with brass milk-churns. Bryn is now in his early eighties and lives in retirement on Merthyr Road with his wife Linlay. While a young lad Bryn lived at 6 Sion Street alongside the River Taff when Nos 1 to 5 were known as Clive Terrace. The whole of the street was once known as Hopkins Row.

John Roberts is an eager magpie for relics of the town's heritage, such as the pocket watches he owns that were made by Eugene Bauman and Francis Joseph Kaltenbach, prominent watchmakers in Market Street and Taff Street in Victorian Pontypridd. His more recent interests and sports include vintage cars—those made between 1916 and 1930—and also car rallying. He once owned a 1935 Austin 12; a friend and fellow marketman Kerry Greenaway (the fish) had a 1936 Austin 10; and another friend Alan James (cooked-meats) had a 1936 Austin 7. All three cars looked the same but stepped down in size; and when on the road, while John peered through the windscreen of the rearguard car, they were overtaken by intrigued motorists who tooted their horns in fly-past salutes as the magnificent three moved along in sedate and dignified procession, not unlike occasional sightings in the town during the war years if enough petrol could be found.

Many characters brightened the streets of Pontypridd in the years leading up to and including the war: you would always see a big, smiling man of Middle Eastern appearance walking from his home close to the old Volunteer Cottages by the then main post office on the Tumble and make his way down the High Street with its throng of increasing motor traffic and into Market Square. As always, he puffed on a pungent cigarette held in his cupped hand. A silk handkerchief fluttered from his other hand as Kushi Mohammad called out, 'Tuppence today, fourpence tomorrow!' Kushi made his living by selling handkerchiefs and silks and haberdashery in the streets and pubs of Pontypridd. He would step down into the seamy and notorious 'two foot nine' bar of the old Victoria Hotel in the High Street and supply highly personal requisites to the needy—singly or by the packet depending on the natural intensity of his regular and his occasional customers.

There was Vetta, of Jewish faith, who used to stand outside the market and also tout round the houses to buy gold. His gold teeth made him instantly recognisable. He was an auctioneer and regularly collected hampers of second-hand clothes from the GWR station or the goods depot off Gelliwastad Road (now the bowls centre), wheeling them to the raised auction-stalls in the market avenue. Vetta rummaged in the hampers at fast speed and threw trousers and jackets at the raised hands of his customers while an assistant standing down in the crowd raked in the twopences and threepences settled for the bids.

Amos Ashong, a West Indian, stood in Market Street selling 'pills for all ills' and started his 'pitching' to attract the crowds by proclaiming that his old father was one of a long line of cannibal chiefs who had passed down a secret formulae for his well-proven toothpaste—which closely resembled a pasty mixture of salt and soot in texture. Alfred S. John, the previous chairman of the Pontypridd Market Company whose son David S. John is the present chairman, once recalled:

> I remember that Amos had the most brilliant set of teeth I've ever seen. They were like ivory. He naturally cashed in on this asset by proclaiming to everyone that he owed his own teeth to the toothpaste for which he had the sole concession. The onlookers— half of them almost totally toothless in those years of depress- ion—would line up to buy the wonder paste, trusting that soon they, too, would have teeth like those of the man.

Bronco, one of the aptly named Strong brothers, was a short and stocky man who always had a threepenny-bit or 'joey' stuck on his forehead. He sold stomach powders and pills from his stall outside Lloyds Bank in Market Square. To demonstrate and propound the evils of infection from undercooked beef and pork, he displayed jars of tapeworms. He extracted the worms from the jars with a pair of tweezers and held them high up to show what his faithful cures had expelled from human intestines. Most of the worms came from the local knacker's yard. Bronco, whose wife was a wrestler, used to strip to the waist to reveal the massive torso his pills had created and kept in good shape.

And there was Dai Swch (Dai Pig) the tramp. In the 1920s and 1930s he slept rough in barns and scrounged for food round local farms. He was always swathed in two or three old coats. His persistent begging for pennies in the town brought complaints; and Police Sergeant Roberts was detailed to arrest him and bring him before the local magistrates if he were seen begging again at the top of the Arcade by the St Catherine Street police station. The sergeant spotted him doing so one day but at that moment Dai Swch approached a passing magistrate who pressed a shilling into the old tramp's grubby hand and ended any idea of an arrest on that occasion.

Butter Market

For many years until recently, the Butter Market had two long delica-tessen stalls but both are now closed. One business was opened in 1937 by Mrs Kate Griffiths who with the help of her son William (Billy) then rented two tables for 5s. 6d. a week. Meat, poultry and dairy produce were bought from outlying farms and from this small beginning grew the stall that adjoined the Thomas cafe in the Butter Market. Billy, one of the best liked personalities of Pontypridd Market and the town, ran his own milk round, too: he obtained churns of milk from a farm at Upper Boat or from a supplier in Cardiff. He poured the milk into three- and four-gallon containers which he carried on his round to houses in Treforest. He knocked on the door, a jug was fetched, and filled from a small pewter measuring-can.

Billy used to run from school in Treforest on Wednesdays at the age of 12 to work in the market until 7 p.m. for Albert Seymour, a fishmon-ger who kept one of fish stalls in the market avenue in 1934. Saturdays were filled with long and hard hours for Billy: at 7 a.m. he waited at Pontypridd GWR passenger station with a horse and cart to collect consignments of fish packed in ice which he took to the market and unloaded. He went back to the station to meet the train from Carmarthen to collect boxes and baskets of eggs and rabbits for a stall on the other side of the avenue. He worked in the market until 9 p.m. and then trundled the unsold perishables in a handcart to the Scudamore cold stores down Gas Lane and waited in the queue for his turn to place the goods in the ice-chamber where they stayed until the following Wednesday. He would finish at 10 p.m. and pocket his weekly wage of 2*s*., which remained the same for two years.

School days ended for Billy in 1936 when he was 14 and he started on the road to success in his own business. He worked in the Butter Market on the stall of Gordon Williams who also had a milk round. Billy worked on the round in the morning and spent the rest of the day serving on the stall. He then kept an egg stall outside the Gwilym Evans shop in Market Street. There were few outside stalls at this time and cars and carts could be parked in the street which was lit by gaslight and some naphtha or oil flares, as in Victorian times. Within a year his wage had risen to 7*s*. a week. He enjoyed spending some of it at the Royal Clarence or New Theatre (from 1938 the County Cinema) where he always sat in the gallery which was guarded by small wire-mesh netting and was popularly known as 'the chicken run'.

In the late 1930s Billy and other traders at Pontypridd market shared the hire of a tarpaulin-covered lorry and for a cost of 10*s*. each they could all load up with a selected half-ton of produce from the market at Hay-on-Wye. They pulled into Hay, cold and hungry, at six o'clock often on pitch-black and frosty mornings and first made for a small cafe where a hot breakfast and a log fire took the chill from their bones. Outside, cars and lorries filled the main street and a great farm cart known as a gambo came by filled with chickens and geese laid out neatly and covered with a white sheet. After some haggling over prices between farmers and marketmen the lorry was loaded and turned for the long journey back home to Pontypridd. Kate and Billy sold poultry at Christmas in the late 1930s and early 1940s. 'If you bought 1,000 birds you could count yourself lucky if you had, say, only 100 left over.' Billy said. 'Poultry cost the customer a shilling a pound and rabbits sold at fivepence each. Baby rabbits, caught up in the nets, cost just a penny.'

Billy joined the Royal Air Force as a flight mechanic in 1941 and his wife Elunid carried on part of the business until he was demobbed in 1946 at RAF Kirkham in Lancashire, a station with happy memories for many local RAF ex-servicemen who were fitted there with a probably blue, wide pin-stripe suit and other items of civilian clothes, at last. Elunid kept the shop, situated half-way along Queen Street in Treforest, from where she took baskets of eggs and other farm produce by bus to Pontypridd market for sale. Meat was obtained from Arthur Lougher, a local pork butcher. Everything was in short supply during the war years and Elunid supplemented sales with garden and wild flowers, watercress and locally grown fruit and vegetables. After the war Billy and Elunid sold garden flowers, eggs, poultry and rabbits; but the trade in rabbits died out because of the national outbreak of the myxomatosis disease in 1953 and much of the market's poultry trade was eventually lost to competition from supermarkets. So Billy diversified into cooked meats which were carefully prepared at their shop on the Broadway at the upper corner of Windsor Road and their market stall became the delicatessen.

Billy bought the bakery at Shepherd Street in Pwllgwaun in 1982 where Elunid baked bread, cobs, teisen lap, Welshcakes, sausage rolls, pies, pasties and other delights. She had little time to relax on her market-day round: from midnight to 7 a.m. she worked at the bakery. Morning broke with her dash home to prepare breakfast, freshen-up and get to the market by 9 a.m. to serve for long hours through the day and then home to the household chores and a short sleep before back to the bakery by midnight. Billy and Elunid are now enjoying quiet and hard-earned retirement in Graigwen. Their son Peter Griffiths who helped in the market from the time he was eight years old gave up his business in Cardiff to continue the family delicatessen in the market with the same high standards of quality foods and personal service.

The other delicatessen stall that stood in the Butter Market belonged to Dennis Oscar Evans and his wife, Gloria. Oscar remembers celebrating his fiftieth birthday about 20 years ago: his family had prepared a party for him at Efail Isaf Hall on that champagne August evening. Presents were set out on a mock market-stall and while Oscar concentrated on the mysterious wrappings and packages a figure stepped from the shadows to confront him with a replica of the big red book and surprise him with the memorable words, 'Dennis Oscar Evans—This is Your Life!' The presenter opened many lively pages of the 'Evans the Black Pudding' association with Pontypridd Market.

The family business started in 1847 when Oscar Evans's great-grandfather, who was a founder of Saron Chapel in Treforest, came to the old market in Pontypridd. Then in 1878 Oscar's grandfather, David Evans, came to the market and became known locally and at five other Welsh markets where he stood as 'Dai Black Pudding'. He discovered a tasty and unique recipe for black pudding and, in keeping with the best traditions of Welsh folklore, the secret recipe has been handed down from father to son through the generations. Nothing has been written down. Grandfather David Evans served as a member of Pontypridd UDC from 1901 to 1919 and was chairman of the council at the ceremonial opening in April 1909 of the reinforced-concrete White Bridge over the

Taff at the Berw. Then Oscar's father, David Idris Evans, followed the family black pudding recipe and cooked the sausage-shaped delicacy to perfection. He was a licensed slaughterman and he auctioned meat at markets in Neath, Ystradyfera and Caerphilly, driving to and fro in his old and familiar Chevrolet van. During the years 1917–34 the Evans family had six butchers shops within a 50-mile radius of Pontypridd, one of them in Park Street, Treforest. David Idris was a very keen member of the Treforest Tennis Club, under captain Windsor Roper, which was then situated a hundred yards or so from the gasometer near Glyntaff Cemetery.

Oscar, who was born in Dynea, took over from his father in 1968 but confined his own trading to Pontypridd Market. Traditionally using a wooden spoon and a wooden mixer, both nearly 140 years old, Oscar stayed true to the family recipe and every week he cooked about a hundredweight (112 lb) of basic pudding mixture which was then prepared in 2 lb rings for sale in the market. The recipe includes a special mix of blood, flour, oatmeal, pearl barley, and herbs. His art of black pudding making and a record of his long family history were included in an exhibition in the Museum of Welsh Life at St Fagans. In more recent years, Oscar and Gloria ran a delicatessen there.

How do you treat a decent black pudding? Oscar Evans knows:

> You must fry it with mushrooms and home-cured bacon. It has to be fried in the bacon fat. It was the old miners' traditional breakfast and always served that way in the valleys. There isn't a breakfast to match it. I believe that black pudding has much nutritional value. Wasn't it the staple diet of a great rugby number eight for Wales? Russell Robins of Pontypridd, of course. Try it with laver bread—the Welsh caviar which we also make. Delicious!

Not many lumps of fat were noticeable in the black pudding rings displayed on the stall. 'That's because we put in the dripping instead,' Gloria said. 'I suppose it looks more like brown pudding, doesn't it?' Visitors from overseas, too, praised the black pudding and asked for the recipe. Not likely—that's been passed on to schoolteacher son Gareth David Evans.

32. Outdoor market in Market Street in the 1950s. The large building centre left with windows facing is Market Chambers with the Scudamore butcher shop on the corner of Church Street. The next large building along was known as the Silver Teapot building and today houses the Market Tavern and an upstairs restaurant.

33. From the 1930s the aristocrat of the six fish market stalls was the Williamses' which had iron gates. It is the only one remaining today. Photo shows William J. Williams and his wife in the 1950s. Stall now kept by Kerry Greenaway and his mother, Nora.

Faggots and peas

A dish of faggots and peas still retains its traditional and popular appeal
in Pontypridd Market today after more than a century. At one time, the
dish was served on long tables in the Lesser Hall. But tens of thousands
of market shoppers have popped in for their faggots and peas at the two
cafes situated in what was the original fruit and vegetable market. And
enjoyed the dish, too, in the tiny Thomas Cafe at the inner end of the
Butter Market. Mrs Elizabeth Lettice Thomas opened the cafe in 1924
and finished in the market when she was over 80 years old. The cafe has
kept the Thomas name, known to some of the customers' families for
four generations, although it is run by daughter Mrs Glenys Amblin who
has worked there all her busy life. Glenys is a stickler for hygiene and
the cafe tables, worktops, cooking bins, trays and utensils are kept
spotlessly clean. It's an early morning start at 6.15 for Glenys and it's
well into the afternoon before she can take off her apron. She still cooks
about a thousand faggots a week; and in past times two thousand, when
she cooked for her daughter Mrs Christine Harper who runs The Copper
Kettle, one of the nearby cafes. There are large nets of onions to peel,
the liver to mince, and some 56 lb of peas to boil. Everything was
cooked on oil stoves until well after the war but has been cooked since
on a large gas stove (spotless of course).

In addition to faggots and peas Glenys still cooks trayfuls of corned
beef pasties, steak and kidney pies, jam suet roly poly, apple tarts and
blackcurrant tarts. She finds time at Christmas to make puddings and
cakes to traditional recipes for her family and the cafe staff. 'Many
visitors from the United States and Canada enjoy a trip to Pontypridd
Market and tell me that they make a bee-line for the cafe,' Glenys said,
as she prepared meat for her pies. 'They leave here well satisfied. Isn't
that nice to know?' She has a collection of greetings postcards from
places all over the world. Before moving to Llantwit Fardre, Glenys
lived on Merthyr Road. She kept her close connections with the area as
a staunch member of St Matthew's Church in Trallwn where she was a
churchwarden. Her daughter Christine Harper has run the Copper Kettle
for more than 14 years. Faggots and peas at the market please: 'Well,
great!' said the big ex-USAF crewman. 'I heard about the traditional
faggots and peas dish served here at Pontypridd Market back home in
San Diego, California. I just had to taste it on my trip here.' Camera
clicking, the man walked off, but turned. 'Hey, what's laver bread?' he
said.

Mrs Gladys Hooper of Cilfynydd kept a stall in the market, at first for
a Mrs Lipscombe, and served fruit and vegetables there for 40 years

from 1928. The stall was situated near one of the faggots and peas cafes. Behind the stall, where second-hand clothes were sold was an old fireplace. In Victorian times faggots and peas were cooked in the market on an open fire and the smoke and smells pervaded the whole market hall. Gladys Hooper's daughter Mrs Glenys James helped out from the time she was nine years old and left school at 14 to work full-time on the stall. Glenys left the market to begin a small business venture by forming Valley Crafts in the old, unused Methodist chapel in Howell Street, Cilfynydd, and manufactured high-quality brassware in a small foundry near the one-time Farmers Arms in Pentrebach Road. Welsh-cakes are sold on several stalls in Pontypridd Market and there are numerous favourite recipes. Glenys James has a taste for Welshcakes. When she exhibited brassware at a National Welsh Ideal Home Exhibition at Sophia Gardens in Cardiff she also baked Welshcakes in a caravan behind the stand. They sold by the queue. A hundredweight of flour was used in three days. Glenys said:

> To make a good Welshcake you've got to mix the ingredients by hand. Many failures are due to cooks putting in the egg before they finish mixing thoroughly. You must pick up the mix and sort of let it run through your fingers to let in the air and make for a lighter cake. Use one pound of self-raising flour (or plain flour with one teaspoon baking powder); 4 oz margarine; 4 oz lard; 4 oz currants; 6 oz sugar; ½ teaspoon mixed spice; 1 egg; pinch of salt; 2 tablespoons milk. Sift the flour and salt together, rub in the fat and add the dry ingredients. Beat the egg lightly and add to the mix. Gradually add enough milk to make a firm dough. Roll out on a floured board to a thickness of ¼ inch and cut into rounds. Cook on a greased bakestone (a girdle—circular iron plate) for about three minutes each side.

Meat Market

Allan Scudamore lives near the Llanover Arms in Pontypridd. An uncle opened a butcher's shop in Taff Street in 1887 opposite the narrow alleyway of steps up to Market Street. Allan's grandfather came from Hereford to take over the business. Then in February 1927 Allan's father, T. Allan Scudamore, leased the vacant Hepworth clothiers shop on the corner of Market Street and Church Street (across from Lloyds Bank) where his butcher's business was well known for many years. The arched doorway of the Town Hall Chambers, now the offices of the Pontypridd

Market Company and an entrance to the Lesser Hall or Clothes Market, separated the shops of Hipps the tailors from his premises. He was a director of the markets company from August 1920 for more than 20 years and was active in local affairs until his death in 1947, aged 70.

Allan Scudamore took over the business from 1935 to 1976 and also rented the two stalls, at one time belonging to Bobby Pring, in one corner of the meat and provisions market on the Church Street side. The Scudamore family owned the old slaughterhouse at the rear of Boots the chemist. Allan was managing director of the Pontypridd Pure Ice Stores in Gas Lane at a time when the chairman was businessman Tudor Jeremy. Hundreds of lambs and turkeys for the Pontypridd market and town shops and the alternate Monday markets at Monmouth and Usk were placed in the cold storage. The Scudamore family had the only significant ice-chamber in Pontypridd in late Victorian times and Allan's mother started making one hundredweight blocks of ice on an early model ice-making machine at the cold stores in 1912. She loved playing the piano and did so right up until she died in her 96th year.

From his home, Allan Scudamore has views of Ynysangharad Park. He lived when a boy in Ynysangharad House, a large early nineteenth-century building with a small farmyard and outbuildings set in Ynys-angharad Fields, later Ynysangharad Memorial Park. The house was occupied in Victorian times by George William Lenox and Lewis Gordon Lenox JP, partners of the Brown Lenox chainworks, and by the firm's manager George James Penn. The house (along with nearby Kenver House) was demolished in the 1930s and a clinic (now also demolished) was built on part of the site, near the present greenhouses in the park. Allan recalls: 'The house was reputed to be haunted although I did not experience any ghostly happenings myself. But some local people in earlier times thought that the old house breathed an eerie atmosphere chilled by deep shadows in its rooms of Victorian gaslight.'

Allan Scudamore remembers the John Scarrott pleasure fairs held in Market Street in the 1930s when a grand merry-go-round would be set up outside his shop, ribbons used to seal off the access roads to the market area, and the street and its shops decked out for the festivities. The front of the large Market Chambers building housing his shop was decorated with red, white and blue bunting; large flags hanging from poles jammed into the attic windows; and large portraits of King George V and Queen Mary, displayed in celebration of their Silver Jubilee in May 1935. The adjacent 'Silver Teapot' building (so named from the prestigious Victorian grocery within it—now the Market Tavern of the latest New Inn Hotel) was also gaily decorated. Jubilee tea-parties, paid for by the Pontypridd Tea Party Fund, lined the streets of the town and all the villages on a glorious summer's day. That night, beacon fires blazed on the hills and mountains round Pontypridd and hundreds of people climbed to vantage points from where they could watch fires twinkling as far away as those on the Somerset coast.

Gwyn Mitchell was at the market for many years and sold beef, pork and lamb on his stall. At Christmas, orders for turkeys, geese, ducks and chickens were made ready for traditional roasts. He started work in the market at the age of 12 by helping butcher Emlyn John part-time and then worked at the Star Supply Stores in Taff Street. The butchers at the Star, who dressed in blue and white striped aprons, scrubbed the meat counters white every day and sprinkled sawdust over the floor ready for the next morning. Gwyn went full-time in 1944 with market butcher George Hadley.

During the wartime years of rationing when packets of tea were little treasure chests of their own, Gwyn Mitchell and other boys working in the market enjoyed playing a prank of filling empty tea packets with sawdust and placing some of them on a deserted stall to appear as though they had been overlooked. The boys watched the furtive glances of people passing by who lifted the packets and then sauntered off with an air of triumph which indicated that it served the careless stallholder right. The boys also dropped some packets on the floor in front of an occupied stall. An honest shopper would pick up a packet, look at it longingly, and then pass it reluctantly to the stallholder. Others, more desperate, would soft-shoe-shuffle the packets away for a short and safe distance before bending down to tie a bootlace or pick up their handkerchief before scarpering further into the market.

One character that Gwyn remembers serving with her meat ration was Mrs 'Gypsy' Lee who lived for decades in one of the caravans parked under the railway arches in Millfield, along Mill Street. Movement of gypsy travellers was confined to the local area during the war. Gwyn's brother, Howard Mitchell, also worked in the market until he joined the Royal Navy in 1945. Many local people will remember Howard as the wartime drum major of the town's 1004 Squadron Air Training Corps band.

Herbert (Sherby) Rowlands of Cae Nant, Rhydyfelin, started work in the market in 1922 at the age of eight as an apprentice to an uncle, butcher Alf Huntley. Sherby, an uncle of present-day market butcher John Bevan, dressed freshly killed lambs when he was just 11. Later, he hired a pony and a governess cart for a shilling and trotted about Pontypridd in the evenings and weekends selling ice cream bought from the Woolford market stall. Sherby left the market in 1939 to join the army and still enjoys a pint of beer in the Rhydyfelin Non-Political Club in Poplar Road. Another club member was the late Sonny Coles who also sold ice cream in the town in the 1930s. Member Percy Wilkes is a descendant of John Wilkes who was a horse-cab proprietor well known on the streets of Victorian Pontypridd.

A past chairman of the 'Non-Pol' was Gordon (Jakey) Durham who lived at one time near the Llanbradach Arms in Glyntaff close to the Glamorganshire Canal. There were always sides of bacon hanging in the pub until the war. In a handcart, Jakey regularly fetched pig feed such as discarded fruit and vegetables from the market to boil up for piggeries on allotments beside the River Taff, which also flowed past the pub. Floodwaters sometimes inundated the allotments and Jakey and the grim-faced allotment holders once watched helplessly as their crops were ruined and so many potential breakfast rashers swirled about in the black and muddy waters of the Taff as the pigs were washed away among the hens laid out or still cackling on the roofs of smashed sheds that floated by swiftly on their way to the river weir and to Cardiff.

Eddie Baldwin, another Rhydyfelin man, worked in the market in 1929 at the age of 13 to help butcher and Pwllgwaun shopkeeper Eddie Griffiths whose stall was then in the Lesser Hall. The hall was used as a meat market from 1921 but a trade depression undermined efforts to establish the building as a market hall. Clifford Dillon and his wife Hilda of Pwllgwaun had a stall there from 1928, selling gramophone records at 6*d*. each and repairing wind-up gramophones that were equipped with loudspeaker horns. There was a plan to convert the hall for dancing but instead, in 1932, all the clothing stalls situated in the vegetable market were transferred to the Lesser Hall, before the second-hand clothes were sold there in wartime. The hall was later occupied by Leslie's Stores to supplement their shops in Taff Street and Market Street.

Eddie left the market to work underground at the Maritime Colliery at Maesycoed. Among his memories are Wednesday crowds at the cattle market when the nearby Tredegar Arms in Taff Street was open all day to serve the farmers and buyers. He recalls Bert Mitchell's band that played regularly at the Star Ballroom in Mill Street; and nearby at the Palais de Danse which was also a roller-skating rink. There was another skating rink in Upper Church Street behind the Colliers Arms and near the Victorian police station and small courthouse. These four buildings are now demolished.

In Gas Road in early Edwardian days there was the old Alexandra Hall skating rink which re-opened in December 1910 and, from July of that year, the eight-table Lucania billiard hall which together became the Tudor Williams salesrooms and later Gingers night club, today a car park. Eddie Baldwin is a keen snooker player and enjoys playing at the

Labour Club in Dyffryn Road, Rhydyfelin. He used to play regularly at the Celtic Club in Mill Street. Open snooker and billiards competitions were held at Welsh professional Joe Ball's Park Billiards Hall above Burton's shop in Taff Street, although Eddie learned to play at the Regent, the workmen's hall and cinema in Hopkinstown which opened in 1926. He played exhibition matches against Joyce Gardner, the world billiards champion, at the Regent in 1932 and against Melbourne Inman, the men's world billiards champion. Eddie remembers with pride playing the great Joe Davis at billiards and snooker at the YMCA in 1946 and playing Fred Davis there in 1951–2. Another fine local snooker and billiards player in the 1930s was miner Bert Toomey who was killed in an accident at the Albion Colliery in Cilfynydd. Frank Thomas of the Graig, the local amateur champion, is also well remembered.

Ralph Perkins started in the market in the 1920s with butcher Ernie Richardson who later kept the Danygraig Arms on the Broadway, where today the famous 'Groggs' are sculptured at the John Hughes pottery. Ralph Perkins was of an era of many unforgettable market butchers of character, among them William Hale, Ted Huntley, Alf Huntley, Billy Thomas, brothers Danny and Lemmie Griffiths, Gitto Gibbon, Arthur Lougher, Edwin Phillips, Bobby Pring, Connie Knott, and George Hadley, father of Frank Hadley who had a butcher's stall from 1940 until recent years in a corner of the meat market by the alleyway leading into the avenue. Ralph Perkins established his stall, centrally situated and with its back to Church Street, after the war. He bought his supplies in livestock markets at Cowbridge and Bridgend. Mansel Perkins, a nephew, started helping in the market 70 years ago when he was a boy of ten. He later attended Pontypridd Grammar School. He joined the Royal Navy in the Second World War as an able seaman and afterwards held the rank of lieutenant, RNVR. He served on motor torpedo boats out of the Shetland Islands and then went out to Freetown in Sierra Leone, West Africa, where he was Naval Provost Marshal.

'Bara'r wlad a theisen flasus fel yr oedd Mam yn eu gwneud' read the fascia board above the old Ceiriog Williams stall in the meat and provisions market. 'Visitors and holidaymakers returning to the town show much pleasure that the stall is still here in the Meat Market hall,' Miss Enid Jenkins said a few years ago. 'The stall was first celebrated more than 50 years ago for the home-made bread and cake like Mam used to make.'

Enid lived all her life in Hopkinstown and was a pupil of the Pontypridd Girls' Grammar School alongside the Glyntaff Cemetery (the school now houses the art department of the University of Glamorgan). She started work in the Ceiriog Williams office and the firm's cafe next

door to the Cecil Cinema in Fothergill Street, Treforest, before coming
to the Wednesday and Saturday markets in 1939. The cafe was a sheer
delight for Treforest residents during the war. It offered home-made flaky
jam puffs, jam tarts, Chelsea buns and Banbury cakes, Dundee cake,
cream doughnuts, fairy cakes, scones, muffins, crumpets or pikelets,
scotch pancakes, large round teacakes and lots more. Mrs Evelyn Davies
of nearby Old Park Terrace used to go to the cafe every Monday for six
cream doughnuts as a treat for her children and herself: a typical weekly
treat for many local families during the dreary days of food rationing in
the war. Enid Jenkins remembered many of those families, some of
whom she still saw regularly at the Pontypridd Market stall until her
death in late 1997.

Shortly after the war, Ceiriog and Maude Williams had a fleet of 13
small vans delivering bread and cakes all over the Pontypridd district: to
the Treforest cafe, a shop in Taff Street where the offices of Alfred S.
John are now situated, and a bakery and a shop at Barry. The bakery at
Barry used to supply the Barry Island traders who served thousands of
day trippers from Pontypridd and the valleys. When large numbers of
packed excursion trains arrived at the resort, the Barry bakery had to call
on the other Ceiriog Williams family bakery behind the one-time Queen
Adelaide Hotel (now a private residence) kept by Haydn Doran in
Fothergill Street. Several residents of the village talk of the smell of
freshly baked bread from loaves of all shapes such as the bakery's split
tin or sandwich loaf, the Swansea or 'bloomer' baked without a tin, the
farmhouse with its attractive crispy crust, round Coburg singles,
two-tiered cottage loaves with the smaller top portion spiked or dimpled,
and twisted 'long toms'—named after some Boer War guns, or the long
swivel-guns mounted on the deck of old sailing ships. These loaves
could also be obtained at the market.

The old bakery, which stopped baking in 1954, had some of the first
gas-fired ovens installed in the Pontypridd area. Previously, they were
coke-fired. Ceiriog Williams, who started his business in the early 1930s,
died in 1974 aged 74. His brother was the highly respected teacher Ellis
Williams—popularly known as 'Shimp'—who taught at Mill Street
School (now Ysgol Gymraeg Evan James) and became the headmaster
at Hopkinstown. Ellis Williams was a Liberal Party candidate at the 1945
General Election and Enid Jenkins recalled the party rallies held with
great fervour in Ynysangharad Park at the time. Ceiriog Williams's
father, W.A. Williams, was a minister at Tabernacle Chapel (now the
Historical Centre).

Blaenclydach-born William Islwyn Griffiths, who later lived at
Heddfan in Rhydyfelin, was a bread-van driver for Ceiriog Williams for

many years. His father, J.W. Griffiths, was a chairman of the Pontypridd Cricket Club. Ceiriog Williams also loved cricket and presented the club with a cup which is still played for. Enid Jenkins bought the Ceiriog Williams market stall in 1965 and expanded the business by buying the well-known Coole's soft drinks stall in 1976 from Mrs Margaret Toms, the daughter of Walter Coole. The Coole pop stall is of Victorian market vintage and thousands of market shoppers of today have stopped by for a refreshing and reviving drink and a chat with Enid while buying their bread, baps, cake and fresh yeast. Enid had many memories of crowded market days with a panorama of passing shoppers—happy shoppers, grim-faced shoppers, and some shoppers looking weary and harassed and loaded with baskets and bags and restless children. She could look back clearly over the years and see the faces of anxious shoppers as the clouds rolled by over Pontypridd on that first Saturday in September 1939 which was to be the last day of peace.

On the Avenue

Kerry Greenaway has the fish stall in the Avenue. He first came to the market 30 years ago and was joined by his mother, Mrs Nora Greenaway, who worked originally for Charlie Williams 40 years ago. In the 1930s, the Williams stall with its white-tiled walls and its iron gates was one of the six stalls of the famous Fish Market. The stall was run later by William J. Williams. 'Hake, cod and haddock are the best value in fresh fish,' says Kerry. 'Although people go for exotic varieties like swordfish and shark, too.' The counter gave a commendable display of fish such as bream, halibut, mackerel, mullet, plaice, salmon, sole, trout, whiting, and much else as appropriate. And there were cockles and muscles, crawfish and crayfish, crab, lobsters, oysters, prawns, scampi and shrimps. Sir Edward Heath, the ex-Prime Minister, was drawn to the array of fresh fish at Greenaway's when he visited the market and stopped for a chat and a photograph with Nora.

'Hake was a popular fish for many years,' Nora said. 'Cod came generally after the war and hake was then in short supply here. Some came from the United States and that was very nice but warm-water fish from around the States was never very popular in Pontypridd Market.' Nora wrapped some fillets for a regular Friday customer. 'People no longer stick rigidly to the devout tradition of always eating fish on Fridays. At one time there were queues in Ponty market for fish on a Friday, particularly on Good Friday. But there are no Friday queues at fishmongers any more.'

Kerry enjoys restoring old cars as a hobby and some time ago he restored a 1969 Daimler that belonged to Alfred S. John. Kerry makes up the marketmen trio of car-rallying enthusiasts with John Roberts and Alan James. Alan is on the Jones and James 'cooked meats' stall by the old McTavish stall. He, too, restores vintage and old cars and about ten years ago restored a 1933 Morris Cowley to its former glory. Alan started at the market 30 years ago to follow his father, Edward James, once a butcher in Weston-Super-Mare who came to Pontypridd Market in 1930.

Near the Church Street entrance to the market avenue, a stall that sold curtain materials and second-hand clothes at various times was run until recent years by William H. (Bill) Davies who supplied a range of spare parts for domestic appliances and repaired all types of vacuum cleaner for some 25 years. Bill served in the army for 22 years and is a keen member of the Korea Veterans Association. He was stationed at Crickhowell at the time of the Aberfan disaster in October 1966 when 116 children and 28 adults died in the slurry of the coal tip which slid down the mountainside and engulfed the village school. He took troops from Crickhowell to help in the rescue and cooks to prepare meals for the many rescuers. The soldiers stayed at the disaster scene from the Friday to the Tuesday. Bill Davies was awarded the British Empire Medal in the Queen's Birthday Honours List of June 1957 for his 'outstanding military service'. He and his wife Phyllis hail from Gertrude Street, Abercynon.

An electricity-based business like Bill's would not have been known in earlier market years: at about the turn of the century the few vacuum cleaners to be found in Pontypridd and used by domestic servants in some of the 'upstairs downstairs' houses in the area were hand operated. Some electricity was installed in Pontypridd homes and the market in Edwardian years, and the market had both electricity and gaslight up to the 1920s. Throughout this time, some stallholders used Humphrey and Blanchard lamps and oil lanterns which were also used in the market place during emergencies like electricity failure or greatly reduced gas pressure. Many of the old arc lamps and gas pipes were removed from the market in 1922 and electric lamps replaced the gas lights at the market entrances in 1923. By October 1926, the only gas supply in the market was for cooking purposes.

The egg stall has been on the same spot in the market since the 1920s. It stands in the fruit and vegetable area opposite the Cambrian Lane entrance to the market where the old roadway once bordered the rear of Penuel Chapel. Many people recall the times when day-old chicks were sold on the stall. Their frantic cheeping made a familiar sound in the market as the chicks milled around in the warmth of an artificial breeder before being packed into ventilated cardboard boxes. Edward Orchard would pedal on his bicycle all the way to Abergavenny market to fetch the chicks and return with the boxes strapped over his shoulder. Later, he had an old Jowett car and used to load it up at Carmarthen with rabbits and poultry. Every spring, Edward Orchard bought a 'golden host' field of daffodils at Carmarthen and brought them to Pontypridd Market to be bunched up for sale.

Mrs Kay Cadwallader sells flowers from her shelved stall opposite the Penuel Lane entrance to the market. Her grandfather Ted James and her father, Bob James, both served in the fruit and vegetable market for many years. Kay tells of some of the market tricks of years ago. They are unlikely to happen today, for customers and traders know better. In the depression years of the 1920s and 1930s, Pontypridd Markets Company needed on occasions to send stern letters to those stallholders held to be guilty of bringing fruit and vegetables in generally unsound condition into the market. Were poorer quality fruit and vegetables placed at the back of a display?:

> Maybe so [said Kay]. But if a stall-holder today bought in the number of boxes of fresh fruit likely to be sold, they would probably soon go; and there would be little sense in deliberately placing any bad fruit at the back to slip into a bag. Cheats get found out and quickly lose their customers. One old trick—after a rabbit was selected by a customer it was taken below the line of her sight and ringed, or switched, for an inferior rabbit.

Another trick Kay told of with her keen sense of humour: one customer bought eight bananas—they sold for 2*s.*—but when unwrapped there were only six in the bunch. When the duped customer came back to the market she was told, 'Yes, luv, two of them were bad so I threw them away for you to save you the bother!'

CHAPTER NINE

Taking it Easy

Those radio times

In the wartime years, before television came into their homes, the people
of Pontypridd often sat by candlelight or in darkness while they listened
to the wireless—to sets such as the Philips model 634A which had a
bakelite loudspeaker and dial surround and was made from natural wood
and plastic. They have become known as Ovaltiney sets after the fondly
remembered children's song from the 1930s ('We are the Ovaltineys,
little girls and boys'). In late 1937, more than a thousand wireless
enthusiasts attended Pontypridd's Great Exhibition at the Arcade to see
particularly a 10-valve Marconi set with 12-valve output. Wartime
wireless programmes presented a long serenade of songs like 'This Is a
Lovely Way to Spend an Evening' or 'I'll Be Seeing You' and the music
of the big bands. There were shows named *Bandwagon*; *ITMA*, which
featured 'It's That Man Again' Tommy Handley; *Garrison Theatre* with
'Mind My Bike' Jack Warner; bandleader *Henry Hall's Guest Night*; and
Hi Gang, which included Ben Lyon, Bebe Daniels and Vic Oliver.
Ack-Ack Beer-Beer was a variety series for men and women serving in
the anti-aircraft and balloon barrage units.

The variety show *Monday Night at Eight* invited you in its opening
signature tune to 'take an easy chair and settle by the fireside'. The show
included 'Puzzle Corner', the first really popular quiz for radio listeners,
and 'Inspector Hornleigh Investigates', featuring a detective who looked
into and solved a crime by cleverly uncovering the criminal's one
mistake which was revealed later in the programme. Another popular
series featured a 'Penny on the Drum' contest, the pennies being a
penalty for wrongly guessing the titles of popular songs played in aid of
a fictitious Spitfire Fund. It prompted donations to the real thing.

Sincerely Yours starred Vera Lynn. The show started in November
1941 and was a letter from the 'Sweetheart of the Forces' to servicemen
and women telling them about things back home; and a rendering of
sentimental ballads like 'Yours', 'We'll Meet Again', 'That Lovely
Weekend', and 'The White Cliffs of Dover'. Her voice coming through
the wireless to a background of wailing air raid sirens with the noise of
threatening enemy bombers and sounds of battle won the hearts of a

nation at war. Another top vocalist who helped keep up morale during some of the dark days of the war was Anne Shelton, dubbed 'The Golden Voice of Radio'. She included a number of simple marching songs in her repertoire along with love songs like 'You'll Never Know', 'You Rhyme with Everything that's Beautiful' and 'Silver Wings in the Moonlight' with the Ambrose orchestra. In a tribute to the singer when she died in 1994, Dame Vera Lynn said Anne Shelton was only 12 in 1940 but became the 'Forces' Favourite'. The War Office was concerned that British troops in North Africa were listening to Lala Anderson singing 'Lili Marlene' on German radio. Winston Churchill said that Anne Shelton's voice was so warm and compelling that it should be used to counteract the German rendering. Soon she was the British Lili Marlene for thousands of 'Desert Rats'. Her record sold a million copies and the Germans listened to it too.

Glenn Miller wanted Anne Shelton to do a show with his orchestra and offered her a place on his flight to France in 1944. But her bandleader Ambrose had three *Workers' Playtime* programmes to record and refused to let her go. Miller's plane disappeared, probably over the Channel. Popular vocalists and bands were often broadcast at certain times to try to induce the many listeners not to switch over to hear the enemy propaganda broadcasts of William Joyce, dubbed Lord Haw-Haw. Despite this, his 'Gairmany calling, Gairmany calling' voice was known to millions of unmoved listeners in Britain. In one broadcast he reputedly said that Taff Street in Pontypridd is very narrow—'but we shall widen it' and 'the River Taff will flow with blood'.

The variety show *Workers' Playtime* was broadcast several times a week during the lunch hour—particularly from factory canteens round the country. *Music While You Work* gave a half an hour of music for factory workers twice daily from June 1940 which was relayed in many factories, including those on the Treforest Trading Estate, by tannoy public address systems. The broadcasts featured dance music and sing-along tunes from the bands of Billy Cotton, Billy Ternent, Geraldo, Joe Loss, Mantovani, Jack Payne and many others whose theme songs or signature tuncs and music were instantly recognised. There was music, too, from the American Forces Network with hit songs by bands like 'In the Mood' Glenn Miller. Pianists Charlie Kunz and Carroll Gibbons with his Savoy Orpheans had a huge following on the wireless and on the 78 rpm shellac records of the time. Frank Sinatra made his fans swoon or helped keep the flame of love burning for parted lovers with 'I Fall in Love too Easily', 'Kiss me Again', 'Try a Little Tenderness' and others. There was always a 'White Christmas' welcome by Bing Crosby from among his souvenirs. Some of the most popular songs in 1943 and 1944 were 'Sunday, Monday or Always', 'Moonlight Becomes You', 'Paper Doll', 'I Had the Craziest Dream', 'Long Ago and Far Away', 'I'll Get By' and 'I'll be Seeing You'.

You could tune in to the *Brains Trust* from January 1941 with its contributions from Professor Julian Huxley, Commander A.B. Campbell, Dr Cyril Joad and others. Or perhaps you preferred listening out for the signature tune 'Coronation Scot' which introduced the compelling mystery encounters of Paul Temple through the wartime and post-war years. *Housewife's Choice* was on the air every weekday morning after the nine o'clock news bulletin. The wireless was a constant companion of the age. Until 1940 news bulletins were broadcast anonymously; but senior announcer John Snagge thought that the newsreaders should be identified to the public who would get to know them and so prevent the possibility of hoax news reports by the enemy. News readers then gave their names: among them Bruce Belfrage, Alvar Liddell, Joseph McLoed, Frank Phillips. They became famous. The well-known V-sign name given to Churchill's two-finger wartime salute of defiance was also the name of the campaign launched by the BBC in 1941 to encourage resistance in the occupied countries of Europe, when the letter V (for Victory) was painted and chalked bravely on walls to taunt the enemy. Broadcasts from Britain to those countries were introduced with great atmosphere by the opening bars of Beethoven's Fifth Symphony (dit, dit, dit, dah) which sound like the morse code for the letter V. At home, people listened to regular war reports from correspondents or dramatised stories of heroism which were broadcast in BBC programmes like *Marching On* or *Into Battle*, with its stirring signature tune of 'Lillibulero'.

In town tonight

Cinemas in Pontypridd were closed by law at the outbreak of war but soon reopened until 10 p.m. The foyers were bound by strict blackout regulations and showed only dimly lit signs. The County, Palladium, White Palace, Town Hall and Park cinemas were nearly always filled to capacity, and few people left their seats when the notice 'Air Raid Sirens Have Sounded' was flashed on the screen. The audiences were too absorbed in such films as *One of Our Aircraft is Missing*, a propaganda film about a shot-down Wellington bomber crew helped by the Dutch resistance; Noel Coward's flagwaving and proud achievement *In Which We Serve*, based on the story of the destroyer HMS *Kelly*; *Target for Tonight*, a Crown Film Unit semi-documentary of a bombing raid on

Germany; *The Next of Kin*, another successful propaganda instructional film about how careless talk caused loss of life on a commando raid; the cartoons of Walt Disney, and hundreds more.

The glamorous, red-haired Irish actress Greer Garson was one of Hollywood's biggest names in the 1940s. She starred in 1942 with Ronald Colman in *Random Harvest*, a 'weepie' film about a First World War army veteran's loss of memory and love, considered by many filmgoers to be one of the most romantic films of the time. Also in 1942, Greer Garson won an Oscar for best actress in the morale-raising *Mrs Miniver*, in which she starred with Walter Pidgeon. The film is now often criticised for sentimentalism. Winston Churchill interrupted a meeting of the War Cabinet to see it and said with tears in his eyes that the propaganda value of the film to Britain was worth a hundred battleships: in the final scene the vicar stands in his bomb-damaged church to tell his congregation:

> This is not only a war of soldiers in uniforms. It is a war of the people—of all the people—and it must be fought not only on the battlefield but in the cities and in the villages, in the factories and on the farms, in the home and in the heart of every man, woman and child who loves freedom. Well, we have buried our dead, but we shall not forget them. Instead, they will inspire us with an unbreakable determination to free ourselves and those who come after us from the tyranny and terror that threaten to strike us down. This is the people's war. It is our war. We are the fighters. Fight it, then. Fight it with all that is in us. And may God defend the Right.

The sermon so impressed President Roosevelt that he ordered the film to be shown across the United States and thousands of copies of the sermon to be dropped over all the countries of occupied Europe. The film, in its portrayal of a middle-class English housewife who was an inspiration to all mothers struggling against the terrors and ordeals of the war, had critics then because of some of the sentiments and melodramatic scenes; but it captured the hearts of the British and American people and became a symbol of all that the Allied forces were fighting for, and so beyond criticism. Queen Elizabeth, now the Queen Mother, was one of the film's greatest fans and told Greer Garson of its important contribution to keeping people's spirits up in wartime Britain: 'It was such a morale booster for us when we most needed it. We had no idea that we were quite so brave and we were very pleased to be told that we were so heroic.' In 1993, at the age of 90, Greer Garson was made an honorary CBE for her role in the war effort.

A top box office star of musicals was pin-up girl Betty Grable who was married at one time to trumpeter and bandleader Harry James. Her legs were said then to be insured for a million dollars. One of her songs invited you to 'Cuddle Up a Little Closer'. Another favourite was Dorothy Lamour, known as the Sarong Girl and remembered in films filled with swaying palm trees and South Sea island magic. She was the No 1 pin-up girl of US servicemen, for her voice told them of home. She starred in the 'Road' shows with Bing Crosby and Bob Hope.

Still photographs, or scenes from the films showing 'All Next Week' or 'Coming Shortly' beckoned (usually in black and white) from glass frames outside the cinemas as you passed in the street, or when you entered the enticing atmosphere of the foyers and stairways leading to the darkness of the hall. Such familiar nightly scenes are now mere memories in Pontypridd. The film had probably started and your pleasure mounted as the usherette led you down the aisle and her torch flashed on your seats, unless you were among the other rascals she kept searching for who had 'pinched in for nothing' and were looking intently and innocently at the screen. And maybe trembling. You watched the 'big picture' through to the point where you came in, and then left; or sometimes decided to see it through to the end again and perhaps wait for the National Anthem.

Cinema organists played popular music on a few occasions during interludes and the audiences often had a sing-song while, high up on the roof of the County, the firewatchers kept a sharp look out for falling incendiary bombs during air raid alerts. Programmes often changed twice-weekly at some of the local cinemas. Sometimes, short Ministry of Information films and stirring newsreels appeared in between the big picture and the supporting B film.

Did the troops want cinemas on a Sunday? In October 1940 Ponty-pridd UDC discussed the issue at a special meeting at which Cllr D.T. Jones presided. Views were that they could attend cinemas anytime on weekdays. He would agree to Sunday cinema if he could receive an assurance that the troops could find no other time. In 1943 the council were criticised for refusing applications for the opening of any cinemas on that bleak wartime Christmas Day. So Pontypridd would be without Christmas entertainment for the first time in fifty years. The council argued, 'Christmas Day is a day which rightly should be spent at home.' They cancelled all the buses that day and public complaints about the attitude of some councillors in restricting public entertainment over the holiday period provoked the *Pontypridd Observer* to respond that 'the council is certainly making big strides towards Puritanism'.

Local seat prices ranged from 6*d.* to 1*s.*, and those posh seats downstairs, usually the one-and-ninepennies, where courting couples kissed in the back row with its more embracing darkness far from the screen. If you could really afford to impress on a night out, there were the two-and-threepenny seats in the balcony at the County Cinema. The building, which became a cinema in 1938 ('Pontypridd's Luxury Cinema'), was built in Victorian times as the first theatre in the South Wales coalfield and was called the Royal Clarence Theatre until it changed its name to the New Theatre in 1901. It is now the Castle Leisure bingo hall. The popular Cecil Cinema in Fothergill Street, Treforest, is now a snooker hall. The Regent in Hopkinstown is still used for various activities. The cinema projectionist and manager at the Regent during the war and for many decades was Gwyn Davies of Thompson Street, Hopkinstown. He was also an ARP warden and later a special constable. His father was Gomer Davies, a well-known colliery overman of Castle Ivor Street in the village.

The Palladium ('Pontypridd's Cosy Cinema'), Park Cinema, and the White Palace have been demolished. All three had shown silent films before the First World War. Edgar Bevan was an organist at the Palladium. He was also an accomplished pianist and at one time he ran his own dance band in Pontypridd. The Palladium site is now occupied by the Somerfield supermarket. The tiny Park Cinema, which closed in 1957, was at the rear of today's Midland Bank in Joseph Studt the showman's field where horses and locally made carts, carriages, and hansom cabs were sold in Victorian times; although a small cinema (Wadbrook's) showing silent films stood on the site before the Park Cinema came. The White Palace, now cleared with other buildings in Sardis Road at the Tumble end of town, was long considered to be a real family hall. Many cinemagoers will remember the cinema ground floor prices of 6*d.*, 9*d.* and 1*s.* and the balcony seats at 1*s.* 3*d.* Mrs Mona Gray, one of the town's best loved personalities, started at the cinema in 1918 and later managed it until she gave up her work in 1984 at the age of 91, when the cinema closed. Mona Gray died four years later, preceded by her husband Jack who was photographer to the famous explorer Ernest Shackleton. The White Palace was demolished in 1991 along with all the shops leading to it from the railway station.

The Town Hall, at one time a cinema and a theatre at the market, is currently being extensively renovated. The Town Hall Theatre was built in 1890 to replace a smaller hall (known until recently as the Clothes Hall) and had a large stage and seating for 1,700. Many famous personalities appeared there in Victorian and later days, including William Booth, the founder of the Salvation Army, and David Lloyd

George. Winston Churchill held a meeting there in 1905. Royal Canadian pictures started screening silent films at the Town Hall in 1910. In 1932, M. Solomon and Alfred Withers, a Bargoed cinema proprietor, negotiated with the Pontypridd Markets Company to install 'talking picture' apparatus. In 1934, Will Stone of Tonypandy was granted a lease and the hall was used regularly as a cinema. A later lessee of the Town Hall was Mrs Wyn Bloomer. Her husband, Emanuel (Manny) Bloomer had been employed at the theatre for some years before he became a long-serving market superintendent in 1928. Through the war years and the post-war era, Manny Bloomer was well known as a theatre impresario.

The Town Hall continued to present Sunday concerts, and meetings such as the public meetings from 1933 of the town's Jewish community. The British Union of Fascists sought permission from the Pontypridd Markets Company to hold a public meeting to be addressed by Sir Oswald Mosley at the Town Hall on 24 April 1936. They were granted hire at the usual scale charge subject to their furnishing a guarantee to pay for any damage caused to the hall. A further application from them at the end of the year to hold another public meeting at the hall on 24 January 1937 was not approved.

A generation of men and women of Pontypridd in the Second World War could recall and reminisce with their children about the many memorable events that took place in the Town Hall in the turbulent and depressed years of the 1920s and 1930s, years that ruled their lives harshly and shaped part of their heritage through the time leading to the outbreak of war. In 1921, the secretary of the Great Western Miners Lodge, Bryn Davies, asked the Pontypridd Markets Company to forgo the eight guineas hiring charge for the Town Hall so that it could be used on a night in June for a meeting of locked-out miners. The charge was waived, for lodge funds were practically swallowed up after help was given to local distress funds. The incensed miners crowded defiantly past the two cannon at the hall entrance to hear a blistering attack on the coalowners. Meanwhile, troops were virtually in earshot with guns, bayonets and swords, and ready for their orders. It was not the first time that troops had been deployed in Pontypridd during coalfield disputes.

The Town Hall staged many concerts, theatrical productions and variety shows through the 1920s although aerobatic acts were cancelled from 1921 when it was thought that the daring young men and women high-fliers had caused strain on the roof supports. Societies paid their eight guineas a night or 33 guineas a week hire charge for the hall and there were regular performances by Cymrodorian Society Drama, Hopkinstown Male Voice Choir, Pontypridd & District Male Voice Choir, Pontypridd Operatic Society, Pontypridd Repertory Players,

Pontypridd Symphonic Orchestra and other groups. The Great Western Colliery Silver Band gave some seasonal concerts, such as the festival of carols on Christmas Eve in 1922. And many concert parties gave performances to aid the Pontypridd Miners Relief Fund set up during the 1926 General Strike. From 1927 and through the 1930s the Annual Police Boxing Tournaments were held there in addition to other boxing promotions in aid of charities, including one in 1929 to raise money for the Llwynypia Hospital Wireless Fund.

On Sunday 12 May 1929 Lady Haig and Earl Jellicoe, the famed admiral at the Battle of Jutland fought 13 years earlier, addressed members of the British Legion to honour the memory of the many Pontypridd servicemen who died in the Great War. Madame Muriel Jones and her Pontypridd Welsh Ladies Choir also performed there on 3 November 1929, some two years after its formation, to raise money for expenses after being invited to sing at the Albert Hall in London on Armistice Day. The choir sang many times before royalty over the ensuing years. A concert in 1929 raised funds to help families distressed by floods in Trehafod. On 30 October 1938 a concert was held to raise money for yet another Trehafod Flood Appeal Fund to relieve the new plight of the villagers.

While shoppers filled the town and market on a Saturday, children came to the Town Hall side entrance near the top of Penuel Lane for afternoon matinees featuring films fraught with fast-drawing cowboys, scalp-hunting red indians and last-minute cavalry; not forgetting the jungle adventures of Tarzan: when he cupped hands to project his mighty calls, most of the cinema audience did the same. When entering the cinema, all the children very often received a small gift of an apple or an orange or a bag of sweets; perhaps even a toy, especially at magical Walt Disney cartoons like *Snow White and the Seven Dwarfs*. Many local people well remember with some nostalgia the Sunday evening variety shows held in the Town Hall in the 1940s when famous artistes and rising stars stood in the spotlights. The Town Hall closed as a cinema and was converted for the inevitable bingo sessions. The hall may yet again offer a place for entertainment.

Among many well-attended performances at the Town Hall were those by the Ovaltineys, who came about three months before the war; the pantomime *Ali Baba and the Forty Thieves* in January 1940, with the cast featuring a 'promising young baritone' named Geraint Evans; a police boxing tournament on 6 October 1941; a variety show, *Starlights of the Ack-Ack* on 19 October 1941 from 7.45 to 11 with ticket prices of 9*d*. to 2*s*.; Joy Clarke and her Accordion Band at the end of 1941 with tickets at the same prices; Madame Gertrude Beaton who ran the

Pontypridd School of Dancing and in March 1943 presented her fifth annual pantomime at the Town Hall—*Jack and Jill*—starring members of the school; the 39th Annual Brass Band Contest in May 1943, won by Cory Brothers' Workmen's Band conducted by R. Little; or a concert by the London Symphony Orchestra in August 1943. Soon afterwards, Communist party leader Harry Pollitt spoke on 'Fascism—It Can Be Smashed This Year'; he also spoke there on 15 March 1942 when the Williamstown Social Gleemen sang Red Army and Welsh songs. In October 1943 a drama week raised money from a presentation of six plays for the building fund of St Luke's Church in Rhydyfelin; children filled the hall in February 1944 when the Shirley Morris School of Dancing presented *Dick Whittington and his Cat*, with all proceeds in aid of the Pontypridd Troops Comfort Fund. Among many activities, the fund sent postal orders to troops and £1 vouchers to families to help them send parcels to prisoners of war.

Scores of concerts and drama productions were held in Pontypridd during the war, one highlight being a performance of *Macbeth* with Sybil Thorndike and Lewis Casson held on the nights of 23–25 October 1940 in the New Assembly Hall of Pontypridd Boys' Grammar School. At the end of May 1940 Geraint Evans, destined for knighthood and opera fame throughout the world, appeared in *Lilac Time* at the Workmen's Hall in his home village of Cilfynydd. At the same hall in March 1943 proceeds of a Grand Russian Celebrity Concert went to the Red Army, fresh from its victory at the Battle of Stalingrad. The Shelley Players performed the drama *Robert's Wife* at the hall in November 1943 and the talented Cilfynydd Dramatic Society performed *Poison Pen*, a three-act play by Richard Llewellyn, for two nights in January 1945 at the Workmen's Hall. On 20 January 1945 at the Deaf and Dumb Centre in Tyfica Road the Pontypridd & District Powell Duffryn Male Choir entertained wounded patients from the Royal Air Force Hospital, Church Village. The choir, conducted by Gwilym T. Jones, could be heard as they practised every Saturday night at the Graig Infants' School in Courthouse Street.

Time for dancing

Dance hall lights were soft and low and the blackout did not spoil the romance of ballroom dancing in wartime Pontypridd. Many of the ladies' dance dresses were imaginatively and attractively created from blackout material in the 'make do and mend' years of clothes rationing. The ladies coped well with difficulties caused by the shortages of things like dancing shoes, lipstick, and stockings. But nothing could stop the wartime pleasure and happiness of dancing 'Cheek to Cheek' with your partner.

The Star Ballroom in Mill Street held several Spitfire Fund dances. The ballroom was above McGregor's where in recent years the South Wales Electricity had its showroom. The large bow window of the ballroom can still be seen above what is now the new main post office there. In October 1940, for instance, Bert Mitchell's orchestra provided the music at the Star on Tuesdays, Thursdays and Saturdays from 7.30 to 10.30, entrance 1*s*. The Blue Aces dance band was one of several in the town that played at special dances held occasionally by organisations like the Fire Service and the Home Guard. Another popular dance venue was the New Inn Hotel, where the ballroom was approached by the hotel's magnificent wide staircase of 1922. A happy evening was spent by 250 dancers at the New Inn on 9 April 1940 when the annual dance of the Morgan Bakeries Welfare Club took place. Music was supplied by the Harmony Boys' Swing Quintette, under the direction of Bernard Elkan and the duties of M.C. were efficiently undertaken by George Ashman. All proceeds were handed to the funds of the local Red Cross Association.

There were regular dances at the Park Hotel, renamed in 1901 from the Butchers Arms; both the top room and the Shelley Hall of the YMCA; the Ranch at Graigwen; and the Catholic Hall (known as Patsy's) in Treforest. Further afield, but often visited by dance lovers from Pontypridd, were the Empress Ballroom in Abercynon and the Rink at Porth.

The most popular of the local dance halls was probably the Coronation Ballroom on the corner of Church Street and St Catherine Street (above the now demolished Co-operative store at the Arcade). In earlier times the hall was the Liberal Club, where George Nash was steward. A jitterbugging contest was featured in the 'Coro' in April 1940 when that dance craze came to town. A grand whist drive (a rare scene in Pontypridd today but at one time well patronised) and dance organised by the Pontypridd Hebrew Congregation, in aid of the Central War Comforts Fund, was held at the Coronation Hall on 18 April 1940, with. tickets at 2*s*. and music by the Harmony Boys' Swing Quintette. The evening started with whist at 6.30, followed by dancing from 8 to 1 a.m. The hall was closed 'for the duration of war' when a string of high explosive bombs fell along nearby Tyfica Road in August 1940 but it soon opened again. Those whisperings after a dance was over of 'Who's taking you home tonight?', as the song goes, started romance for many of the boys and girls and men and women of Pontypridd who recall the great happiness they found in the war years. Many couples who met at the Coro those 50 years ago are nowadays celebrating their golden wedding anniversary.

There was still a shyness about boy and girl introductions in the wartime years: the start of dancing time usually meant girls sitting or standing at one end of the dance floor smiling and chatting away watched by boys standing in groups here and there towards the other end of the hall and seemingly not particularly interested in wanting to dance. But there would be furtive glances and the quick turning away of the head if eyes should meet; and then at last the more brave among the boys would saunter over to invite that special girl for a dance— sometimes to shuffle back with dashed hopes—or a couple of boys would break in on two girls dancing with each other and soon the floor would fill and the band seemed to play more happily: for such dances as the modern waltz, slow foxtrot, quickstep, gypsy tango and many other 'Once again, please'. invitations, with popular tunes like 'Jealousy' or 'La Cumparsita' and others more gentle where the melody lingered on.

A distinguished master of ceremonies at many dances and other events in Pontypridd was tall, moustached Peter Morgan of Oakland Crescent, Cilfynydd. One of his sons was Harry Morgan, well remembered (together with Elvet Cullen) as a hairdresser at the Maison Samuels Salon near the Fountain in Taff Street before his service in the RAF, and for years afterwards when he ran his barber shop in Richard Street in Cilfynydd. He was a staunch member and player of the post-war Cilfynydd & District Amateur Dramatic Society whose memorable performances included *The Deep Blue Sea* and *Waiting for Gillian*.

One moonlit night a young couple with stars in their eyes strolled home after a dance to the strict tempo gramophone records of Victor Silvester in a hut near the Queens Head Inn at Penycoedcae. Between embraces, they thought that some fluffy light clouds seen through the trees were the white billows of parachutes slowly descending. A loud burst of what sounded like chattering machine-gun fire startled them as they came to the top of the Graig. Their hearts pounded when some hob-nailed boots scurried by—worn by a clodhopping youth spinning an ARP 'gas warning' rattle whose loud staccato sounds closely resembled rapid gunfire. However, the sweethearts apparently calmed down after a satisfactory number of goodnight kisses before parting.

34. *Above:* Gwyn Davies of Thompson Street, Hopkinstown, projectionist and manager for decades at the Regent Cinema, with the Pontypridd UDC chairman, Cllr George Paget, when two new projectors were installed. *Below:* Gwyn Davies showing the projectors to an unknown audience. Both photos 1930s.

35. *Above:* Town park and the bluff of Coed Craig-yr-Hesg, 1950s, with the Monument on the Common and the villages of Trallwn, Coedpenmaen and Cilfynydd in the distance; also the pools, tennis courts, bowling greens, cricket ground and miniature golf course. *Below:* The bandstand and the 1930 Evan James and James James Memorial to the father and son composers of 'Hen Wlad Fy Nhadau'. The memorial comprises two bronze figures: a male harpist representing music, and a woman representing poetry. 1950s.

Out and about

Everyone made the most from the entertainment laid on for them in the war: there was roller skating at the Palais de Danse in Mill Street—a large hall which at one time was used for boxing contests and also the 'dole' office. It was later Terry Badman's furniture warehouse. Pontypridd had another roller skating rink, the Alexandra Rink, in Upper Church Street behind the now-demolished Colliers Arms. Snooker champion Joe Davis came to Pontypridd on 2 May in 1945 for a few days visit and played two sessions daily at the YMCA in Crossbrook Street with selected opponents from South Wales.

The Fairfield, opposite the YMCA and now part of the temporary Gas Road car park, was the home on many holiday seasons from the 1930s to the pleasure fair of Edward Danter & Sons, which came with its familiar festoons of coloured lights, blaring dance band music on records, barrel organ music, merry-go-rounds or carousels with wooden horses or motor vehicles, dodgem rides, and siren sounds and screams. In Pontypridd in late May 1942 Danter's featured the thrills of the Moonrocket—the only ride of its kind in the country. The fair was always a big draw to people of all ages during the war: at the great Easter Fair at the fairground in 1943 all monies from the dodgem and Noah's Arc rides were donated to the Pontypridd Cottage Hospital.

One envied ATC cadet spent long evenings in a caravan at the fairground earning half-a-crown for playing the gramophone records relayed to the loud speakers. Most of the dance band music, ballads, swingtime and jazz came from the many big bands of the time—the term 'pop' mainly applied then to those soft drinks consumed, along with milk shakes or frothy coffee, by the young people who gathered nightly in the town's Italian cafes (generally known as 'Bracchis') like Marenghi's and Franchi's and the Clarence and others in town before strolling in small groups up and down the length of Taff Street and the High Street, particularly on a Sunday night, hoping to 'click' with a date. 'On the monkey walk' it was called.

Many other events were held at the Fairfield: towards the end of the First World War, on 27 May 1918 an army tank named 'Julian' was on display after it had arrived by rail and been paraded through the town to boost the £¼ million raised in War Certificates and War Loan savings. J. Gess had a boxing pavilion there in 1926 and tournaments which promoted some of the famous names in the sport were held in the field in later years. Circuses set up their big tops there in the 1920s and 1930s, especially Bostock & Wombwell's circus and menagerie. A tiger was actually born in Pontypridd in 1920. Side shows and small retail stalls under striped canopies sometimes spilled out from the jostling, bursting fairground on to both sides of Taff Street from the Palladium Cinema down to the Fountain, close to the market place. The council wanted to buy the Fairfield in 1935 for use as a bus centre but fairs continued to be an attraction there. Pontypridd Markets Company drew up plans in 1937 to build a cinema on the site but these were shelved with the approach of the Second World War. The detailed plans for the cinema are still held at the offices of the company.

A Whitsun fete was held in June 1943 at the Hawthorn Greyhound Track (the field in front of today's Hawthorn Leisure Centre) in aid of the Upper Boat and Hawthorn Troops Comfort Fund. Large crowds attended the fete opened by the local MP, Arthur Pearson. The council organised a horse show, military tattoo and bowls and football tournaments to support the Stay At Home Holiday Week campaign in July 1943, and gave permission to Miss Wynne Davies to hold keep fit and some games classes on the park rugby field. The *Pontypridd Observer* reported at the time that Ynysangharad Park was a popular destination for Sunday School outings from all over South Wales and asked 'What seaside resort can offer such wonderful facilities for clean and healthy recreation?' On Whitsun Monday 1945 Beryl Morgan was crowned Queen of the Hawthorn Fete. The following week the Pontypridd & District Powell Duffryn Male Choir of 100 voices performed in a celebrity concert at the Town Hall. The artistes included contralto Kathleen Ferrier.

Iestyn Williams opened the new Treforest Boys' clubhouse in Queen Street in December 1939. Among the keen lads interested in boxing there were Ted Davies and the brothers Fred and Tony Fackrell. An Old Boys' football match at Taff Vale Park on Boxing Day in 1941 raised the princely sum of threepence short of £3 which went to the Help for Russia Fund. An increasing number of events were arranged as the war went on. On August Bank Holiday in 1943 several thousand people at Taff Vale Park watched a Home Guard display included in one of the greatest military pageants held in Britain. An RAF band provided the music; and the displays included changing of the guard, bayonet fighting, tank destruction, camouflage, tug-of-war and 16 boxing contests. All proceeds went to charity.

The second annual fete and carnival in aid of the local Troops Comfort Fund took place in the grounds of Dyffryn Ffrwd, Nantgarw, in July 1943. Some highlights were a ladies' tug-of-war and bright and lively entertainment by the Tongwynlais Silver Band. Also in July, a Horse Show, Gymkhana and Fete held in Ynysangharad Park raised £800. At a presentation at the Queens Hotel £400 was given to

Pontypridd Cottage Hospital and £400 to Mrs Churchill's Aid To Russia Fund. Evening entertainment at the ceremony was provided by Corporal Ivor Humphreys, a baritone often heard on the wireless, and Jack Lewis the blind tenor of Griffin's Hill in Cilfynydd. Another local tenor of this period was Hansel Vaughan of the Graig, then serving in the RAF. Joyce Alderman was a popular local vocalist, as was Howard Jones of Cilfynydd who sang with the Joe Loss orchestra. In 1945 Geraint Evans was singing in the Forces overseas, and Bette Caddy, aged 15 from Mill Street, joined the well-known Ivy Benson all girls big band. She played the saxophone and the piano accordion.

Various local clubs raised £164 for the Welsh Services Club (London) Appeal in 1943. A rugby match played at Ynysangharad Park on Saturday 15 May between a Stanley Evans XV and a South Wales XV was reportedly one of the best ever seen on the ground. The organisers, Tudor Jeremy, Police Sergeant Tom Davies and PC Jack Davies, were pleased by the proceeds that were shared between the Welsh Services Club and the Glamorgan Troops Comfort Fund. Also in that year, Trallwn Ward Good Deed Committee raised £227 which they presented to seven local charities one evening at the Central Hotel. A bridge drive under the auspices of the Town Ward Troops Comfort Fund was held at the Shelley Hall on 21 May. There were about a hundred players present and the M.C. was Allan Scudamore. The prizes were presented to the winners by Councillor Morgan Phillips, president of the Town Ward Fund, and proceeds of £20 handed to treasurer John Humphreys.

The new Shelley Hall at the Pontypridd Educational Settlement (YMCA) was filled with an enthusiastic audience when Mrs Ashley Cooper, wife of the governor of the Hudson Bay Company, gave an interesting account and showed views of her recent visit with her husband to the company's trading posts and the two occasions when their ship was caught in the ice for a week. She was the daughter of solicitor James E. Spickett and Mrs Sarah Spickett of Merthyr Road. The proceeds of the lecture went to the Old Bridge Unemployment Club off Taff Street (now Clwb-y-Bont) of which Miss Daisy Spickett was president. Miss Spickett said that the rebuilding and equipping of the club had been carried out by the members themselves. The owners of the premises, Messrs Thomas & Evans, had been very generous and had given them the premises for the term of their lease. During the evening several solos were rendered by soprano Madame Blodwen Evans.

Sadly, despite the community spirit throughout the town and district in the wartime years and the many efforts made to bring interesting, varied entertainment to everyone to counter the sometimes grim war news in the newspapers, there were less happy reports too, such as the one from the manager of Pwllgwaun Colliery who told of serious acts of vandalism at the colliery and said, 'We regret the war effort is being hindered by sabotage by such culprits who are helping Hitler and acting as Fifth Columnists. They should be charged with sabotaging the war effort.' The culprits turned out to be children who were trespassing there and at the brickworks. But positive things went on: a fund was opened to repair the grave of William Edwards, the builder of Pontypridd's Old Bridge, near the south door of the church at Eglwysilan. Rhydyfelin Ward Labour Party entertained 32 wounded RAF men at the Unemployed Social Institute in the town with tea in the afternoon and a concert in the evening. Each airman was given cigarettes and half-a-crown. In her extensive programme of wartime entertainment, Madame Muriel Jones and her Pontypridd Welsh Ladies Choir gave a concert at the RAF station at St Athan in the Vale.

For quiet reading at home women had a choice of many magazines. They included, to meet all tastes: *Everywoman, Family Star, Glamour, Good Housekeeping, Good Taste, Home Chat, Home Journal, Home Notes, Housewife, Lucky Star, Modern Woman, My Home, My Weekly, Red Letter, Red Star Weekly, Secrets, Silver Star, Woman, Woman and Home, Woman's Friend, Woman's Pictorial, Woman's Magazine, Woman's Own* and *Woman's Weekly*. Some magazines popular with men and women which could be consulted in the upstairs Reading Room of Pontypridd Library if you wished were *Everybody's, Illustrated, Illustrated London News, John Bull, Lilliput, Picture Post, Radio Times, The Sphere, Tit Bits* and *War Illustrated*. Boys' papers and comics always eagerly bought or swapped included *Adventure, Beano, Boy's Own, Champion, Dandy, Film Fun, Girl's Crystal, Hotspur, Jester, Magnet, Meccano Magazine, Radio Fun, Rainbow, Rover, Sunny, Tiny Tots, Triumph* and *Wizard*.

The green green grass

At Christmas in 1920, in the grieving aftermath of the First World War, Pontypridd Urban District Council sought donations to help purchase Ynysangharad Fields for use as a public park. Ynysangharad Memorial Park was opened on 6 August 1923 by Field Marshall Lord Allenby. On that day, too, he unveiled the 5th Welch War Memorial on the Common in remembrance of Pontypridd's 28 officers, three warrant officers, 51 NCOs and 279 men of the battalion who died in the Great War. The park gleamed like a jewel in the town for people seeking rest and relaxation and comfort, or walks in the spacious greenery. There were flower gardens to bring gladness. A magnificent avenue of trees, planted in the early 1930s alongside the new tennis courts, led from the 1923 concrete bridge which had replaced the late Victorian bridge over the River Taff opposite Mill Street. Grand memorial gates of iron (no longer there) stood at the park's main entrance in Bridge Street. On 23 July 1930 Lord Treowen, watched by 10,000 people, unveiled the memorial with its two bronze figures, a woman representing poetry and a male harpist repre-senting music, to honour Evan James and James James, composers of 'Hen Wlad Fy Nhadau'.

Bowling greens were opened in the park in May 1924 and new greens with many improvements opened in April 1929. In July 1945 the Pontypridd Bowls Club won the championship of the Cardiff Municipal Bowls League in a game with Heath, Cardiff, on Fair Oak Green, Roath Park. When the first score was called at the fifth head, Pontypridd were ten ahead and held the lead right to the roll up of the last wood when the score was shouted 86–80. The team captain, J.C. Miles, received the trophy. Bowls fixtures were always popular in the park. The secretary of the Pontypridd Bowls Club at this time was Herbert (Bert) Hughes.

The elegant bandstand was opened on 24 July 1926 on a Victorian playing field of Pontypridd Rugby Football Club. The prize-winning Great Western Colliery Silver Band gave a rousing performance at an afternoon celebration concert in the bandstand for the crowds of people in the park. Throughout the evening Bert Mitchell's band played music for dancing held in the bandstand circle. Similar events were held in the park on summer evenings through the thirties when thoughts of another war seemed far away in the interlude of peace. The chairman of the urban district council opened the large open-air swimming pool on 30 July 1927. For decades and through the wartime years, thousands of young and hardy not-so-young people of Pontypridd and its villages and the valleys had splashed in its cold waters, swallowed some of them, raced to the fountains, and shivered and dripped in the long lines of wooden dressing-cubicles or chilled at the poolside with a towel concealing their goose pimples. Then up on the diving board again in the scorching sunshine and the sounds of babbling voices and laughter to plunge with prowess from the hot planks into the muffled sounds of surging air bubbles and then the deep silence of the waters.

The park is crowded with memories of fetes and galas and many rugby and soccer matches; the greensward of Pontypridd Cricket Club field has seen countless runs and boundaries and first class teams have played matches there. Pontypridd Cricket Club was formed in May 1870 and played its first match, against the 'Publicans Eleven', in the grounds of Gelliwastad House, thanks to the interest of the owner, Mr Rea.

Afterwards, he allowed the team to use the ground regularly. In the 1896 season the club was undefeated in the league and were league champions. The club moved to Ynysangharad Park in 1924 where the ground had been laid out with turf cut from the mountainside at Cilfynydd. Some seasons later, the club affiliated to the Glamorgan County Cricket Club, who had paid half the £800 cost of a new pavilion, and the first county match was played in the park, with Derbyshire the opponents. The Pontypridd followers enjoyed many first and second eleven games at wartime Ynysangharad Park. Dr Kingsley Lewis of Gelliwastad Road became president of the cricket club in March 1938. He was one of the best known medical practitioners in Pontypridd but died suddenly in September 1943. The Ceiriog Williams cup was donated in 1951 for a knock-out competition. The first open-air community hymn-singing service by the united churches of Pontypridd was held in June 1943 in front of the cricket pavilion. More than a thousand people turned up in the evening to sing under conductor W.D. Evans of Maerdy.

The miniature golf-course in the park opened in May 1929 and was extended after 1937 when the Ivor Arms Hotel and the tiny houses of Ivor Court and Llewellyn Court off Bridge Street were pulled down. Golf was enjoyed at the Pontypridd Golf Club at Ty Gwyn, where in 1945 Owen Thomas was elected secretary for the 39th year in succession.

Cilfynydd Welfare Committee added to their achievements on 5 May 1930 when, in bad weather, Captain C.S. Mason MC opened a new pavilion costing £950 on the rugby ground. Chairman of the committee Henry Holley said that in the last seven or eight years they had acquired bowling greens and putting greens, a children's corner and pavilion, a football ground and central pavilion. Captain Mason said that the rugby ground would be level if the lumps were removed from the centre. He wished success to the rugby, cricket and tennis clubs. Then to mark the occasion a large crowd watched Cilfynydd play and lose 12–18 to a strong Cardiff side (S.C. Cravo's XV) which included seven international players. Walter E. Rees, the secretary of the WRU who kicked off, thought the pavilion was one of the best on any sports ground in Wales.

Cilfynydd played their home games at the Welfare grounds by the Albion Colliery. In March 1940 the result was Cilfynydd 3, Ebbw Vale 6, in a match in aid of Cilfynydd Troops Comforts Fund administered by the Welcome Home and Comforts Committee. Cilfynydd maintained their brilliant wartime rugby football by scoring two substantial wins over Easter 1941. The *Pontypridd Observer* reported that Cilfynydd kept the flag flying more than any other second class club in South Wales. McVicar's XV (Cil) played Superintendent William McDonald's XV at Ynysangharad Park in May 1941 in aid of the Pontypridd Spitfire Fund and won 28–6. Bleddyn Williams (Rydal Mount) and W. Cleaver (University College, Cardiff) were in the Cilfynydd backs. Bleddyn Williams scored three tries and W. Cleaver two. On 20 September Cilfynydd met Pontypridd at Ynysangharad Park in one of their regular fixtures. On Christmas morning 1941 Ynysybwl Home Guard met Cilfynydd C Company Home Guard in a match which brought in £16 10s. 8d. for PoW funds. Cilfynydd played an Army XV from Bridgend in May 1942, winning 20 points to 6. Another game that month ended Cilfynydd 18 v Army XV 9 at Cilfynydd. In April 1943 a lemon was the prize in a raffle at the Cilfynydd v Select Cardiff XV game to help PoW funds. It was reported in July 1945 that Cilfynydd RFC and Pontypridd RFC were going to amalgamate. The proposed merger caused controversy and many protests throughout the month until the merger scheme was scrapped.

In October 1945 Pontypridd RFC were anxious to obtain a set of jerseys in the club colours but were up against a clothing ration coupon difficulty. They needed 62 coupons and asked their supporters to donate them. Rhydyfelin RFC proved a strong side in the 1940s when Trevor Davies was the team captain. Full histories or shorter records exist or are being written about the activities of rugby and association football clubs and sports clubs in Pontypridd and its villages during the 1930s and 1940s.

CHAPTER TEN

The Last All Clear

Allied advances in Europe following the D-Day landings in Normandy in June 1944 brought the war with Germany to an end within a year. Many scenes and activities in Pontypridd in the times leading up to the landings gave everyone the confident hope of ultimate victory.

The Yanks are coming

The first of the 1.5 million American troops (the GIs, meaning Government Issue) came over here in 1942 and word soon spread that some of them would be coming to Pontypridd. They brought gifts of nylon stockings, perfume and chocolate for their girlfriends; strong cigarettes which they passed round; and chewing gum which answered the hopes of many children who boldly called out the catchphrase 'Got any gum, chum?' There were white soldiers here, and also black soldiers with their own officers. Troops were billeted in private houses and in virtually every suitable hall that could be found throughout Pontypridd, including St Matthew's Church hall in Trallwn, with their cookhouse in the metal-sheeted building in the field that is now the site of Plas yr Eglwys houses alongside Thurston Road; a 1920s club in Sion Street; the old Unemployed Club (now Clwb y Bont) off Taff Street; above Kendall's umbrella shop on the corner from where they exchanged many waves with girls who worked in the nearby Leslie's Stores warehouse; on Merthyr Road; in Treforest at the Catholic Hall just opposite Saron Street, and another place on the White Tips; and at Oddfellows Hall in Old Park Terrace. Their 'stage door canteen' was in the vestry of Penuel Chapel at the Fountain in Taff Street. Bryn Roberts of Merthyr Road, and other townspeople, remember seeing the Yanks singing on their march there, when all that seemed to be lacking was the Glenn Miller or some other big band to accompany them.

The Americans had plenty of money—a GI was paid £3 8s. 9d. a week while a British private was paid 14s.—and were generous with it: young lads in Cilfynydd could earn big pocket money of maybe two bob or even a half-a-crown by collecting from the local shop an order for often twenty packs or more of fish and chips, which troops billeted at the

Social Club or one-time Boy Scouts' hut in Park Place consumed eagerly from the newspaper wrappings. Troops billeted at the St Mary's Church hall at Glyntaff enjoyed their parcels of fish and chips too. They also discovered the large slab cakes sold at Charlie Farmer's grocery shop by the humpbacked bridge over the canal and quickly got hooked on them. American and other Allied soldiers were welcomed to special entertainment in every village hall. Stanley Wells of Middle Street remembers black American soldiers and their officers being well received one night at the nearby Central Hotel in Central Square, Trallwn. There were also many Canadian soldiers in Pontypridd, who were known as the 'Polar Bears' from the large shoulder flashes they wore. They were billeted in part of the large Lucania Billiard Hall in Gas Road. In the town, and also known as the Polar Bears, were soldiers of the 49th Division of the British Army which included several local men.

Colin Gibbon of Park Prospect, Graigwen, remembers a soldier giving him a football which became his greatest treasure for months until it ended up spiked on a railing. He had better luck he says when, 'I saw a black American selling grapefruit—the first I had seen of either—and rushed home for a shilling to buy the very last fruit. It made a great treat for the family.' He recalls the American troops stationed at Merthyr Road and Cilfynydd. They were the 94th Medical Gas Treatment Battalion from Indiana, part of General George Patton's 3rd Army which liberated Paris in August 1944. There is a copy of the wartime history of the battalion, written by its commanding officer, Col. William C. Burry, at the Pontypridd Historical and Cultural Centre, who described thus their stay in the town in 1944:

> On weekends members of the 94th could draw their rations in kind to share with their hosts. Each officer and man could draw his piece of meat, a can of fruit and a can of vegetables instead of eating at the mess halls. These items were strictly rationed for the British and so a welcome addition to their meager store of food. We shared each other's food and enjoyed each other's company.
>
> To take up slack time the 94th drew some fifes and drums from the Quartermaster. There were a number of talented officers and men who practiced together as a 94th Fife and Drums Corps. When they became proficient the 94th advertised and put on a Battalion parade complete with music and our Battalion Colors. The Welsh enjoyed it. Most of the men who attended with their wives were World War I Veterans and they wore their medals on their lapels in honor of the occasion.
>
> We had been in Pontypridd since 25 May and on the 31st of

July we received orders to move to the coast and take part in the invasion, after crossing the English Channel.

We had enjoyed our stay in 'Ponty'. We understood most of what was said to us when they spoke English, but did not know Welch, which is a Gaelic language still taught in their schools and spoken among themselves at that time. The Welch were a proud people who didn't care for either the English or the Scots, which went a long way back in history.

It was somewhat difficult to adjust to their overhead pull chain toilets, and shiny toilet paper. We marvelled at how much heat they could get out of their coal fireplaces with 3 lumps of coal the size of baseballs. The evenings were chilly, and we sat in a semi-circle about the fireplace sipping tea, prepared in a kettle that sat on a stand next to the fire. When it became bedtime our host put a brick near the heat of the fire, and gave it to the guest for warming the cold bed for the guest's feet. The sheets were flannel, and most of us had bought flannel pajamas at the U.S.A. clothing store for the cold damp climate of Wales even in late spring and early summer.

The afternoon of 31 July the CO ordered a battalion formation and explained all we had trained for would soon be an operation, and finished off by saying, 'This is it!'. We all hurried back to our billets and explained we would be off early in the morning and packed our personal gear, and loaded our trucks and Jeeps for early morning departure.

On August 1st we moved out in convoy from Pontypridd under forced march conditions to arrive at the marshalling area at Romsey early on 2 August and were fed our last hot meal for quite a spell. We were loaded in combat formation (first on last off), with every man assigned a specific vehicle where all his personal gear was stowed and where he could locate his material with which he would function in combat support.

Our experiences in Pontypridd were mostly all very favorable impressions. At first our personnel were not knowledgable of the strict rationing imposed on the British. A few days following the Battalion's arrival and billeting the CO was visited by a local delegation of Pub owners. They had a complaint that members of our unit had drunk their entire ration of beer and ale for the month in a couple of nights.

The CO sent some of his headquarters staff officers to the local rationing board and obtained a ration of kegs of beer and the 94th set up its own operation in the basement of a large building. Here we operated a small bar serving beer and soft drinks. We obtained authority to operate a small exchange with candy bars, cigarettes, cigars and small snack purchases. In order to maintain control we mimeographed ration slips which were issued to each officer and man. This satisfied the Pub owners who then knew they did not have to serve members of our unit who were readily identifiable by their uniforms as none of us had brought civilian clothes along.

This was a mining town and there were many young miners exempt from military service because of their occupation. Our young men in uniform apparently competed with these young miners for the young ladies of Pontypridd. There were some altercations, a few bloody noses and shiners occasionally seen among members of the 94th, but no incident of complaint was ever forwarded to HQ by the Glamorgan Constabulary, which were our local civilian police. The CO called upon the Superintendent shortly after arrival to establish a liaison and our relationships were excellent.

After the war some American soldiers (and some Canadians) came back to Pontypridd and married local girls. Two of the GIs were R. Fegley and A. Mietk. Their brides were two of the 70,000 British GI brides who went to the United States when the war was over. In 1988, one of the former GIs, Emil C. Evancich, of Carmel, Indiana, made a nostalgic visit to Pontypridd to show it to his family. Another, Morris 'Mickey' Weiner, told that he came over here in an Atlantic convoy and landed after twelve days at Liverpool on 24 May 1944. Then straight on to Pontypridd in a convoy of trucks for a few months. The advance party had been working with the Glamorgan Constabulary and had worked out a plan where the officers and enlisted men of the 94th would be billeted with families who resided in Pontypridd. Many of the homes did not have bathrooms and men wanting baths were allowed to use local pithead baths.

Until they loaded up and left for Utah Beach in Normandy, they were given provisions for a mess and indoor areas in two buildings: one building for headquarters 'belonged to the British Legion, and the other in a different part of town was a church' (the canteen at Penuel Chapel). Relations with the people of Pontypridd were excellent. They made many friends, were invited to many concerts and made welcome guests at churches and clubs. Mickey recalled that the CO stayed in Pontypridd with Jack Edwards and Mrs Edwards at 'their home on a hill'. A photograph shows it to be in one of the streets off Llantwit Road in Treforest.

36. American locomotives stockpiled on the line from Tonteg to the Graig in readiness for the D-Day invasion. View shows Llantwit Road at the Devil's Bridge, and Upper Boat power station. 1944.

37. Edna Raybould of Rhydyfelin, the 20-year-old winner of the beauty contest at the Treforest Trading Estate to celebrate Victory in Europe, 1945.

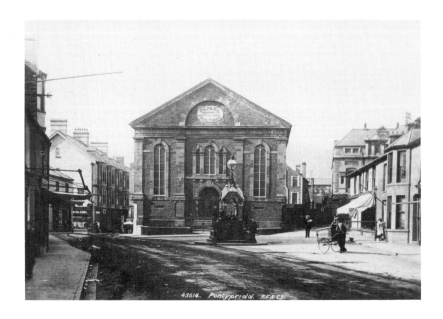

38. *Above:* Penuel Chapel, now demolished, and the Fountain in Taff Street. The American GIs used the vestry of the chapel as their canteen. Photo 1899. *Below:* View of Trallwn with the White Bridge at the Berw at centre bottom. St Matthew's Church is at centre right. American troops were billeted in the church hall. Photo *c.* 1950.

39. War Memorial in Ynysangharad Park in 1994. The Remembrance Day services ending with buglers sounding the Last Post were held at this spot and at the Memorial on the Common during the Second World War.

American locomotive works were shipping to Britain many of their powerful 'invasion' engines—utility engines to supplement the engines built by British companies—their final destination being across the Channel. They were designed for use on both British and continental rail systems and were a great help in moving the huge amount of wartime traffic here. Bert Wilcockson of Llanover Road recalled:

> I was a steam locomotive fireman during the war for the Great Western Railway, based at the large Newport engine shed. Towards D-Day 1944, America was sending over large numbers of brand new locomotives, to be used in France later. The up Barry Railway line from Tonteg to Kirkhouse Street Station (Graig) was closed and given up to storage of these huge locomotives. After their salty sea journey the locomotives were stiff and needed running-in again. They came through the Newport shed for this to be done, and the Yanks had a typically American way of doing it: they would couple a locomotive in steam to a stop block and then station a soldier armed with a large oil can at each of its eight driving wheels. The engineer, or driver, would open up and the loco would do about 30 mph standing still—with the soldiers squirting oil under the wheels. The Americans would also lend the GWR these locos for use on freight trains. I well remember they were beautiful and powerful to work, with a high regard for crew comfort, and with 'U.S. ARMY' emblazoned on the engine tender. We drew many admiring waves of hankies from the female population en route.

The American soldiers were often seen driving by in their jeeps and bren gun carriers. During a training exercise, one carrier sank deep in one of the bogs along the road to Llanwonno some miles past Penygraigwen.

Those American troops stationed in Pontypridd in the New Year of 1945 shivered with the community through a week of exceptionally cold weather. They woke on a Thursday morning at the end of January to find the town snowbound after the heaviest fall for some years. The snow was more than two feet deep in the main streets of the town and considerably deeper in Graigwen and Maesycoed and on the Graig. Many workers with large socks pulled over their shoes walked miles to their factories on the Treforest Trading Estate. Trains from Cardiff took two hours for the journey to Pontypridd and four hours to Merthyr. Two trolley buses ran all night on the Treforest-Cilfynydd route in the fast-falling snowflakes to help keep the roads clear and to preserve the overhead power cables. Production in the pits was severely affected as workmen could not travel from any distance to the Albion, Cwm, Maritime, Lewis Merthyr, Tymawr and other local collieries. All schools were closed and housewives found it very hard to collect food rations or stand in queues for whatever was on offer. W. Cecil Evans, the UDC surveyor, said that 40,000 tons of snow had fallen on Pontypridd and more than one million tons on the urban area with an average depth of 18 inches. The council's two snow-ploughs kept going and a bus was adapted to take the larger plough. It was just as bad on the Friday, with few buses and a severe frost to make walking dangerous. More than 120 of the American troops helped to clear the snow and could be seen shovelling away in the town.

Home Guard sunset

The Home Guard nationally stood down on 1 November 1944 and finally disbanded on 31 December 1945. Their last parade in Pontypridd was held on 15 October 1944 when thousands of people assembled at Ynysangharad Park to watch the four battalions in the Pontypridd sector Home Guard (1st Battalion, Aberdare; 2nd Battalion, Pontypridd; 7th Battalion, Rhondda; and 25th Battalion, Treforest Trading Estate) take part in a drumhead service. The *Pontypridd Observer* reported that more than 1,500 officers and other ranks were on parade in one of the most spectacular military processions ever seen in the town. The band of the Welch Regiment, under Bandmaster T. Clegg, attended.

The salute was taken in the park by Maj.-Gen. J.G. Halstead (Commanding Officer, South Wales District), accompanied by Maj. A. Hall-Maxwell (aide-de-camp), Col. A.P. Carey Evans (Glamorgan Home Guard advisor), Col. W. Lester Lewis (commanding officer of the Pontypridd Home Guard Sector), Lt-Col. W.H. Edwards (second in command, Pontypridd Sector), Lt-Col. W.J. Hodges (1st Batt., Aberdare), Lt-Col. Willis Walker (2nd Batt., Pontypridd), Lt-Col. John Evans (7th Batt., Rhondda), Lt-Col. R.S. de Burgh (25th Batt., Treforest Trading Estate), and Maj. H. Ware (sector training officer).

In his address to the parade, Gen. Halstead said that quite a number would be sorry, in a way, when the final dismissal was given, because of the good feeling and comradeship in the Home Guard. He had been a very fortunate general indeed: having in all parts of South Wales an organised, efficient and well-led body of men for any emergency. This was fully borne out during the preparations for the dispatch of the expeditionary force across the Channel, for some members of the Home Guard actually took part by performing duty round and about South

Wales which otherwise would have had to be done by regular troops. That duty was done willingly and efficiently; and he felt confident that the Home Guard would have proved equal to doing much more than that if it had proved necessary. He had learned to be confident because he had noted the Home Guard progress—a vast progress from the days of pikes, clubs and shotguns to the days when it became an army unique in history. He hoped that those on parade would not allow the spirit engendered by the Home Guard to be lost, and suggested that the men might find it possible to perpetuate it in clubs, associations or some other means. He thanked all officers, NCOs and men of the four battalions 'for your admirable service to the country and the South Wales District Command'.

Capt. the Revd T. Emlyn Rogers (vicar of St John's, Graig, and chaplain to the Pontypridd battalion) said in his address that when the call came for men to man the breaches there was no lack of answer. The Home Guard showed the loyalty, courage and firm endeavour of men who have something worthy of fighting for. Men gathered in the Home Guard because they were aroused by the threat of danger:

> The threat of invasion is now passed and a new dawn was breaking. The daylight would be full of question marks which would call from us a deeper resolve than had ever been summoned before. The country had passed through strenuous times, many changes had taken place, and men and women would need a loyalty and courage which had marked past years to meet the changes of the future.

The minister's closing remarks of more than 50 years ago are in tune today with the thoughts expressed by some Pontypridd residents both young and old who face the dangers of today and yearn for a more comforting community spirit. He said:

> There is one thought I would like to leave with you. It is this. What is that day to be like? The answer depends upon each one of you. We want to carry into our future living all those magnificent qualities which had birth in dangers through which we have passed. We want to live the full, really vital life we have lived in past years when dangers hung over us. It will need all your courage and loyalty of the very best to preserve what I call the Christian way of living in this land of ours.

Gen. Halstead presented certificates of merit and gallantry awarded by the General Officer Commander-in-Chief Western Command to 16 members of the four battalions in the Pontypridd Sector. The awards included certificates 'for good and meritorious service' to Sgt F.C. Sparrow and and Sgt E. Punter of the 25th Battalion; and awards 'for gallantry and meritorious service' to Cpl E.T. James and Pte T.J. Davies of the 2nd Battalion, who together rendered heroic service in an attempt to rescue the crew of a crashed aircraft. After the service, the Home Guard were inspected by Maj.-Gen. Halstead and his aide-de-camp together with Cllr Hopkin Smith (vice-chairman Pontypridd Urban District Council), H. Leonard Porcher (clerk of the council), Joseph Jones (chief constable of Glamorgan) and Superintendent Howell Rees. The parade marched through the town accompanied by the band of the Welch Regiment and the drum and bugle band of the Pontypridd Army Cadet Force.

Victory celebrations

VE Day (Victory in Europe Day) was proclaimed throughout the land on Tuesday 8 May 1945. Church bells pealed all over Britain and the victory celebrations held in Pontypridd reflected the jubilation in the towns and villages of Wales.

People congregated in Pontypridd early on that Tuesday, the first day of a two-day public holiday. Crowds packed Market Street, the Square, and Taff Street for the 3 p.m. broadcast by Winston Churchill, which was amplified through loudspeakers from Rediffusion Ltd at 10 Market Street, now the offices of the *Pontypridd Observer*. Churchill told of the unconditional surrender the previous day of all German land, sea and air forces in Europe. But he was in a forceful and serious mood and his words made it clear that Britain could not rest content: Japan remained unbeaten. But this was a day for rejoicing to mark the defeat of Nazism. There was laughter of relief and joy for the family reunions to come when men and women returned from the battlefields and prisoner of war camps. There were tears, too, for the loved ones who would never come home to Pontypridd. The red poppies would remember their sacrifice. In the evening, crowds applauded the broadcast by the King.

An evening of revelry switched on with the bright illuminations. Strings of multicoloured lights sparkled from the Tumble end of town and along Taff Street to the Old Bridge. They culminated there in a huge crown scintillating with red, white, blue and green lamps and supported on brightly lit arms which formed an arch over the adjacent Victoria Bridge across the River Taff.

British, American and Russian flags, streamers, banners and bunting decked the streets and many shop-window displays cast warm light across the pavements filled with happy people. Two large V for Victory signs lit the front of the Municipal Buildings. Sardis Road was judged to be the best-dressed street in South Wales. Men wore red, white and blue rosettes; women dressed in patriotic coloured clothes; young girls clipped flowers in their hair and waved small flags; high-spirited boys made the most of the chances for fun.

Bands of the Air Training Corps, Sea Cadets and Army Cadets marched through the town playing their rousing music from bugles, fifes and drums. Loud applause greeted them for their part in the festivities. Couples danced in the streets to music from gramophone records of Glenn Miller and Victor Silvester, or kissed in the dark to love songs from Sinatra. In Tabernacle Square, a lantern glowed on a shepherd's staff inviting hundreds to join the hymn singing which praised and gave thanks with traditional Welsh fervour. In the early hours, hands were linked as hoarse voices sang 'Auld Lang Syne' and national anthems before the crowds drifted home.

Throughout Pontypridd and the district many churches and chapels held thanksgiving services. Villages made merry to music from pianos in the streets and from a whole orchestra of other instruments. Air raid sirens sounded the last 'All Clear'. Bonfires crackled near gaily decorated houses in many terraces or flamed on the hillsides while effigies of Hitler and other Nazis, which had hung all day from lamp posts, burned amid great rejoicing.

Down our street

Despite food rationing, Wednesday 9 May 1945 brought sumptuous street parties and continued merrymaking to nearly every street in the town and in all the villages. The residents of Henry Street in Hopkins-town celebrated with relief that no more bombs would fall on the village. In the more outlying areas, the older inhabitants of Tynant well remember the competition between Mildred Street and Commercial Street for their delightful decorations. A huge bonfire blazed at the end of Commercial Street. Children in Beddau were entertained and given gifts at parties in Wingfield Avenue, Castellmynach Street and Llantrisant Road, and took part in foot races in the early evening.

In 1995 the inimitable Harry Hartill of Elm Street, Rhydyfelin, wrote a poem to celebrate the 50th anniversary of the VE Day celebrations, which was published in the *Pontypridd Observer*:

Celebration

We owe our freedom
So we are told
To the memory of people
Who never grow old
Like the young air force pilots
We never knew
In the Battle of Britain
They named them 'The Few'
To the mothers in factories
Doing the jobs of the men
Who suffered the air raids
Again and again
Many worked in the fields
Sowing the seeds
Knowing in death camps
People had to be freed
Men died in the jungle
In the desert and the sea
That children like us
Could always be free
We celebrate their victory
The future is ours
We thank them with prayers
As we lay down these flowers

Harry Hartill

Thanksgiving services for victory in Europe were held in many churches and chapels in Pontypridd and its villages. One programme, typical for the area, said:

> The United Thanksgiving Service of the people of Cilfynydd. This service was held on the day following the cessation of Hostilities in Europe and was sponsored by the Committee of the Cilfynydd Welcome Home, Comforts, and Prisoners of War Fund, on behalf of the Churches, Chapels and other organisations in the village.

The service embraced the Cilfynydd churches and chapels of St Luke's, Bethel, Beulah, Moriah, Rehoboth, Bethany, English Methodist and

Wesleyan Methodist. The service consisted of prayers by the Revd J. Francis, scripture readings by him and the Revd D. Eden Davies, thanksgiving prayers by the Revd D. Emlyn Lewis, community singing, and contributions by Bethel Choral Society (conducted by Madame Phillips Howells) and Handel Glee Party (conducted by W.J. Evans).

There was an afternoon 'Cilfynydd United Children's Armistice Thanksgiving Service' with prayers and hymns in Welsh and English, a prayer for thanksgiving service composed by C.C. Evans; a scripture reading by Russel Pearce, and a solo by a young Stuart Burrows, destined for fame as an international star of opera. He broadcast on 31 October 1945. As everywhere else locally in 1945 the churches and chapels were filled for their morning and evening services and Sunday School. And the quiet Sundays were marked by the peal of church bells and the scenes of many people dressed in their best clothes, and walking to their chosen place of worship. At Christmas 1945 'Messiah' was performed at Calvary English Baptist Church on Wood Road.

Thanksgiving Sunday on 13 May heralded a special Victory Parade by a host of local defence and other organisations. All servicemen and women who were home on leave were asked to join the parade. Superintendent Howell Rees and Inspector D.R. Watkins marshalled the parade which included contingents from the Royal Navy, Army and Royal Air Force, Glamorgan County Constabulary, Sea Cadets and Sea Rangers, Army Cadets, the Air Training Corps and Women's Junior Air Corps, Royal Observer Corps, Boy Scouts, Girl Guides, Church Lads Brigade, and the Simmonds Aero Works Fire Brigade. Led by bands, the parade started at the *Observer* offices on the Broadway and marched up to the Tumble, or Station Square, through the town to Bridge Street to Ynysangharad Park where everyone gathered for a memorable service. The victory was won and Pontypridd had proudly played a part in the valiant years.

Coming home

The end of the war in Europe meant demobilisation for millions of British servicemen and women. Demobilisation began on 18 June 1945 with priority going to builders and other men needed for construction work. Others, longing for home, were to be released at intervals depending on age and length of service, two months service equalling a year of age. They returned at last to 'Civvy Street' with a demob suit, a set of clothes and a ration book. 'Welcome Home' banners flew in nearly every village street in Pontypridd to greet them. Many children wondered who was that strange man in their house.

The men had to readjust to civilian life and try to settle down. And after their 56 days 'demob leave' it was back to work. The law required that all ex-servicemen had their old jobs back. The women of Pontypridd who had worked for years in transport and in factories and offices now had to change their way of life again. The war years had brought dramatic changes in the lives of the people and many did not want to return to their old way of life. Their expectations were high and they sought greater opportunities for independence. And women, many of them with a different outlook, would soon be home from the Forces. Welcome home presentations were made in most villages to men returning from the fronts and the sea and the camps, such as the presentation by the Treforest Prisoner of War Welcome Home Committee to returning PoWs arranged in late June by Mrs Zenus Thomas, friend and organiser of an active group, with Miss L. Jenkins as secretary and Mrs G.W. Parke as treasurer.

In the first weeks after the end of the war in Europe the Queen, then Princess Elizabeth, visited Cardiff on 2 June. The Guard of Honour at Cathays Park for the Princess (who was Commodore of the Sea Rangers) included Sea Rangers Pauline Jones of the 2nd Pontypridd Company and Marjorie Warburton of the 1st Treforest Company. Sea Ranger Irene Tallis was given the honour of seconding the vote of thanks, and to the surprise of Sea Ranger Mary Holder, one of the bosuns of the crew, the princess spoke to her.

Monday 18 June heralded the visit of 250 men of the 1st Battalion Welsh Guards under Maj. J.M. Miller DSO, MC, headed by their drum and fife band. The marched through Cilfynydd, through Taff Street for the salute taken at 3 p.m. near the Fountain by the new chairman of the council, Cllr Hopkin Smith of Rhydyfelin, who was supported by many dignitaries. The guardsmen then marched along Mill Street and Gelliwastad Road, and through the Treforest Trading Estate to pay tribute to the war workers and received an ovation from many thousands of people there.

On 6 August 1945 an American B29 Super-Fortress flying at 30,000 feet dropped an atomic bomb on the Japanese city of Hiroshima. Three days later another bomb was dropped on the city of Nagasaki. Japan surrendered. Flags flew again among the miles of colourful bunting in Pontypridd and all the villages in celebration of VJ Day, Victory over Japan, and the end of the Second World War. The Victory Arch surmounted by its crown was again placed over the Old Bridge and fairy lights lit the town from the GWR station on the Tumble and through High Street and Taff Street to the bridge. Happy crowds milled through the town shortly before midnight on Tuesday, 14 August. After listening to the midnight news and the broadcast by the new Prime Minister, Clement Attlee, the revellers sang and danced in the streets for hours. And it was the same in in every village.

The next day was a market day and the local buses kept running for the shoppers but there were no buses from the valleys into town. Collieries and factories closed for the day. For their celebration parade through Taff Street, the bands of the three cadet forces abandoned the traditional order of march of navy, army, air force. They massed, with the three drum majors in echelon and the drum and bugle bands of the army cadets and air cadets mingling with the drum and fife band of the sea cadets. Huge crowds applauded the ceremony. Cllr Hopkin Smith broadcast an afternoon message saying there would dancing at the bandstand in the park until 10 p.m., and music for dancing relayed over loudspeakers in Market Square until two o'clock in the morning. Thousands cheered! A large crowd packed the Old Bridge and square where the Revd Ken Matthew led the community hymn singing with his piano accordion accompaniment. Thanksgiving services were arranged by all churches and chapels and others were held in the open air.

There were street teas and celebrations everywhere in the area on Wednesday. A huge bonfire was lit at King Street in Treforest, though some rain in the afternoon meant the teas had to be held in the Boys' Club nearby. The first prize for the best decorated street in Tynant, promoted by the Cwm Welfare Association, was Mildred Street.

Towards the end of the month, 28 cadets of the Air Training Corps under F/O D.G. Lewis returned from their annual camp at St Athan aerodrome where they enjoyed long flights in service aircraft. The squadron band under W/O Tom Green had led some 3,000 cheering airmen and WAAFs through the camp and the village. F/O Rogers was there with support from Cadet Sgt Bernard Brennan and Sgt W. Elsmore. The Air Officer Commanding gave praise and thanks at the passing out parade on the Saturday and said that the cadets upheld the tradition built up by the first ATC cadets, who were now scattered all over the world and had helped to win the victory. The news was related that ex-ATC cadet 19-year-old AC2 Mervyn Oliver of Middle Street, who had worked at Brown Lenox Chainworks, had died in India the previous month.

In late September many local families were receiving official cablegrams informing them that their loved ones had been released from PoW camps in the Far East. October saw the return of the some of the British prisoners of war from the Japanese horror camps. Among them were men of Cardiff's own 77th Heavy Ack-Ack Regiment of the Royal Artillery. Many of them docked at Liverpool on 29 October. After disembarking from the SS *Cilicia* they were taken to a transit camp at Aintree to prepare for dispersal and the train journey home. When they arrived at Cardiff General Station on 30 October the men of Pontypridd were greeted by their relatives and friends and by Cllr J.R. Clayton who represented the Cilfynydd Welcome Home Committee and Prisoner of War Fund. The first man he greeted off the train was Gunner Tom Powell, husband of Mrs May Powell of Oakland Crescent, Cilfynydd, who had been imprisoned in Java for 3½ years. 'Welcome Home' banners were draped on the homes of the survivors and flags and bunting brightened many streets.

The welcome to ex-PoWs in Treforest was typical of the bright and cheerful receptions in the other villages. Among the men coming home in November was Lance-Bombardier Albert Jones, Royal Artillery, husband of Mrs Mabel Jones of Cliff Terrace. He was captured at Singapore when it fell in 1942. He came home to Liverpool on the SS *Orduna*. In his imprisonment he worked on the notorious Thailand–Burma railway for 15 months. Elsewhere in the town, Gunner Walter Mear of the 77th Ack-Ack Regiment, whose mother lived at Ty Mawr Cottages in Hopkinstown, spent years in camps in Java, Sumatra and Singapore. He also worked on a railway line and was forced to carry on until it linked with another line five days after the war had ended. 'Ever since we were set free the Red Cross have done all they can for us,' he said. When he reached Liverpool the SS *Antenor*, frustratingly, could not dock for two days owing to gales. Able Seaman Thomas Henry Chapple of Bonvilston Road, Coedpenmaen, came home on the same ship and thought that treatment was 'pretty bad' in his camp in Sumatra.

When he was a prisoner of the Japanese, QMS Bert Reakes of the Royal Artillery, husband of Mrs Pat Reakes of Thurston Road in Trallwn, met Stanley Davies formerly of Trallwn and later of Ynysybwl. When QMS Reakes came home on the *Ile de France*, via Canada, he had served in the army for 24 years. Also home on the same ship was Pte Joseph Berry of Middle Street, Trallwn, who had worked on the Thailand railway. He said that ex-prisoners had a marvellous welcome when the ship docked in Canada. When the PoWs from the Japanese camps reached Liverpool they were issued with 'don't talk' leaflets. The men were reluctant to tell of their gruelling horror anyway.

A number of competitions were held in the town and district as part of the victory celebrations. In October 1945 a Victory Queen competition was held for Thanksgiving Week, for which a target of £200,000 was set, which was passed by only a small amount, unlike the earlier savings campaigns. There was a dance on 5 October with Milton Mace's band. For the next week, Brenda Plummer of Leyshon Street, Graig, was the

Victory Queen. Her court ladies were Betty Jennings of Collins Terrace, Treforest, and Elaine Lewis of Hinkley's Terrace, Merthyr Road. The main organisers of the event were Stanley Evans, W. Elvet Hughes; and D.R. Owen of the New Cecil Cinema.

On 8 November 1945 the children of the Cottage Homes at Church Village, some evacuees among them, celebrated VJ Day. There was keen rivalry among the 'cottages' (the large buildings that nowadays comprise Garth Olwg) in providing the best treat for the children. The *Pontypridd Observer* reported that the master and matron of the homes, Joseph Jones and his wife, who had served at the homes for 22 years, and the foster mothers and their assistants made the day memorable for their charges at every table. The newspaper reporter and the visiting group were greeted by rows of happy faces. There were ten cottage homes (five for boys and five for girls) containing a total of 150 children from four to 15 years old, and a mixed nursery with 19 toddlers from 18 months to four years. In the nursery the kiddies gave the visitors the greatest thrill with cheers of welcome for them and the foster mothers; and the master and matron who knew the name of every child. The reporter could see that they reigned by love and not fear. The children were taught the essential things of life and the fact that many of the tables were attended by old boys and girls was a proof of the affection they had for those who had taken care of them. One man was an ex-soldier just home to Penygraig after 3½ years service in India and Burma who said he was proud of the training he had received at the Homes in his younger days. After tea the children watched a cinema show from Herbert Davies of Church Village.

Remembrance Sunday on 11 November 1945 was observed in Pontypridd when the British Legion held its annual parade and service. The parade comprised British Legion ex-servicemen and women, 5th Welch Old Comrades Association, chairman and members of the urban district council, police and the special police, National Fire Service, Sea Cadet Corps, Air Training Corps, Women's Junior Air Corps, British Red Cross, St John Ambulance Brigade, WVS, Pontypridd Chamber of Trade and members of the public. Headed by the St John Ambulance Band, the parade marched through the town to St Catherine's Church for a moving service. The Revd T. Derwent Davies read part of the Scripture and led in prayer. The Revd T. Emlyn Rogers, vicar of St John's, Graig, gave an address. After the parade had reassembled and marched to Ynysangharad Park he conducted the service there. Wreaths were placed on the Garden of Remembrance and the parade later dispersed by units at the main gate of the park while some marched to the watchful 5th Welch Monument on the Common.

A Victory Dance with spot prizes was held in Helliwell's factory canteen at the Treforest Trading Estate on 28 November with music until midnight by Billy Butler's band from Aberdare. The important event of the evening was the selection in the interval of the beauty queen and court ladies for the Estate Thanksgiving Week, which had set a savings target of £10,000. Eight finalists had been chosen from various factories and they appeared before the judges D. John Williams, committee chairman and managing director of Butter Candies, and the factory managers J. Ransom of Helliwell's, L.G. Oxford of Simmonds Aerocessories, and E.B. Thomas of Standard Telephones and Cables. E.E. Evans compered the selection ceremony and the close contest was decided with loud applause from the large attendance.

An unanimous decision of the judges chose 20-year-old Edna Raybould of Sycamore Street in Rhydyfelin as Victory Queen. She had been nominated by the men of the thermometer department of the H.J. Elliot glass factory. Second place was awarded to Mrs Margaret Cairns of Tongwynlais, who was the queen of Simmonds Aero's victory social in the previous month; and third place went to Molly Warne of Dyffryn Crescent, Rhydyfelin, who worked at General Paper and Box. D. John Williams then presented Edna Raybould and the court ladies with prizes of savings certificates. Proceeds of the dance, voted a huge success, were in aid of Pontypridd Cottage Hospital. In September 1947, Edna married Reginald Phillips of the Common at St Mary's Church, Glyntaff, and they spent the early months of their married life at Pencoed Farm. They have three sons and a daughter, and celebrated their golden wedding anniversary at their home in Raymond Terrace, Treforest.

Army Cadets assembled at the Drill Hall in Treforest on 21 December when Col. R.G. Llewellyn presented a silver bugle to A Company for winning the band championship held at Porthcawl in August. Col. S.B. Watkins presided, supported by Maj. Clifton, Maj. H.W.Davies, Maj. Howard Griffiths and Maj. J.G. Wordgates. Councillor Herbert Gardner represented the Pontypridd UDC. Cadet Cpl Downing received the silver bugle and expressed thanks on behalf of the cadets; and then Mrs S.B. Watkins presented a mace to Drum Major W.H.Payne. The Air Training Corps was represented by W/O Symons and W/O Green; and the Sea Cadets by Lt-Cdr J. Hastings, CPO Dickson, Sub-Lt Ash and Sub-Lt Lewis.

The turmoil of war was ending for the people at home and for the men and women of the services. The people returning to their homes in Pontypridd had longed for a silence of guns, and a merciful end to the brutality and callousness witnessed in some evils of inhumanity. They sought an inner serenity, and the tranquillity of another world about us.

One soldier just wanted to walk in the hills of home. After the steamy jungle prisoner of war camp of the vicious Japanese for long war years, he did not care that it was raining here in Wales on that first day he was able to look again for an uplifting hand from the beauty at home. He found an inner peace in his walk in the tangling heather and wimberries clinging right down from the moorland of Eglwysilan mountain to the clear spring of Paddy's Well which has long held a welcome for walkers and ramblers. Drenched cohorts of Roman soldiers, too, might have halted there in the autumn of their occupancy. He could quench his thirst now or follow the road to the beckoning Rose and Crown. The clouds overhead threatened with a wash of Indian ink. There was a mellow lighting and warmth in the oak-beamed inn.

CHAPTER ELEVEN

Aftermath of War

General Election

The wartime national coalition government resigned on 23 May 1945 and the first general election for ten years was called for 5 July. It was thought that the prestige of the victorious war leader Winston Churchill would bring the Conservatives a good majority. Public opinion polls predicted a Labour victory: the issue that concerned most people was housing, and Labour had presented itself as the party most committed to the task of much needed social reform. And there had been a growing mood in the war for radical change. It was several weeks before the election results were known because of the great difficulties of collecting and counting the votes of all servicemen and women. Labour reaped a landslide majority. The figures were: Labour 393, Conservatives 213, Liberals 12, others 19. Labour took 47.8 per cent of the votes cast, Conservatives 39.8 per cent, Liberals 9 per cent, and others 3.4 per cent. Clement Attlee became Prime Minister.

Local candidates for the Pontypridd division at the General Election were Arthur Pearson, the sitting Labour member since 1938, when he had a majority of 7,349 over the Liberal contender Lady Rhys Williams; for the Conservatives, Capt. Cennydd Traherne; for the Liberals, J. Ellis Williams of Mackintosh Road, a senior teacher at Mill Street School. The votes cast were: Arthur Pearson 27,823, Capt. Traherne 7,260, and J. Ellis Williams 5,464; a Labour majority over the National Conservative of 20,563. Two other local men were also elected to parliament, D.T. Jones of Llanover Road gained Hartlepools for Labour with a 275 majority, and A.J. Champion of Lanelay Terrace, Maesycoed, gained South Derbyshire for Labour with a 22,950 majority. When Arthur Pearson took his seat in 1938 he succeeded D.L. Davies who had served from 1931.

Politicians had promised that every family would have a home after the war was over. Housing the homeless was the giant problem facing the new government. Millions of homes needed bomb damage repair, and shortages of materials meant there was little private building for years. There was a great housing shortage in Pontypridd and young married couples, for example, had to wait many years for a place of their own after putting their names on the council waiting list. As a temporary measure a national programme started in 1945 and 1946 on the erection of 40,000 aluminium prefabricated houses or 'prefabs'. They were built in many areas of Britain. At last the occupiers had a key to their very own homes and found them to be little palaces. The prefabs were set in small gardens and were fitted with a folding kitchen table, a gas or electric cooking stove, a small refrigerator and a thermostat switch for hot water. Prefabs were intended to last for ten years but the little estate of Pinewood Avenue and other streets in Rhydyfelin were demolished only in recent years and replaced with brick-built houses.

Britain faced a grave economic crisis when on 20 August 1945, five days after the war, the new American president Harry S. Truman ended without warning the Lend-Lease Act introduced in 1941 by President Franklin D. Roosevelt which enabled him to lend or lease arms and supplies to countries whose defence was considered vital to United States security. Most of the supplies came to Britain which obtained them without down payments of cash. Food imports were now drastically reduced.

The government announced plans to create a welfare state with free health services. In June it introduced family allowance of 5*s*. a week for every child excepting the first. It told of intentions to nationalise the coal, railway and other industries.

Schools were to be better, brighter places of learning. The minimum school leaving age was to be raised from 14 to 15 with a deadline of April 1947 as the top priority of the Butler Education Act. Thousands of 'emergency trained' teachers had a one-year intensive course. Before 1945 most children knew only one school during their education years: they started at five years and stayed there, often in the same classroom, with the teacher covering all subjects, until they left at 14. Secondary school places were a privilege and parents had to pay fees, though some free places—and a free uniform—were reserved for pupils who won scholarships. Pupils had to pass an 'eleven plus' examination to get into a grammar school, free. In Pontypridd, you could win a place to Mill Street Intermediate School through examination and go on from there at the age of twelve to Pontypridd Grammar School.

Snows and strikes

The war effort in industry had wiped out unemployment and much of the poverty of pre-war years. For nearly six years people had worked closely together for the common aim of victory and the wartime spirit continued for a time. But workers' attitudes had changed and orders were not taken easily. A national campaign urged for increased production and exports to pay our way out of our difficulties. By 1947, women who earlier had been forced to stop working and return to the home were now persuaded to go back to work.

Much of industry depended on coal supplies and it was hoped in 1945 that the proposed state ownership of the coal, electricity, gas, transport and other industries would help put an end to strikes, considered to be the 'British' disease of the time. The average number of stoppages due to strikes and lock-outs was 903 for the years 1927–45 with 371,000 workers involved and 2,765,000 working days lost; between 1945 and 1955 there were 1,803 stoppages involving 557,600 workers and 2,163,000 days lost.

'Unofficial' strikes were rampant during the years of war which seemed to indicate that not all was well with industrial relations. The year 1944 saw great discontent in the coalfields and the falling output caused a severe coal shortage. Miners had left themselves open to the charge that they placed their own interests before those of the country. Military control was considered; and the Trades Union Congress issued a statement that unauthorised stoppages of work had gravely impeded preparations for the attack on Europe and if continued might produce a national disaster and imperil victory. There were many grumbles that miners still received their traditional free coal allowance, and in 1942 the government acted during one strike which was deemed unreasonable, when the ringleaders were jailed and 1,000 miners were fined, though the prison sentences were not served nor the fines paid. The Bevin Boy conscripts first went down the pits in 1944. That year, the year of the D-Day landings in Normandy, strikes by South Wales miners spread, with 156 of the 200 pits then idle. Miners from Poland were recruited in 1947 and those who came to Pontypridd pits lived at the hostel at Fairfield House in Miles's Lane, now the site of the Hawthorn Leisure Centre.

A petty dispute of dockers at Birkenhead early in 1945 led to an extended unofficial strike of dock workers in most of the large ports: 40,000 were on strike and 20,000 soldiers had to take their place. The Minister of Labour, after consultation with the TUC and the British Employers' Confederation in 1944, had issued a defence regulation giving him strong powers for dealing with those responsible for inciting strikes or lock-outs which interfered with essential services. He refused to intervene until the men returned to work. After the war, demands for wage rises caused numerous strikes, both official and unofficial. Unrest continued among dock workers. Great hardship was again the lot of the housewife in those years of austerity and shortages. In late 1947 a crisis plea from the Chancellor of the Exchequer, Sir Stafford Cripps, for 'a steady pace and a long pull with our hearts in our work' won TUC support for a wages freeze.

Coal was nationalised and the National Coal Board created on 1 January 1947. Just three weeks later, the worst winter since 1880–1 brought Britain to a standstill. Production was badly affected and two million people were put out of work or worked short time. Only a few thousand of the 106,000 South Wales miners were working, for many of the men could not get to the pits. The bitterly cold weather in Pontypridd started on Monday 20 January 1947 and temperatures stayed low for a week. When classes started in Treforest Park Schools the temperature was 45 degrees Fahrenheit (7.22 degrees Celsius) and then dropped rapidly. At nine o'clock one morning at Hawthorn School it was 26 F (six degrees of frost, -3.33 C) and that was the average temperature in the town for several weeks. E.G. Mort, geography master at the Boys' Grammar School, said that one temperature recorded in Pontypridd was 17.5 F (14.5 degrees of frost, -8 C). On 26 January Cardiff was the coldest place in Britain.

The snow came down three days later to shroud South Wales. Then came two months of heavy falls which virtually crippled the country. Snow blocked all the streets in Pontypridd and the villages and the valleys. Shivering householders were to be seen everywhere collecting coal from local dumps in buckets or in sacks pulled on sleds (as they did in the snowfalls of 1940 and 1945) and coal was frozen in railway trucks for weeks. To add to the trials of rationing of foods and much else there was a severe shortage of bread and milk. If you were in the Forces you couldn't get home on leave; if you were at home you couldn't get back. Heavy snow began to fall on 29 January. Pontypridd Transport buses were in the grip of thick snow and ice and there was a big drop in the number of passengers. The streets were empty of shoppers. Several more inches of snow fell the next day and the freezing north-east wind created large drifts in the local streets.

After two weeks of Arctic conditions that were worse than those in Pontypridd during the same week of January 1945, the transport manager John Powell said that it had been impossible to maintain ordinary services, especially during the very bad weather of the previous week. Early morning services were maintained and all workpeople were taken to their factories and collieries. The abnormally low temperatures had affected the trolley buses which were withdrawn and replaced by motor buses. After a bitterly cold morning on 1 February it started to snow heavily in the high winds and the *Pontypridd Observer* reported that 'people had to battle their way blindly along'. In the town, women hurried to finish their shopping, and before six o'clock there was a 'deserted village' air about the main streets and districts. It snowed steadily for about five hours until there was a over a foot on the ground, with drifts very much deeper in places. Post Office engineers were called out on the Saturday night to repair telephone lines damaged by the snow storms. On the Sunday they found 300 faults and 22 junctions out of order. Many of the faults were repaired before subscribers knew their lines were damaged.

Ynysangharad Park was said to be 'breath-taking in its austere beauty' on the Sunday morning. By Wednesday, two-thirds of the snow had been cleared—ready for the next blizzard. February was a harsh month alternating between heavy snowfalls and treacherous thaws: big efforts were made to keep the Pontypridd GWR station and its approaches clear of snow but it was sometimes a losing battle. Several hillside bus services were suspended. Thousands of workers walked miles to and from work in the appalling conditions. Gilbert K. Sutton, school attendance officer, said that headmasters had the right to close schools if pupil attendance fell below 40 per cent. On the Friday of one week, for example, an average of 17 per cent of pupils attended in the morning and 14 per cent in the afternoon at schools in the Pontypridd district. Children had fun though with their sleighs and toboggans on every hillside. Despite the first snows it was reported that 'a good crowd' of worshippers braved Graigwen Hill to reach Carmel Baptist Church to hear the minister, the Revd B. David Jones, conduct the service. And some worshippers made it to the 8 a.m. Holy Communion at St Mary's, Glyntaff, and St John's on the Graig. The bleak midwinter revived the story of a famous preacher who always began the service with a prayer of thanksgiving. One perishing morning, when conditions were at their worst, the congregation wondered what he would say. He began: 'We thank Thee, O Lord, that every day is not like this one.'

With every thaw the local roads and pavements changed into rivers of slush. The milder weather raised everyone's hopes, though by evening the temperature dropped to below zero again. And of course the slush froze and the icy roads and pavements were hazardous and there were accidents and hardships. Leslie Joshua of the Park Street ironmongery in Treforest said they had been inundated for aid as there was damage to many water tanks and pipes. The main roads were often cleared for a time but conditions in the villages were very bad. The *Pontypridd Observer* reporters and other witnesses told that the Graig Hill was in a dreadful state for weeks and no buses could travel there. The residents of the Graig and those of Penycoedcae had to walk to and from work and the women had a hard time carrying their heavy shopping bags up the slippery hill. It was the same in Maesycoed with Mound Round particularly bad. A temporary bus service ran from the town, through Pwllgwaun, up Maesycoed Hill and along Woodland Terrace, where it turned back to Taff Street. Graigwen Hill was dangerous and people living on the Rock found it impossible to go down to the town. Sand and salt on the hill to the Common enabled a bus to reach the Cottage Hospital. At one time, six operations (non-emergency) were postponed there because surgeons could not get to the Cottage. And more hardship: the *South Wales Echo* told that a Pontypridd councillor placed his false teeth in a glass of water overnight and woke to find them encased, mammoth-style, in a block of ice.

In February the government ordered power cuts to homes and industry. Pontypridd suffered along with rest of the country. More warm clothing was desperately needed by many people but clothing coupons were necessary. An extra ration of fats helped. Electricity supplies were rationed to homes and restaurants and you were chilled to the bone without a fire in the grate because coal could not be delivered. Electricity was not to be used between the hours of 9 a.m. and noon and between 2 p.m. and 4 p.m. except in essential industries. It was difficult to work in cold offices and dimly lit shops. Woolworth's store in Taff Street was lit by eight gas lights. The manager, W. Ellis, said that every candle in stock had been sold. Marks & Spencer also had eight gas lights, instead of the 80 electric lights normally used. Their manager, R. Howell, said that even during the times that lights were allowed on they used only the absolute minimum. They felt it was their duty to help, and it was in that spirit the assistants were taking it. At Hodge's shop, a reporter found the manager and his staff wearing overcoats and scarves, there were no lights and it was freezing cold. It was the same in the drapery department of the Co-operative store in Market Square and most of the shops in town. The assistants stayed cheerful and helpful and worked by candlelight, as they did during the power cuts and three-day working week of the 1970s.

In the first week of March 1947, after a thaw and two days of springtime, came one of the worst blizzards ever to hit South Wales and snowdrifts in parts of the Valleys reached the telegraph wires. In Pontypridd it brought severe dislocation of rail and road transport and affected trade in the town. Except for a short break, it snowed for two days. High winds caused great drifts and people living in the hilly areas of Cilfynydd, Maesycoed, the Graig and Graigwen had to dig themselves out. It was not possible to operate most buses. Some ran between Pontypridd and Porth; and motor buses took over from trolley buses between Treforest and Cilfynydd. But housewives had to queue at the shops for food every day and tradesmen fought to deliver food, milk, bread and coal. You were given no promise at the GWR station that any train would arrive or depart. Snowdrifts on the lines were reported in many places and those at Nantgarw and Groeswen prevented any trains running from Pontypridd to Caerphilly. Coal production plummeted with up to 70 per cent absenteeism in the Albion, Cwm, Lewis Merthyr and Tymawr collieries. Absenteeism among the nearly 10,000 workers on the Treforest Trading Estate ranged from 50 to 90 per cent on the worst two days. There were ten-foot drifts or more all over the country.

The *South Wales Echo* told that during the blizzards, a hearse was not able to get up Graigwen Hill and a coffin had to be pulled on a sleigh to the Glyntaff Cemetery. Snow fell relentlessly on 7 March and road and rail routes were cut for the third successive day. It was 15 feet deep at Stormy Down near Bridgend and reports came from the Brecon Beacons of thousands of sheep frozen to death. The thaw began on 10 March and caused thousands of burst water pipes in South Wales.

March 1947 was all set to go out like a lion. On the Saturday of another weekend the blizzard returned in all its fury and became a memory of the wildest and most severe days in Pontypridd history. It snowed heavily until nightfall. All sport was called off again and traffic was disrupted. There was little hope of getting to the cinemas or the dance halls or the pubs. At about 4.30 in the afternoon, when the blizzard was at its height, fire totally destroyed Elim Church in Thurston Road, Trallwn. The *Pontypridd Observer* reported that a neighbour, seeing smoke coming from the building told the church secretary, D.J. Ingram, who lived opposite. He phoned the fire brigade and then the Revd Ken Matthew, the church pastor. They and several deacons and neighbours and friends made gallant attempts to salvage some of the church furniture but were driven back by smoke and fumes. The National Fire Service under Divisional Officer T.F. Hogg did their best to save the church from destruction but the task proved hopeless and by 6.30 p.m. the building was completely gutted. Only three weeks earlier the church had opened after renovations and redecorations costing over £1,000. Mr Matthew estimated the damage at about £3,000, a very substantial sum in those years. The cause of the fire remained a mystery.

Later in the night, a thaw set in and heavy rain washed most streets clear of snow by Sunday morning. But a gale late in the afternoon and then winds of hurricane force left a trail of damage everywhere and the River Taff at flood level. Scores of houses in the villages lost roof slates and chutes, and several chimneys collapsed through roofs. The chimney of one house in Middle Street, Trallwn, crashed through the kitchen roof of the house next door causing considerable damage. Shop signs were ripped away in Taff Street and hoardings demolished outside the Fairfield opposite the YMCA. At Oaklands allotments in Cilfynydd a shed was blown into a brook 50 yards away. Corrugated iron sheets were torn from the roof and sides of the Stand at the Hawthorn Greyhound Racing Track. A wall blew down near the Queens Hotel by the canal in Trallwn.

In the early hours of Saturday 29 March, PC Arthur was on duty near the disused Glamorganshire Canal near the park gates and entrance to the Brown Lenox Chainworks. In the blackout (this one caused by electricity cuts and fuel shortages) he noticed a beam of light. On investigation he discovered a large car, a Lanchester 14, on the roadway and perched at right angles to the canal with the rear wheels overhanging the muddy waters that filled the canal at this point. The car's engine was running and its lights were on. Soon after the officer had obtained help from several employees of the chainworks, the body of a man was found in the water about four feet away from the bank. Artificial respiration was applied but when Dr Alfred Feiner arrived he pronounced life extinct.

The driver, a company director from Llandaff, had spent some time at the nearby Queens Hotel early in the evening, and the police believed that he had taken the wrong turning in the blackout and driven up to the chainworks. When near the canal he realised his mistake and so reversed the car to get back to Bridge Street, but in the darkness he misjudged the distance and the rear wheels dropped over the edge of the canal. The man left the car to see what could be done, missed his step and fell into the canal. In the early 1930s a small Austin or Morris car plunged into the then busy canal at the very same spot after the driver had taken a wrong turning in the dark.

The cupboard was bare

Food supplies and other needs in wartime Pontypridd had been reduced to mere essentials. When peace came, people expected a speedy end to the Mother Hubbard pantry and to austerity and shortages. But Britain was almost bankrupt and two particularly bad harvests brought harsh warnings that wartime restrictions would have to stay. Pontypriddians hoped to get increased food supplies but instead they got less. And even more cuts could be expected. There was little change in rationed foods between VJ Day in 1945 and the end of 1949. You did get an extra one ounce of bacon, three ounces of fat, and 4*d*. worth of meat. In June 1948 the meat ration was reduced again and consisted of six pennyworth of corned beef and six pennyworth of meat: it was too little for a family Sunday joint and butchers found difficulties in cutting such small portions to suit their customers.

There was a public outcry in July 1946 when John Strachey, the Minister of Food, announced that bread—not rationed during the war years—was to be rationed from 21 July because of a shortage of wheat. The Minister of Fuel at this time was Emmanuel Shinwell, and the Conservative opposition taunted Labour with the slogan 'Shiver with Shinwell, and starve with Strachey'. The loaf was now a darker grey in colour, owing to a 95 per cent extraction rate of flour from wheat. The adult daily ration was nine ounces, female manual workers had eleven ounces, and male manual workers had 15 ounces. This was nearly a whole loaf and was more than people normally used, which proved to campaigners with a loss of faith in the rationing system that bread rationing was unnecessary. It ended in July 1948, along with the restrictions on serving bread in restaurants; but deliveries from mills were still controlled to prevent any bread or flour being fed to livestock.

Housewives found shopping an ordeal and wondered what to get for the family to eat. It was far worse than during the war. Potatoes were rationed towards the end of 1947 and this caused great difficulties until the scheme ended nearly six months later. Although housewives did not have to queue for rationed foods, they joined any queues for whatever other food was available. They stood for perhaps an hour for a pound of sausages. They still had a raw deal from some shopkeepers who, as in the war years, waited for a queue to form and then opened up the shop to sell a little before closing up again for the day.

Ministry of Food broadcasts called 'Kitchen Front' gave recipes for housewives to try to make rations more interesting, and possibly appetising. Newspapers carried 'Food Facts' every week. Tinned snoek fish, a kind of mackerel, was imported from South Africa: it was very salty. Whale meat appeared: when grilled it tasted like steak but the taste soon gave a strong flavour of cod liver oil. Horse meat became part of the sorry British diet. This was the year of the Berlin Airlift, when the RAF began hundreds of flights to deliver two million tons of food and essentials to the city to counter the Russian blockade at the start of the Cold War. Supplies of vegetables were still grown in local gardens, though Anderson shelters were being removed and the dug out pits made into ponds or filled in to make plots for flowers or rock gardens. Garden drabness was disappearing and border colours were predominantly red, white and blue. There was now DDT insecticide to help fight the bugs. *Gardeners Question Time* was on the wireless from 1947 and the Peace rose came at this time to tell of hope for the future.

Clothing coupons were fewer than ever in 1946 and the black market thrived. Hawkers, known as 'Spivs', sold their wares from suitcases on the pavements in Taff Street, especially in front of Barclays Bank, and around the Tumble area. A spiv would buy your clothing coupons for 6*d*. or 1*s*. each and sell them for 3*s*. each or more. He offered to buy a man's demob suit for £10 and sold it at a handsome profit. Servicewomen being demobbed could choose to take a demob suit or £12 10*s*. in cash. This would buy a dress or costume suit at £4 15*s*., a blouse at £1, a raincoat at £3 10*s*., stockings at 10*s*., shoes at £1 5*s*., a scarf at 6*s*., and a hat for 10*s*., with about 14*s*. left for minor items. New fashions in ladies' clothes appealed greatly with their attractiveness. In April 1947 Christian Dior created his New Look which captivated thousands of women. Full skirts fell to mid calf, much to the disap-pointment of some government ministers who voiced that the style was an irresponsible waste of cloth and begged that the short skirt should be retained. Women who for years had worn service uniforms or factory dungarees and 'make-do and mend' plain dresses could hardly wait for clothes rationing to end. It did so in 1949, although rationing of footwear ended in 1948.

In his 1948 Budget, Sir Stafford Cripps put up the price of a packet of 20 cigarettes from 3*s*. 4*d*. to 3*s*. 6*d*. and pipe tobacco up by 2½*d*. an ounce. Beer went up by a 1*d*. a pint and a bottle of whisky up by nearly 2*s*. 6*d*. Wines were up from between 6*d*. and 1*s*. a bottle. But there were still the familiar notices greeting you with No Beer, No Cigarettes, No Matches, No Potatoes, No Eggs: no this, no that, not much of anything. More goods started to arrive in the shops by 1950 which marked the beginning of the consumer boom of that decade. Food rationing did not finally disappear until 1954. The basic petrol ration for motorists was restored in June 1945 but rationing continued until June 1950. Although cars with both traditional and new designs were flowing off the production lines, few were seen here as most of them went for export. The Morris Minor was one of the most popular small cars at the 1948 Motor Show.

Enjoying yourself

Because of petrol rationing, post-war buses and trains in Pontypridd were usually packed. The GWR station heaved with people who made once more for the crowded beaches of Barry Island and Porthcawl. British seaside resorts reached the high peak of their popularity in 1948, for strict currency controls made trips abroad almost impossible. Because there were few cars, cycling was very enjoyable on quiet local roads. Cycle picnics were highlights of the time. Many couples, young and old, could now enjoy trips by coach to towns in Wales and the border counties: perhaps to spend a day in Hereford or elsewhere, a day to remember.

Everyone in austere Pontypridd looked for a happy time for the family. Many households had two incomes as more married women were in work. Although average wages in mid 1947 were £7 a week, those of, say, Pontypridd bus conductors at this time were a couple of pounds less. But most workers now had holidays with pay and much of it was spent living it up at Butlin's holiday camps. The standard rate of income tax was raised from 7*s*. in the £ to 7*s*. 6*d*. from Sir John Simon's War Budget introduced on 27 September 1939, 8*s*. 6*d*. in 1940–1, 10*s*. in 1941–2 to 1944–6, and 9*s*. in 1946–7. The Pay As You Earn or PAYE system by which current income tax was deducted from current wages and salaries, which started in 1943, continued after the war. Income tax increased to 9*s*. 6*d*. in 1951–2 to help pay for Britain's rearmament programme.

There was no television in local homes and so wireless broadcasts were an attraction. The 14th Olympic Games was held in London in 1948 and you listened to the particular achievements of two famous names: Czech distance runner Emil Zatopeck and the personal triple-gold Dutch housewife Fanny Blankers-Koen. Popular songs at this time included 'There's a Tree in the Meadow' (Dorothy Squires) and 'I Wonder Who's Kissing Her Now' (Perry Como); and wireless shows *Top of the Form* with question master Wynford Vaughan Thomas, and *Take it From Here* with Jimmy Edwards. At 6.45 p.m. on 7 October 1946, the musical signature tune of 'The Devil's Gallop' introduced a 15-minute programme which went out on every weekday evening for several years: children and a great many adults listened to the thrilling adventures of *Dick Barton—Special Agent*. Two Cilfynydd men, who later achieved international fame, began to make their mark: Stuart Burrows, then a well-known boy soprano, broadcast on 31 October 1945, and Geraint Evans starred in opera at Covent Garden in January 1949.

Pontypridd cinemas and theatres and dance halls were magnets of enjoyment. Many couples went to the 'pictures' twice a week to cuddle in the back row or to escape briefly with their favourite film stars from the real world outside. At the cinema in 1948 or so you could see films like the colourful musicals *Oklahoma!*, *Annie Get Your Gun* and *South Pacific*. There was *Whisky Galore!*, *Scott of the Antarctic* and *The Blue Lagoon* with Tonypandy-born Donald Houston. His brother Glyn Houston appeared in many films in these years. Sunday night variety shows drew packed audiences to the Town Hall Theatre in the early post-war years. In January 1947 the pantomime *Snow White and the Seven Dwarfs* looked promising entertainment at the Town Hall. And scantily-clad 'Jane' of the *Daily Mirror* strip cartoon, who revealed all for the Victory in Europe celebrations, appeared at the theatre in February 1948. Winston Churchill said that she was the secret weapon of the British Forces in wartime. There was interest in local drama and the Pontypridd Theatre Club met at the Community Hall in Sion Street and in later times, as Stanley Wells recalls, in the upstairs room of Queens Hotel by the old canal lock.

Reading was a widespread interest locally and the Pontypridd Public Library with its large number of books, free lending services, and a small but comprehensive reference section and local collection (then situated downstairs) was well used, as is the extensively renovated interior today. Wilfred Cowdry was the well-known and highly respected librarian of the war years. Residents were saddened to learn soon into the New Year of 1947 that Miss Sarah Crute had died. She kept the Chain Library (near the Fifty Shilling Tailors shop in the Fountain area of Taff Street) where a good selection of books could be borrowed for a small charge, particularly fiction, including many of the Just William and the Biggles stories so much sought after by young people. She and her likewise elegantly tall sister Elizabeth, who worked for Leslie's Stores, were also well-known and respected in the town. Both were faithful members of Park Chapel in Treforest for many years.

Cradle to grave

The National Health Service had its roots in a report produced in 1942 by Sir William Beveridge, which was a plan for something to look forward to when the war was over and, in his words, 'a scheme of social insurance against interruption and destruction of earning power and for special expenditure arising at birth, marriage and death'. It showed how to begin to overthrow the five evils: Want, Disease, Ignorance, Squalor, Idleness. And 'the many' were to care for 'the few'. Beveridge worked out how much it would cost for insurance benefits to rid the sick, the old and the unemployed from the fear of poverty. People must receive enough income to keep them fed, clothed and housed properly.

When Labour came to power after the General Election in 1945 their policies were even more radical than those Beveridge had planned. Part of this plan became law in 1946. Welshman James Griffiths was appointed Minister of Labour and promised one National Insurance for all 'from the cradle to the grave'. He introduced weekly unemployment and sickness benefits of 26s. a week for a single man and 42s. for a married couple. Employees paid 11d. a week from their pay packets and employers paid the other half as contributions to the scheme. The first Family Allowances, paid on 6 August 1946, gave 5*s*. a week for every child after the first. Everyone received a stamp contribution card and a National Insurance number which covered every benefit.

The new Health Minister, Aneurin Bevan, the MP for Tredegar, faced a medical profession suspicious of his plans for a National Health Service. As Bevan said, 'No society can legitimately call itself civilised if a sick person is denied medical aid because of a lack of means.' His aim was to prevent inequality in medical treatment and to change a system in which hospitals were funded largely by public generosity or by local authorities and had a wide variation of standards of care.

Before the NHS, if people were ill at home only those on low wages, but not their dependants, were covered. If you qualified for help you were 'put on the panel'. Otherwise you paid 2*s*. a time but this did not cover the cost of all medicines or the services of specialist consultants. Miners and many other workers contributed to a 1*d*. or so a week to schemes for medical treatment and stays in hospital. Back in 1939 more than 16 million workers contributed to national health insurance. Many local children had free school meals through the war years and afterwards and were medically examined at school. Glamorgan County Council introduced a scheme in 1934 to provide dental treatment, spectacles and surgical appliances for people on public assistance. A national midwifery service began in 1937 which provided maternity beds. And there were eye, ear, nose and throat services.

The RAF Hospital at Church Village was 'demobbed' after all RAF staff and patients left in the last months of 1946. It reopened in April 1947 as the East Glamorgan Hospital after the shortage of equipment was made good by generous RAF co-operation. The hospital had two floors with connecting lifts, and eleven wards with 310 beds. Of these, 56 were for maternity cases and 20 were for children, who had a special wing of their own. It had a physiotherapy centre, an out-patients' department, clinics, laboratories, labour theatres, five operating theatres and a large kitchen with staff dining rooms. Behind the hospital block stood the three-storey building with bedrooms for 150 nurses and 50 domestic staff, sitting and recreation rooms, and flats for the administrative sisters. The out-patients' department at Llwynypia was retained as an important unit. The East Glamorgan Hospital, known to so many residents of Pontypridd and district over the years, is to be replaced by a new Royal Glamorgan Hospital sited at Ynys-y-Plwm, near Llantrisant.

Doctors in 1948 were concerned by Nye Bevan's ideas for the nationalisation of hospitals. He wanted to legislate where doctors could practise and to pay them a state salary. Doctors feared they would lose their independence and 56,000 of them voted 9 to 1 against the scheme. The National Health Service was due to start in July 1948; and in February everyone received a leaflet entitled *Your New Health Service*. In May 1948 A ballot of GPs, now reassured that they would not become state employees, voted to cooperate and the BMA ended its boycott of the NHS Act. Most voluntary and municipal hospitals passed into the ownership of the Minister of Health. Bevan told the public to register with a NHS doctor of their choice. A doctor received £1 a year capitation payment for every patient registered with his practice.

Women and children who previously were not covered for medical attention could now be treated for neglected complaints. The payment of maternity benefit brought on a new baby boom. Scores more local mothers collected orange juice, cod liver oil and vitamin tablets from the old local board offices at the bottom of Penuel Lane and elsewhere. Ante-natal welfare services were available from the clinic in Ynysangharad Park.

The National Health service started on 5 July 1948 and the new appointments books of opticians in the town were filled, for free eye care could now be sought. Everybody seemed to need prescription glasses, or spectacles. And free glasses had style compared to the generally rimless ones available previously. More than five million pairs were provided nationally in 1948. Two million bottles of medicines were issued every week and people were urged to return their empty bottles to the chemist to combat shortages. Dentists saw a huge demand for false teeth and other treatments. Yet the days of everything for free were numbered: in 1951 the chancellor of the exchequer, Hugh Gaitskell, introduced charges for glasses and false teeth. But when dental care first became freely available many patients who had put up with years of discomfort could find the courage to sit in the dentist's chair. In so many ways, the 1940s was a decade of courage.

Victory celebrations

Pontypridd Victory Week Celebrations from 8 to 15 June 1946 were marked with a sparkling programme of events. H. Leonard Porcher, clerk of the Pontypridd Urban District Council, stated that the council realised that the final Victory Celebrations were of especial interest to every member of the British Legion and had readily and unanimously decided to co-operate fully with the organisers of the British Legion Victory Celebration Campaign. The council had granted the campaign committee the use of all the amenities available in the Ynysangharad War Memorial

Park. They would spare no effort to ensure that the week's celebration would not only make a lasting impression on the rising generation but would be a great financial success, and help the wise and reasonable ambition of the British Legion to obtain suitable headquarters where its members, in peace and security, should be able to 'fight their battles over again'.

Col. W. Lester Lewis, chairman of the British Legion (Pontypridd) Appeal Committee, told that the month of June also marked the Silver Jubilee of the British Legion which had done such fine work over the years. The committee had accepted the responsibility of organising the programme of events. We were living under restrictions and there was a shortage of much that was required for our welfare and comfort and happiness. But the fact remained that, after the trying and troubled years of war, we had been delivered from great peril. We now knew what our fate would have been had we known defeat. We were surely entitled to celebrate and rejoice in the deliverance we owed to our splendid Forces on land and sea and in the air. His closing remarks were:

> In our rejoicing, let us remember those of our town who made the supreme sacrifice for us and those who are left proudly to mourn their passing. But for the self sacrifice of these—our bravest and our very best—we should not be celebrating today.

Tudor H. Jeremy, president of the Pontypridd and District Chamber of Trade, said that when Pontypridd had set out to do something worth while it usually succeeded, particularly if the object was a deserving one. The British Legion had done wonderful work for the ex-serviceman and his family, in wartime and also in the difficult days that followed. It had taken special care of the disabled and the dependents of those who had made the supreme sacrifice. Members of the Pontypridd Chamber embraced the opportunity to do something for those who had made the week of thanksgiving possible. Having survived the difficult days of war, during which we had done our best to cooperate with the much harassed but very courageous housewife in preserving the Home Front, it was with grateful hearts that we joined in preparing to celebrate victory and to help the British Legion. The previous president, presented with his chain of office on 10 January 1945, was D. Merlin Phillips.

The officials of the Victory Celebrations Committee were Col. W. Lester Lewis, chairman; E.E. Morris, secretary; William Berriman, organiser; T. Emlyn Williams, treasurer. For the Victory Parade: Maj. Vivian Lloyd Thomas, Capt. Ithel Gowan, Capt. W.J. Thomas, Stanley Ashford and James Beech. For motorcycle events: Pontypridd Motor

Cycle and Car Club (secretary, T. Jones). For musical and other events in Ynysanghard Park: Miss Daisy Spickett and Bert Gregory Evans. For the jazz band competition, baseball, boxing and fireworks: George Ball JP, William Berriman, Manny Bloomer, A. Boobyer, F. Dixon, Harry Gale, and T. Lougher. Masters of ceremonies for the Victory Dance: Maj. Vivian Lloyd Thomas, Capt. W.J Thomas, Lt Jerry Evans.

The Victory Parade assembled at the Broadway at 10.30 a.m. on Saturday 8 June and the Great Western Colliery Silver Band led the march through the town to Ynysangharad Park. Fewer uniforms were worn than in past parades. And though flags and bunting fluttered everywhere, decorations in the streets did not reach the grandeur known for the VE and VJ celebrations of the previous year. The chairman of the council, Herbert Gardner, received the parade and addressed them with other ex-service speakers at 11.30. Six Royal British Legion standards were lowered in silent tribute as ex-Sgt Jim Beech spoke the lines of Laurence Binyon:

> They shall grow not old, as we that are left grow old:
> Age shall not weary them, nor the years condemn.
> At the going down of the sun and in the morning
> We will remember them.

Events during the week at Taff Vale Park, some marred by heavy rain, included motorcycle racing with famous aces of racing track and speedway. A boxing tournament of eight contests had two featherweight bouts that featured Pontypridd boxers Gerald Evans and Cliff Morris. There was a Monster Jazz and Character Band Competition with £100 in prizes. And on Saturday 15 June an exhibition baseball match between the pick of Cardiff and Newport schoolboys.

A swimming gala at the Ynysangharad Park swimming baths in the evening of the first Saturday featured the Boys under-16 Diving Championship of Wales (with admission prices merely 1*s*. 6*d*. or 1*s*., and 6*d*. for children). A tennis tournament on the park tennis courts on the Wednesday was organised by Miss Terry Jones of Lan Park Road. For a sixpenny entrance fee you could compete at the miniature golf course for a silver cup given by J. Lewis Thomas. There was a bowls competition at the Park Rinks, and lots of fun and games—including tombola. In matches through the week Pontypridd Cricket Club played teams from Rhondda, Baldwin's C.C. Swansea, Whitchurch, and Cardiff Prudential XI. Glamorgan played Somerset on the last Saturday.

At 8 p.m. on Sunday 9 June there was a United Service of Thanksgiving for Victory (Pontypridd Council of Churches) at Ynysangharad

Park conducted by the Revd C.M. Davies, the Revd E. Austin Evans, the Revd A.F. Harries, the Revd G.J. Matthews and the Revd J. Selwyn Roberts. The Band of the Salvation Army was in attendance.

The bandstand in Ynysangharad Park attracted several performances during the week: on 8 June a concert by the Handel Glee Society, conductor W.J. Evans; on Monday, the Settlement Youth and Junior Choirs (and folk dancing) with artistes including the young Stuart Burrows, conductor Miss Gwyneth Lewis; on Tuesday, the Pontypridd Operatic Society in *Songs from the Shows* with guest conductor Brinley Lewis; on Wednesday, the Settlement Ladies Choir (fresh from the performance of *The Student Prince*) with conductor Madame Phillips Howells; on Thursday, choir Cor-yr-Hen-Bont 'every chorister an artiste' with conductor Ronald Chivers of Cardiff; on Friday, an open-air dance, with dances to suit everyone—Modern and Old English; and in the Grand Finale on Saturday 15 June the Powell Duffryn Male Voice Choir, conductor Gwilym T. Jones. The Victory Celebrations ended with 'The greatest display of fireworks ever presented in South Wales' by the Crystal Palace Fireworks Company.

More than 50 local traders supported the Victory Celebrations souvenir programme with advertisements to help the success of the campaign. The programme was arranged by the Pontypridd and District Chamber of Trade whose officers at this time were Tudor H. Jeremy, president; D. Winton Phillips, chairman; W.R. Boobyer, vice-chairman; R.H. Thomas, treasurer; and F. Smith, secretary. There was a great shortage of bread (rationed from 21 July) and a Battle for Bread Exhibition was held for a week from 12 June at the Lucania Billiard Hall in Gas Road. It was opened by Arthur Pearson MP. It gave a practical demonstration of how to save bread and it was 'everyone's duty to visit the exhibition'.

The remarkable war record of the Pontypridd Boys' Grammar School was included in the programme, which noted that 1,800 past students served in the Forces of whom, it was sad to record, 98 made the supreme sacrifice. Decorations included a Victoria Cross (Major Tasker Watkins, Nelson, 5th Welch), the DSO, DFC and Double Bar (Wing Commander Ivor G. Broom), seven other DFCs and three DFMs, two MCs and one DSC, two George Medals, eight military MBEs and two BEMs, two OBEs, two MMs and one DSM, one Croix de Guerre, one American Bronze Star, and a number of Oak Leaves and Mentions in Despatches.

*   *   *   *

Pontypridd, as it was more than sixty years ago in the 1930s, during the Second World War and immediately afterwards, is too full of memories—sad ones and happy, treasured ones—ever to lose its enchantment for the many people who lived there then. Many are named here, for they and their loved ones before them were part of the town and they represent the thousands of others who honoured Pontypridd and its villages on the Home Front. The town today is struggling to adapt, as it must, to the changes needed to meet the demands of the new millennium ahead. It knows the strengths of its past, and knows that its future strengths and prosperity and joy is in the hands of today's young generation. Pontypridd, together with its villages, can look forward to great things, but to win through to success it needs to bring to bear a sort of blood, toil, tears, and sweat that it knew in its past.

The stories of the men and women of the armed services who saw little of the Home Front in Pontypridd during the wartime years have yet to be told and their names and sacrifices carved in honour. They will tell of happenings in all parts of the world, of Welsh men and women fighting and dying in bloody battles on land and sea and in the air or striving to survive the horrors of captivity so that the freedom and peace of this land and the security and happiness of its people would not be violated again. Today many men and women and boys and girls of those times here in Pontypridd and the villages and the valleys, yearn for a new springtime of glad community spirit worthy of the efforts and sufferings and sacrifices made for their families, their children and their grandchildren in the harsh winter of those valiant years.

List of Wartime Pubs

There were about 140 pubs in Pontypridd and district in Victorian times. Many disappeared in the first half of the twentieth century. This list includes 80 of the more popular pubs in and around Pontypridd which were open during the war or immediately afterwards, or were then of recent fond memory. Some no longer exist: some were demolished to make way for modern development such as flats, shops and business premises, or the construction of the A470 through the heart of the district in the 1970s; some have changed their names (this list uses the names they had in wartime Pontypridd); a small number have reverted to private homes; and some closed and were perhaps pulled down because of the rise of clubs and modern-day economics.

Albion Hotel, Cilfynydd Road, Cilfynydd

Baileys Arms, Graig-yr-Helfa, Glyntaff
Bassett Arms, Merthyr Road, Pontshonnorton
Bonvilston Hotel, Coedpenmaen Road, Coedpenmaen
Bridge Inn, Berw Road, Pontypridd
Bridge Inn, Bridge Street, Treforest
Bunch of Grapes, Ynysangharad Road, Pontypridd
Bush Inn, Main Road, Llantwit Fardre
Bush Inn, Park Street, Treforest

Castle Ivor, Rhondda Road, Hopkinstown
Central Hotel, Central Square, Trallwn
Cilfynydd Inn, Cilfynydd Road, Cilfynydd
Clarence Hotel, High Street, Tumble, Pontypridd
Colliers Arms, Mill Street, Pontypridd
Commercial (Spite), Cilfynydd Road, Cilfynydd
Commercial Hotel, Forest Road, Treforest
Criterion, High Street, Tumble, Pontypridd
Cross Inn, Main Road, Church Village
Cross Keys, Cardiff Road, Nantgarw
Cross Keys, Broadway, Pontypridd
Crown Inn, Cardiff Road, Rhydyfelin

Crown Inn, Fothergill Street, Treforest

Danygraig Arms, Broadway, Treforest
Duke of Bridgewater, Pentrebach Road, Glyntaff
Dyffryn Arms, Cardiff Road, Rhydyfelin

Farmers Arms, Pentrebach Road, Glyntaff
Farmers Arms, St Illtyd's Road, Church Village
Forest Hotel (Cot), Wood Road, Treforest
Fox and Hounds, Cardiff Road, Upper Boat

Globe Hotel, High Street, Graig
Graig Hotel, Llantrisant Road, Graig
Green Meadow, High Street, Graig
Greyhound Hotel, Llanfabon
Greyhound Hotel, Broadway, Tumble, Pontypridd

Half Moon Hotel, High Street, Tumble, Pontypridd
Hawthorn Inn, Cardiff Road, Hawthorn
Hewitts Arms, Llantrisant Road, Penycoedcae
Hollybush Hotel, Main Road, Church Village
Hollybush Hotel, Tymawr Road, Hopkinstown
Horse and Groom, High Street, Graig

Ivor Arms, Bridge Street, Pontypridd

Lamb and Flag, Pentrebach Road, Pontypridd
Llanbradach Arms, Machine Bridge, Glyntaff
Llanover Arms, Bridge Street, Pontypridd

Maltsters Arms, Bridge Street, Pontypridd
Merlin Hotel, Pwllgwaun Road, Pwllgwaun
Morning Star, Llantrisant Road, Graig

Newbridge Arms, Foundry Road, Coedpenmaen
New Inn, Main Road, Llantwit Fardre
New Inn, Cardiff Road, Rhydyfelin
New Inn Hotel, Taff Street, Pontypridd

Park Hotel, Taff Street, Pontypridd
Plough Inn, Cardiff Road, Rhydyfelin

Queen Adelaide, Fothergill Street, Treforest
Queens Head, Llantrisant Road, Penycoedcae
Queens Hotel, Bridge Street, Pontypridd

Railway Inn, Broadway, Treforest
Red Cow, Rhondda Road, Hopkinstown
Rhydyfelin Inn, Cardiff Road, Rhydyfelin
Richards Arms, Cilfynydd Road, Cilfynydd
Rickards Arms, Park Street, Treforest
Rose and Crown, Eglwysilan
Rose and Crown, High Street, Graig
Royal Oak, Rhondda Road, Hopkinstown
Royal Oak, Merthyr Road, Pontshonnorton
Ruperra Arms, Berw Road, Pontypridd

Salmon Arms, Llantwit Road, Treforest

Taff Vale Hotel, High Street, Graig
Three Horse Shoes, High Street, Graig
Three Horse Shoes, Llantwit Road, Tonteg
Tredegar Arms, Taff Street, Pontypridd
Trehafod Hotel, Rhondda Road, Trehafod
Tymawr Hotel, Pantygraigwen, Graigwen

Upper Boat Inn, Cardiff Road, Upper Boat

Victoria Hotel, High Street, Tumble, Pontypridd

Welsh Harp, Mill Street, Pontypridd
Wheatsheaf, Soar Street, Graig
White Cross Inn, Groeswen, Eglwysilan
White Hart Hotel, High Street, Tumble, Pontypridd

Ynysybwl Inn, Old Ynysybwl, Ynysybwl

Note on Sources

Marwick, Arthur, *The Home Front. The British and the Second World War* (Thames & Hudson, 1976).

Civil Defence. Public Information Leaflet, Nos 1 & 2 (Issued from the Lord Privy Seal's Office, July 1939).

If the Invader Comes. What to Do—and How to Do it (Ministry of Information, June 1940).

Beating the Invader. Rules for Civilians (Ministry of Information, May 1941).

Hammerton, Sir John, *The Second Great War* (Waverley Book Co. in association with Amalgamated Press, 1943, 6 vols.).

The World at War (Thames Television series).

Wartime issues of the *Pontypridd Observer, Glamorgan County Times, Western Mail, South Wales Echo* and other newspapers in Pontypridd and Cardiff Libraries.

Documents, magazines, directories, programmes and minute books in the Local Collection, Pontypridd Library; and in school, business, church and other archives.

History of the Third United States Army, operated by the 94th Medical Gas Treatment Battalion in World War II. By its Commanding Officer, William C. Burry, MD. Colonel, US Army, Retired. Copy in Pontypridd Historical and Cultural Centre.

'A Short History of the School, September 1939 to August 1940', *Sir Joseph Williamson Mathematical School, Rochester, Kent, Magazine*, Summer term, 1940.

History. Chatham County School for Girls (n.d., 1940s).

Chatham, Rochester & Gillingham News (May 1940).

Ex-evacuees located by courtesy of *Kent Today* newspaper, August 1998, and Peter R. Hayward (Nonington, Dover), Don Phillips (Chatham) and Winifred Rolfe (St Albans); personal stories gathered from interviews with ex-evacuee children to Pontypridd from Kent and the London area.

Posters. Central Office of Information, Ministry of Agriculture, Fisheries and Food, and the Imperial War Museum.

Information gathered from visits to the Museum of Welsh Life, St Fagans; National Museum & Gallery of Wales, Cardiff; Historical and Cultural Centre, Pontypridd; and elsewhere in Wales.

And, most importantly, the people of Pontypridd and its villages for their memories.

Index

243